AP* HUMAN GEOGRAPHY:
A STUDY GUIDE

3rd Edition

by Ethel Wood

WOODYARD PUBLICATIONS

AP Human Geography: A Study Guide, 3rd edition, by Ethel Wood

Published by
WoodYard Publications
285 Main Street, Germantown, NY, U.S.A.
Ph. 610-207-1366
Fax 610-372-8401
www.woodyardpublications.com
email: ejw@woodyardpublications.com

ISBN 978-0-9831766-6-4

Cover Photo: Sacred Valley, Peru (photo by Claudia Coburn)

TABLE OF CONTENTS

A Note from the Author

Why Human Geography?

I taught social studies classes for many years, mostly at Princeton High School in Princeton, New Jersey. Like most social studies teachers, my experience included classes in United States history and government. I have also published review books, textbooks, readers, and web materials that have required me to do extensive research in various types of American studies. Needless to say, I believe that an education in these areas is incredibly important for high school students, and every secondary curriculum should include them. So why is human geography so important?

The 21st century has taught us that we cannot ignore the world around us. Happenings around the globe now directly impact our lives, and social studies teachers and students around the country face the challenge of interpreting a complex, interactive world. The AP human geography course focuses on spatial organization – the location of places, people, and events, and the connections among places and landscapes that shape virtually all human endeavors on the planet.

It is my hope that this book will help students to grasp something of the complexities of our global environment, and gain some understanding of geographic commonalities and differences. In today's world, we cannot afford *not* to know.

Ethel Wood
Germantown, NY
August 2012

Other Books by Ethel Wood

American Government: A Complete Coursebook (Great Source Books)
AP Comparative Government and Politics: An Essential Coursebook and Study Guide (5 editions)
 (WoodYard Publications)
AP European History: An Essential Coursebook (WoodYard Publications)
AP United States History: An Essential Coursebook (WoodYard Publications)
AP World History: An Essential Coursebook (2 editions) (WoodYard Publications)
The Immigrants: An Historical Reader (Nextext Books)
Introduction to Sociology (Nextext Books)
Multiple Choice and Free-Response Questions in Preparation for the AP United States Government
 and Politics Examination (6 editions) (D&S Marketing Systems)
Multiple Choice and Free-Response Questions in Preparation for the AP World History Examination
 (2 editions) (D&S Marketing Systems)
Teacher's Guide - AP Comparative Government and Politics (College Board)
The Best Test Preparation for the Graduate Record Examination in Political Science (REA)
The Presidency: An Historical Reader (Nextext Books)

PREFACE: THE HUMAN GEOGRAPHY EXAMINATION

No matter whether the Human Geography Exam is your first experience with AP tests or just one of several, it is important to know what you will face when the day of the examination comes. So let's start with an overview of the exam format. The AP Human Geography Examination is approximately 2 hours and 15 minutes long, and it is divided into two basic parts:

- 75 multiple-choice questions (60 minutes allowed; 50% of the exam grade)
- 3 free-response questions (75 minutes allowed; 50% of the exam grade)

The multiple-choice questions cover all the topics listed on the following page in the same proportion as indicated. The questions are challenging. Some points to keep in mind about the multiple-choice section are:

- On the exam, the College Board no longer subtracts one-fourth of the number of questions answered incorrectly from the number of questions answered correctly. So if you have no idea how to answer a question, you might as well choose an answer since there is no penalty for guessing.

- Some questions are based on charts, photographs, and maps, so it is important to carefully consider the visual information provided, including the title and the two axes of a chart or graph. Sometimes these questions just require that you read the chart correctly, but sometimes you must also have some content knowledge in order to answer correctly.

- Be prepared for EXCEPT, NOT, and LEAST questions, such as "All of the following are physical site characteristics of a location EXCEPT:" These are sometimes called "reverse multiple-choice questions," and they require you to identify the only incorrect answer. These questions take practice because you must reverse your thinking practices in order to answer them correctly.

This book has multiple-choice questions that follow each section of the review, as well as 75 multiple-choice questions in each of the two sample exams at the end. The questions are very similar to those that you will encounter on the College Board exam.

In the free-response section, you must answer ALL three equally weighted questions, and you should spend approximately 25 minutes on each one. The questions may concentrate on one topic, but often they require you to interrelate concepts from different areas. Some of the questions are based on stimulus materials – such as maps, charts, graphs, diagrams, or photographs. There are no formal time divisions among the free-response questions. Instead, a total of 75 minutes is allotted to answer all of them, so it is important to keep up with the time, and not spend so long on one question that you don't have time to complete the others. Be sure to answer all parts of each question. Your response will be graded according to a rubric that assigns a certain number of points to each section of the question.

Generally, multiple-choice questions are distributed among these seven topic areas within the percentage range indicated:

As you can see, six of the seven topic areas are weighted exactly the same, so it is important to study all areas as equally as possible.

AP Human Geography: A Study Guide is designed to help you prepare for the exam by giving you a sound footing in human geography concepts and topics. Your best preparation for the exam is to know your stuff. The questions do require reading and writing skills, but the surer you are of the material, the more likely you are to answer the questions correctly. This book provides the concepts and information, as well as plenty of practice questions that will prepare you for the exam. Most importantly, I hope that you learn something about human geography, and that you learn to love it, too!

A note about dates: The dates in this book are defined by either "B.C.E." (Before the Common Era) or "C.E." (Common Era). They correspond to the older system of "B.C." and "A.D."

SECTION ONE: UNIT REVIEWS

This section includes review materials for the seven major topics of the AP Human Geography Course. Each section is followed by a set of multiple-choice questions and one free-response question.

UNIT ONE:
GEOGRAPHY: ITS NATURE
AND PERSPECTIVES

The word "geography" is probably a familiar one to you since most people take geography for granted. Geography is concerned with place and location – two concepts that are inherently important parts of everyday life. However, the Advanced Placement Geography course invites you to see your world through the lens of the geographer, and in doing so encourages you to enlarge your vision to encompass other places and locations and consider them in new ways.

Don't make the mistake of thinking of a geographer as merely someone that can name all the rivers, lakes, cities, and countries of the world. That would take a lot of memorization, and you would have to question the value of the information by itself. Geographers do have this kind of knowledge, but human geographers are much more interested in understanding how those places shape and are shaped by people, and what their location means in the past, present and future. Some key concepts that define geography as a field of study are:

- **Location** – the position of something on earth's surface

- **Space** – the physical gap or distance between two objects

- **Scale** – the relationship between the size of an object or distance between objects on a map and the size of the actual object or distance on earth's surface

- **Place** – a specific point on earth with human and physical characteristics that distinguish it from other points

- **Pattern** – the arrangement of objects on earth's surface in relationship to one another

- **Regionalization** – the organization of earth's surface into distinct areas that are viewed as different from other areas

- **Globalization** – the expansion of economic, political, and cultural activities to the point that they reach and have impact on many areas of the world

All of these concepts help you to understand the importance of **spatial organization** – the location of places, people, and events, and the connections among places and **landscapes** (the overall appearance of an area that is shaped by both human and natural influences). Geographers believe that the "**why of where**" is critical – explanations for why a spatial pattern occurs. Sometimes geographers ask questions about how particular human patterns came about, so that specific places become distinct from all others.

Often these patterns and places combine into regions – large areas that may be compared to other large areas. Some patterns and places may reach many areas of the world so that geographers may comment on the effects of globalization. Spatial organization defines human life on earth, with all of its similarities and differences, and the spatial analysis tradition is an integral part of the geographical perspective.

GEOGRAPHY AS A FIELD OF STUDY

Geography was first given structure as a field of study by the ancient Greeks from the words *geo*, "the earth", and *graphein,* "to write." Several scientists described the parts of the known world, and used a combination of mathematics, explorers' reports, rumors, and assumptions to draw maps of the world. The Greeks also laid the foundations for **cartography,** the art and science of map-making. Of course, the maps were much more accurate for the areas around Greece than they were for other parts of the world. A good example is a reconstructed map by Hecataeus, who lived in the late 6th and early 5th centuries B.C.E. One of the great unsolved mysteries of his day was the shape and extent of the southern part of the African land mass. Some scientists believed that it eventually widened and connected to East Asia. The Greeks understood that the earth was round, with Ptolemy estimating in the 2nd century C.E. that the circumference of the earth was about 16,000 miles. He was about 9,000 miles short of reality, an assumption that led Christopher Columbus to believe that he was near Asia when he first landed in the Americas.

Geography was and still is of interest to people in many lands. For example, the ancient Chinese studied geography, although they apparently did not have contact with Mediterranean geographers until much later. Also, while Europeans during the Middle Ages (500-1400 C.E.) lost touch with Greek and Roman geographical knowledge, Muslim scholars in the Middle East built on that knowledge to describe and analyze their known world. These Arab geographers were often great travellers, and they searched the Eastern Hemisphere for new knowledge. Although they were most interested in practical knowledge of locations, places, and products, these scholars proposed theories about the evolution of mountain ranges.

Geography was reborn in Europe in the 17th century as a broad study of both physical landscapes and the roles that humans play in shaping them. The modern scientific study of geography began in Germany during the 17th century, as European power began to slowly spread over much of the globe. In the 1700s, the German philosopher and geographer **Immanuel Kant** defined geography as the study of interrelated spatial patterns – the description and explanation of differences and similarities between one region and another. By the end of the 18th century, place could be determined and described by using lines of latitude and longitude, and maps were becoming much more accurate and reliable. By the turn of the 20th century, students in universities throughout Europe were studying geography as a distinct discipline.

As geography became more and more specialized throughout the 20th century, many sub-fields emerged, including cultural, social, urban, population, medical, economic, and political geography. However, today the field may be divided into two great branches: physical and human geography.

Human geography focuses on people. Where are they? How are they alike and different? How do they interact? How do they change the natural landscapes, and how do they use them? Because other fields of study – such as history, sociology, economics, and political science – also deal with human behavior, human geography often overlaps and interacts with these disciplines.

Hecataeus's Map of The World. Hecataeus was a Greek historian who lived from about 550 to 476 B.C.E. He described the countries and inhabitants of the known world, and included a map to illustrate where they lived. Hecataeus's map was based on Anaximander's earlier map of the earth, which he corrected and enlarged. Notice how much more accurate the map is in the area around Greece.

Whereas human geography emphasizes people and the way they interact with their natural environment, **physical geography** focuses on the natural environment itself. For example, a physical geographer might study mountains, glaciers, coastlines, climates, soils, plants, and animals. Of course, neither human nor physical geography could exist without the other because the two fields inevitably intersect and interact, making them inextricably bound to one another.

KEY GEOGRAPHICAL SKILLS

In order to understand the geographical perspective, students must learn key skills that help to organize and manipulate concepts. These skills include learning to use the vocabulary of geographers as well as those all-important tools – maps.

MAPS AND SPATIAL DATA

All geographers are very interested in the way places and things are arranged and organized on the surface of the earth. This common bond – the **spatial perspective** – means that they notice patterns of both natural and human environments, distributions of people, and locations of all kinds of objects. Words can describe space, and so some geographical data may be communicated through written and spoken language; however, the map is a powerful geographical tool that is almost as old as geography itself. Why describe something when you can draw a picture of it? Mapmaking (cartography) is a time-honored skill that has developed an incredible degree of precision and adaptability.

Absolute and Relative Location

Maps show us two types of location:

- **Absolute location** – Maps provide the exact location of a place on a mathematical grid of the earth divided by two sets of imaginary arcs: **meridians** and **parallels.** A meridian is an arc drawn between the North and South Poles that measures **longitude,** a numbering system that calculates distance east and west of the **prime meridian**. The prime meridian is located at the observatory in Greenwich, England at 0°. The meridian at the opposite side of the globe is 180°, and all meridians placed in between are designated as either "east" or "west" of the prime meridian. A parallel is a circle drawn around the globe

SOME FAMOUS GEOGRAPHERS

Throughout the centuries, many curious people have studied and written about geography. Below is a list of some geographers that have shaped the way that millions of others have come to see the globe.

Eratosthenes, a Greek scholar who worked in the third century B.C.E., accurately calculated the circumference of the earth by measuring the sun's angles at the summer solstice (June 21) at two points along the Nile River – Alexandria and Syene. He used geometry to conclude the circumference based on the distance between the two cities and the angle of the sun at each place.

Ptolemy, a Greek scholar who lived five hundred years later than Eratosthenes, recalculated the circumference of the earth to be much smaller – by about 9,000 miles. He was wrong, but his mistake was taken as truth for hundreds of years. Despite his famous miscalculations, his *Guide to Geography* included many rough maps of landmasses and bodies of water, and he developed a global grid system that was a forerunner to our modern system of latitude and longitude.

Idrisi, an 11th century Arab geographer, worked for the king of Sicily to collect geographical information into a remarkably accurate representation of the world. Under Idrisi's direction, an academy of geographers gathered maps, consulted mariners and travelers, and went out on their own scientific expeditions. Although the final world map that they assembled is lost, much of the information and many partial and sectional maps have survived.

George Perkins Marsh, a 19th century American geographer, is best known for his classic work, *Man and Nature,* published in 1864. He focused on the impact of human actions on the natural environment, so his thinking is basic to the field of Human Geography. He emphasized human destruction of the environment, and used the conversion of ancient Mesopotamia from a "Fertile Crescent" to a vast barren desert. Marsh's message is a familiar one to us today: Conserve the earth, or live to pay the disastrous consequences.

Carl Sauer, an early 20th century geographer from California, shaped the field of Human Geography by arguing that cultural landscapes (products of interactions between humans and their environments) should be the main focus of geographic study. His methods of landscape analysis provided a lens for interpreting cultural landscapes as directly and indirectly altered over time as a result of human activity. His study is basic to environmental geography, a field that centers on the interaction of human and physical geography.

parallel to the **equator,** an imaginary circle that lies exactly half way between the North and the South Poles. Parallels measure **latitude,** or distance north and south of the equator. The equator is 0° latitude, the North Pole is 90° north latitude, and the South Pole is 90° south latitude. So any absolute location of a place on the surface of earth may be described in terms of longitude and latitude. For example, New York City is located at 74° west longitude and 41° north latitude.

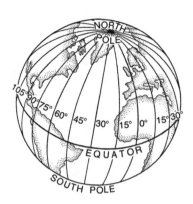

Lines of Latitude. Meridians drawn between the North and South Poles measure longitude, a numbering system that calculates distance east and west of the prime meridian.

- **Relative location** – All places on earth also have relative locations – spots relative to other human and physical features on the landscape. In other words, where does the country of Chile lie relative to Brazil? or Argentina? Where does the Caspian Sea lie in relation to the Black Sea? or the Mediterranean Sea? Relative location is important to think about because it defines a place in terms of how central or isolated it is in relation to other places. For example, if you were to study a map of Central Asia in the 13th Century, you would find an important city called Samarkand that lay on a major trade route called the Silk Road that stretched out in both directions, making the city central to Eurasian trade. Once sea-based trade became faster and more efficient, the Silk Road trade withered away, leaving Samarkand a shrinking, isolated place, far from the center of commerce. So Samarkand's relative location changed, although its absolute location has stayed the same. Today modern cities wax and wane not only in size, but also in levels of prosperity and types of activities as their relative locations change.

Use of Maps

Geographers use maps in two basic ways:

- **Reference material** – Maps are efficient tools for storing information. Once a map is drawn, it may be pulled out to help find relative locations of places. Maps show roads or waterways that connect places, and for centuries travelers have used them. For example, 16th century European explorers used maps to help them cross the Atlantic Ocean, just as 21st century Americans use maps to visit vacation destinations.

- **Communications/education** – Maps may also be used to explain spatial perspectives to others. These maps are often thematic because they are designed to explain a type of geographic information. Examples are maps that show soil types, relative elevations, economic prosperity levels, and spatial arrangements of racial and ethnic groups.

A Changed Relative Location. Although it was once one of the grandest cities in the world due to its location on the Silk Road, today Samarkand is only the third largest city in Uzbekistan.

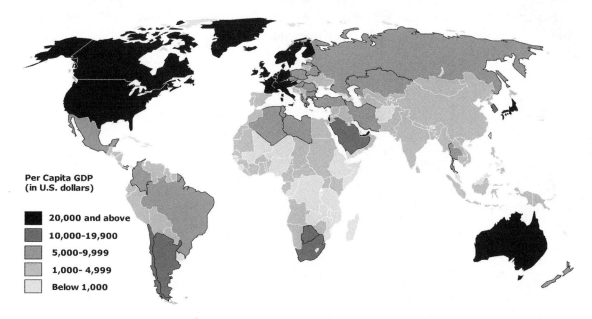

Per Capital GDP. The map above is meant to communicate information about various economic prosperity levels of countries around the world.

(Reference: International Monetary Fund, 2008 estimates)

Map Projections

An important problem with communicating information through maps is that the only accurate representation of earth is a globe. When spatial information is presented on a flat piece of paper, a cartographer immediately faces the issue of **distortion** caused by trying to represent a three-dimensional object (the earth) on a two-dimensional surface (a flat map). Different methods have been devised to increase accuracy, but it is impossible to avoid some type of distortion. Inaccuracies may take several different forms: the shapes of areas, the distances between places, the relative size of different areas, or the direction from one place to another. A correction for one usually results in a distortion of another. For example, if the cartographer concentrates on getting the shapes right, often the distances between the shapes become inaccurate. As a result, the best map **projection** (method of transferring locations on earth's surface to a flat map) depends on how you are using the map.

Three common map projections are:

1. **The Mercator projection** was invented by Flemish cartographer Gerardus Mercator in 1569 for a specific purpose – navigating ships across the Atlantic Ocean between Europe and the Americas. Mercator designed parallels and meridians to cross one another at right angles, just as they do on the globe. As a result, the direction is true everywhere on his map, a very important fact for anyone traveling east to west, or vice versa, on the Atlantic. The Mercator map was designed as an aid to navigators since straight lines on the Mercator projection are loxodromes or rhumb lines – representing lines of constant compass bearing – perfect for "true" direction. If a navigator wishes to sail from Spain to the West Indies, all they have to do is draw a line between the two points and the navigator knows which compass direction to continually sail to reach their destination. However, the Mercator projection distorts size of areas, particularly as you get closer to the North and South Poles. Why? Imagine trying to place a whole orange peel on a flat piece of paper. The middle of the peel (the equator) would stay relative intact, but the ends would have to be stretched or cut to make them lie flat. As a result, Antarctica in the south and Greenland in the north look huge on a Mercator projection. Since 16th century European explorers were generally headed east or west in the middle latitudes, this gross distortion of size in the north and south made little difference to them.

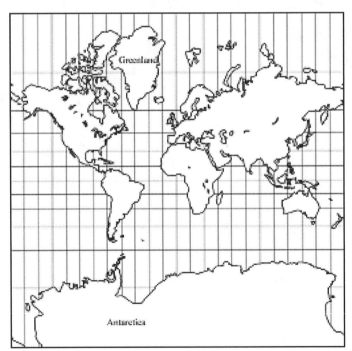

The Mercator Projection: Notice how large Antarctica and Greenland appear.

2. **The Robinson projection** (opposite page) tries to correct for this distortion in the high north and south latitudes by curving these areas inward on the paper. The meridians curve gently, avoiding extremes, but thereby stretch the poles into long lines instead of leaving them as points. As a result, distortion close to the poles is severe but quickly declines to moderate levels

moving away from them. Shapes are not distorted very badly within about 45° north or south of the equator or within about 45° of the map's central meridian. The Robinson projection is an attempt to balance all distortions by making errors in all four ways: shape, size, distance, and direction. As a result, it is a good projection for general use, and is often used for wall maps in classrooms.

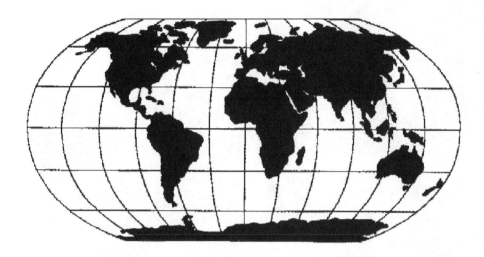

The Robinson Projection. The northernmost and southernmost areas are more true to size than they are on the Mercator Projection, because the lines of longitude have been curved to more closely resemble a globe.

3. **The Peters projection** – This controversial projection was first introduced in 1974 by historian and geographer Arno Peters. The Peters map focuses on keeping land masses equal in area. As a result, the shapes are distorted, resulting in an overall map that seems quite unfamiliar to most viewers. However, other projections have made Africa and Latin America appear to be smaller than they really are, so supporters of the Peters Projection believe that it corrects misconceptions based on the Mercator and Robinson projections.

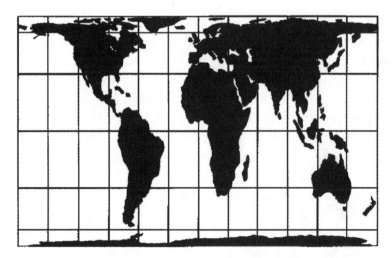

The Peters Projection. This map is controversial largely because it distorts the familiar shapes of the continents and other large landmasses. However, the map accurately compares land masses in terms of area. For example, notice how much larger South America appears in proportion to North America than it does on the other projections. Africa also gains size in comparison to Eurasia.

A special type of map is a **contour map,** designed to reveal the nature of local **topography** (the natural land surface). Contours are lines that are drawn to represent a consistent height above sea level. The spacing between the lines helps the map reader to determine the height of mountains and the depth of valleys, as well as the slopes that lead up to mountain peaks or down to the valleys. The farther apart the contour lines, the gentler the slope. Contour maps are useful for hikers as they make their way through rough terrain, and for engineers or developers as they determine the best place to construct buildings or homes.

Contour Map. The map above shows the topography of the Swamp Canyon Trail in Bryce Canyon National Park, Utah. (***Reference:*** U.S. Government National Park Service)

SCALE

Scale is an important conceptual tool for geography. Generally, it has two meanings:

- **Size of the unit studied** – Geographers refer to phenomena as they exist on different levels from small to large. For example, they may refer to a problem, such as drought, on a **local scale**, **regional scale**, or **global scale**. If the drought is highly localized, with other areas around the place under study being drought-free, it is an entirely different problem from a drought that affects an entire region. A situation may begin as a local phenomenon, but become regional, or even global, as time goes by. For example, when Mount St. Helens in Washington state erupted in 1980, the immediate concern was for the area just around the mountain. However, as ash and rock continued to flow, a cloud of volcanic matter traveled first to the region, and eventually to other areas of the globe. Many scientists argue that volcanic eruptions should be studied on a global scale, because they often affect faraway places.

- **Map scale** – Scale also tells us the mathematical relationship between the size of an area on a map and its actual size on the surface of the earth. Scale is a feature of every map, so it is important for understanding what is shown on the map. A map may show a small area of the earth, such as one town or city, so that every feature – such as a street or a building – appears much larger than it would on a map of a larger area. A map with a smaller scale shows a region or continent, and a map of the entire world is on a smaller scale still. The level of detail that a map shows depends on its scale. When it is important to know specifics, such as which way to turn on a small street, large-scale maps are best. If it is more important to show broad patterns or general relationships, small-scale maps are more helpful. Most maps include the scale in the legend, and it may be presented as a fraction (1/10,000), a ratio (1:10,000), or a graphic bar scale as pictured below.

With both definitions, scale implies the degree of generalization represented. Geographers may ask broad or narrow questions, and the maps they need depend on the questions they have. Scale affects our perceptions of accuracy and truth. For example, a map of the United States that shows population density by state will make the state appear to have an even population distribution within its borders. A map on a larger scale (for example, county by county) will reveal that some areas are more densely settled than others. Likewise, a map of the United States that shows the average income of people who live in each state will disguise the fact that people in some areas of a state are wealthier than others. A map that shows average income by zip code would illustrate the variations within the state. Even though we may separate scale into local, regional, and global levels, in reality the levels interact in a **local-global continuum**, in which phenomena at one level influence those at other levels.

TIME ZONES

Longitude plays an important role in calculating time. The earth is divided into 360 degrees of longitude (180° west of the **prime meridian,** and 180° east). The prime meridian is set by international agreement on a line of longitude that runs through Greenwich, England, and lines of longitude are spaced 15° apart in both directions (east and west) from it. A **time zone** is a region that has adopted the same standard time, usually referred to as the **local time**. Because the sun hits the earth at different times as it spins on its axis, time zones are meant to make time more uniform. Most adjacent time zones are exactly one hour apart, and by convention compute their local time as an offset from **Greenwich Mean Time,** or the standard time at the prime meridian. For example, 12 p.m. is midday everywhere, a time when the sun is high in the sky. Likewise 12 midnight is night everywhere, since the sun is shining on the other side of the earth. This uniformity can only be reached if time zones – and clocks – change as one travels on either side of the prime meridian.

Standard time zones are defined by geometrically subdividing the earth into 24 sections bordered by meridians each 15° of longitude apart. The local time in neighboring zones is then exactly one hour different. Time zones often stray from the meridians for practical purposes, such as following political borders so that people in the same country (or state) follow the same standard time. For example, the People's Republic of China has only one time zone, although the country's borders stretch east to west across many meridians. Many areas have also adopted **daylight savings time**, which pushes the clock forward one hour in the spring in order to allow people to enjoy more sunlight in the afternoon during the warm spring and summer months, especially for people after they get off work. The clock is then set back to the original standard time in the fall.

One consequence of the organization of the world into time zones is that somewhere on the globe the date has to change. This occurs at 180° longitude, also called the **International Date Line** that divides the world from pole to pole through the Pacific Ocean. If a traveler crosses the line headed from Asia to America, she sets the clock back 24 hours; likewise, a traveler crossing the line headed from America to Asia will set the clock ahead 24 hours.

Before the adoption of time zones, people used local **solar time**, based on the position of the sun in the sky as the day progresses. As railways and communications connected people in different regions during the 19th century, differences in local times became problematic. Governments in many countries synchronized the clocks in all localities, so that travellers could more easily adjust to time changes, and so that communications could be standardized. Time zones still allow local time to approximate the mean solar time. For example, four time zones were created in the United States in 1883 – Pacific Standard Time, Mountain Standard Time, Central Standard Time, and Eastern Standard Time – with Pacific Standard Time set three hours earlier than Eastern Standard Time.

INTERPRETATION OF PLACES AND PATTERNS

To geographers, the seemingly simple term "**place**" is deceptively complex. Briefly defined, place is the unique location of a geographic feature. As a result, each point, or place, on earth is different from all others. Its uniqueness may be identified in four ways: place name, site, situation, and absolute location.

- **Place name** – Most places on earth have names or **toponyms** – that distinguish them from others. Some names reflect history. For example, many places in the eastern United States have the word "new" as part of their name. Settlers that came from "England," or "York," or "Jersey" named their new homes "New England," or "New York," or "New Jersey," reflecting the historical migration of people from Britain to North America in the 17th and 18th centuries. Other names are simply – often hopefully – descriptive, like "Springfield," or "Pleasantville," or "Three Rivers." Still others invite a map reader to find out the story behind the name, like "Medicine Hat" or "Yellow Knife." The point is that humans name places to distinguish them from other places, an action that helps to define the uniqueness of each place.
- **Site** – Location may also be defined by site – the physical and human-transformed characteristics of a place. **Physical site characteristics** include climate, topography, soil, water sources, vegetation, and elevation. Site features have usually been important for people in choosing a place to live. Many of the earliest civilizations were centered on rivers, not only for water sources but also for transportation purposes. Rich soil is important for farmers, and hilltops are good choices for people looking for defense from enemy attack. An important site characteristic for Britain is that it is an island off the larger land mass of Europe – a fact that has affected the British people throughout their history. Being an island was quite helpful when Napoleon and Hitler were on the march, since this site characteristic probably saved the British from invasion in both cases. Additionally, being an island has limited Britain's natural resources for growth, a site characteristic that has encouraged British political leaders to take to the seas to find those resources. Humans may transform sites to suit their needs so that the sites are part of the human mosaic, not the physical site itself. Examples are airports, street patterns, public parks, and sports facilities.
- **Situation** – This characteristic refers to relative location. As mentioned earlier, relative location is important in determining the centrality or isolation of a place, a fact that is

highly subject to change. Additionally, situation helps us to find an unfamiliar place by comparing its location to a place that we know. If you are giving directions to a person that does not know a place location, you usually start with what he or she does know. For example, you may start with the main street in town to begin giving directions to a smaller street.

- **Absolute location** – A place may be located by mathematically calculating its location using latitude and longitude. Because meridians and parallels allow us to be very precise, absolute location is unique for every place on earth.

Another important type of spatial data is **pattern**, or the arrangement of objects on earth's surface in relation to other objects. Pattern refers to distribution, like the number of towns that appear along a river and how they are spaced. If the pattern is along straight lines, like rivers, streets, or railroad tracks, the arrangement is **linear.** If objects circle another object, they form a **centralized pattern.** For example, in an Islamic city, houses and public buildings may circle around the mosque, or house of worship. A **random pattern** exists if no regular distribution can be seen.

One type of geographic pattern – a checkerboard rural pattern – may be seen from a plane that is flying above much of the midsection of the United States. The lands are laid out in sections that are separated by types of crops or grazing that takes place, and roads often follow the grid. This **grid** or **rectilinear pattern** reflects a rectangular system of land survey adopted in much of the country under the Ordinance of 1785. Since the towns were laid out in much the same way, many streets form grids, sometimes labeled "1st", "2nd", "3rd" streets, and so on.

REGIONS AND REGIONALIZATION

Even though every place on earth has its own uniqueness, patterns among places lead us to generalize to areas around them. If similarities are apparent, we may conclude that spatial regularities exist within an area that geographers call a **region.** If we begin to compare regions for similarities and differences, then **regionalization** – the organization of earth's surface into distinct areas that are viewed as different from other areas – takes place.

One way to think about regions is to categorize them into **formal, functional,** or **perceptual regions.**

- **Formal regions** – Sometimes called uniform regions, a formal region is an area that has striking similarities in terms of one or a few physical or cultural features. A good example is a formal political region created when a government draws imaginary lines (that may follow natural features like rivers) around an area, calling it a "state," or a "province." One state or province, then, becomes distinct from another. Formal regions may also be defined by cultural characteristics, such as language or religion. For example, in the Middle East, a geographer could regionalize by using political boundaries, and refer to "Iraq," "Iran," and "Saudi Arabia." Another method of regionalizing in the area is to refer to all as "Muslim lands," in contrast to other regions where other religions prevail. On a smaller scale, regionalization could be based on a division of the area between inhabitants who are "Sunni" or "Shiite" Muslims. If the regions are based on religion, the characteristic is predominant, but not universal. In other words, some Shiites might live in Sunni lands and vice versa.

- **Functional regions** – Sometimes called nodal regions, functional regions are areas organized around cores, or nodes. Visually, the space can be seen as having interdependent parts that all operate together and connect, but with a center that directs the movements and characteristics of non-central parts. The **core** area has distinct characteristics that lessen in intensity as one travels into the **periphery**, or the region's margins. A city often forms the core of a region. For example, Denver, a U.S. city in the state of Colorado (a formal region), is the center of trade, transportation, business, and culture for a region that extends beyond the formal borders of the state. People in Wyoming might follow Denver's baseball team (the Rockies), but probably not in as great numbers as people that live in Denver. Likewise, *The Denver Post,* a newspaper produced in Denver is read in many towns and rural areas in its periphery. As you travel west from Denver, you will eventually venture into the peripheral areas of Salt Lake City, a core that exerts its own influences throughout a large area of the formal region known as "Utah."

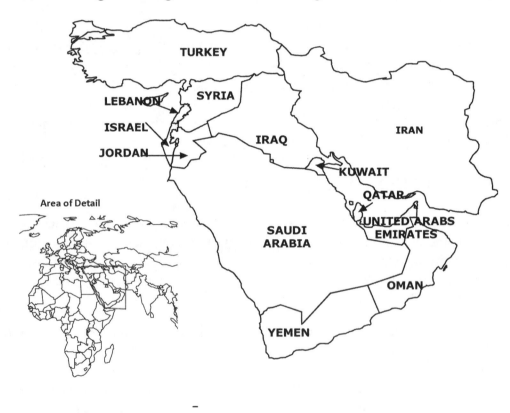

Formal Regions in the Middle East. Formal regions are often designated by governments to mark boundaries that define political authority and differentiate political states from one another.

- **Perceptual regions** – Sometimes called vernacular regions, perceptual regions are not as rigorously structured as formal and functional regions. Instead, they are places that people *believe* to exist as a part of their cultural identity. They reflect feelings and images more than any objective reality, such as physical features, formal political boundaries, or economic centers. Almost all human beings define their lives by thinking about perceptual regions. For example, despite the fact that the Korean peninsula is divided into two formal regions (North Korea and South Korea), the people of the area have a long history of cultural identity as "Koreans" with a common language and similar customs that distinguish them from the nearby region of "Japan." Physical geography certainly has played a role in the development of these perceptions, since Korea is a peninsula and the region called Japan is a series of islands. However, even if Koreans move to Japanese cities, or Japanese move to Korean cities, they shape their new spaces in terms of perceptual regions. Another example on a smaller scale is the appearance of a "Little Italy" or "Little Chinatown" in many American cities. Cultural perceptions shape the way people view their spaces.

INTERCONNECTIONS AMONG PLACES

Places connect to form patterns, and patterns connect to form regions. Likewise, regions connect to form broader regions that eventually connect to other parts of the globe. It's all a matter of scale, and geographers may alter their lens to focus locally, regionally, or globally. For many reasons, global connections are rapidly growing through a process called **globalization** – the expansion of economic, political, and cultural activities to the point that they reach and have impact on many areas of the world. Geographers use the term **space-time compression** to describe the changes that rapid connections among places and regions have brought. Distant places are brought much closer not only through faster transportation and communication, but through new technologies – such as televisions and computers – that bring images from those places into our homes, businesses, and schools.

One type of evidence for globalization in the political realm is the increasing number of international organizations that have appeared in recent decades. Although the world is still organized by national governments, international organizations such as the United Nations and the European Union are now significant players in world politics. Economic globalization is apparent through the proliferation of **multi-national corporations** that have centers of operation in many parts of the globe. Well-known examples are Coca-Cola, McDonald's, and the Disney Corporation. Television broadcast companies, such as CNN and the BBC, also operate internationally. Cultural globalization manifests itself in popular music, television, and film that spread American culture across the globe.

Critics of globalization sometimes fear that globalization is a threat to regional and local uniqueness. For example, a few years ago French farmers dumped manure in the roads leading to EuroDisney outside Paris to protest American influence. On the other hand, local and regional uniqueness show few signs of disappearing. Instead, the spatial view of earth as a web of interconnected places, from local to global, still accurately describes the geographer's lens on the world.

NEW GEOGRAPHIC TECHNOLOGIES

For many years maps have served as important tools for storing and sharing geographic information. In the past few decades, two important technologies – GIS (geographic information system) and GPS (global positioning system) – have been developed to advance geographical knowledge.

A **GIS (geographic information system)** is a computer system that captures, stores, analyzes, and displays data. GIS measures the position of an object on earth and stores it in a computer along with countless other specific measurements. The geographer may manipulate this data to combine them into an image or a map that is more accurate than anything drawn by hand. Each type of information may be stored in a layer, and then layers may be combined to present the overall image. For example, one layer may show soil composition, another may show forest cover, and yet another the road system in an area. Most maps combine several layers and provide a great deal of information that can be altered by adding or subtracting layers. The layers may be analyzed as they interact, and may be used to solve a multitude of problems, such as soil erosion, water pollution, or the viability of building houses on hillsides.

A **GPS (global positioning system)** uses a series of satellites, tracking stations, and receivers to determine precise absolute locations on earth. Remote-sensing satellites orbiting the earth scan the surface, and then transmit digital images to receiving stations on earth. Images of tiny areas are organized by pixels (picture elements) to create larger images or maps. Although the technology has vast untapped potential for geographers, they already use GPS to map vegetation arrangements and gather data for the ice cover around the North and South Poles. GPS technology is also used to navigate airplanes and ships, and most recently, it is used in automobiles to guide drivers as they try to reach their destinations.

HOW GEOGRAPHERS WORK: FIELD AND CENSUS DATA

Geographers gather their data and get their ideas from many different places. Their methods are reflected in the variety of jobs that geographers have. Many teach in secondary schools and universities, and others work for local, state, or national governments where they may analyze water, minerals, weather, climate, or soil. Recently, geographers have helped fill a demand for environmental managers and technicians. They sometimes consult with builders, architects, or politicians on the impact of human projects on the environment. A knowledge of geography is important to people in health care, transportation, population studies, economic development, and international studies.

Field-based skills refer to the ability to gather, assemble, and analyze data that may affirm, alter, or contradict conventional wisdom in the field. Field-based observations are directly made by the geographer, and go beyond simply reading and understanding the observations of others.

Field-based skills include:
- Familiarity with and ability to manipulate and interpret GIS
- Familiarity with GPS and ability to use remote sensing data
- Cartography and computer mapping
- Competence in data analysis and problem-solving

One of the biggest employers of geographers in the United States is the **U.S. Census Bureau.** Every ten years since 1790, the U.S. government has collected information about the country's inhabitants and compiled a census report. In modern day census forms are mailed to millions of homes in all 50 states, the District of Columbia, and Puerto Rico. Census workers try to count people without permanent residences, but this is a difficult task, particularly in large cities. Data collected from the census includes information about age, race, gender, language, education, employment, income, and housing. This data is useful to many social scientists, including geographers. Today geographers analyze massive amounts of data and arrange and display it in many different types of maps that reflect the nation's changing geographical characteristics.

More than anything, geographic skills are based on keen and careful observations of the world at different scales, a curiosity about why objects are where they are, and the desire to see the world through a geographer's eyes.

TERMS AND CONCEPTS

absolute location
cartography
circular pattern
cultural landscapes
daylight savings time
distortion
environmental geography
equator
Eratosthenes
formal regions
functional (nodal) regions
GIS
globalization
Greenwich Mean Time
GPS
grid pattern
Hecataeus
human geography
Idrisi
Kant, Immanuel
landscapes
latitude
linear pattern
local time
location
longitude
Marsh, George Perkins
Mercator projection
meridian
multi-national corporations
parallel
pattern
perceptual (vernacular) regions
periphery
Peters projection
place
physical geography
physical site characteristic
prime meridian
Ptolemy
random pattern
regionalization
Robinson projection

Sauer, Carl
scale
site
situation
solar time
space
space time compression
spatial organization
spatial perspective
time zone
topography
toponym
U.S. Census Bureau
"why of where"

MULTIPLE-CHOICE QUESTIONS
UNIT ONE

Questions 1 and 2 refer to the following statement.

This computer system captures, stores, analyzes, and displays data. It measures the position of an object on earth and stores it in a computer along with countless other specific measurements. Each type of information may be stored in a layer, and then layers may be combined to present the overall image.

1. The statement above refers to which of the following?

   (A) a GIS
   (B) a local-global continuum
   (C) U.S. Census tracting
   (D) a GPS
   (E) a spatial data pattern

2. The computer system identified in #1 would most likely be helpful in solving problems related to

   (A) navigation of airplanes and ships
   (B) identification of ethnic settlement patterns
   (C) core-periphery relationships
   (D) the viability of building houses on hillsides
   (E) determination of precise absolute locations on earth

3. Which of the following is an example of the spatial analysis tradition in geography?

   (A) natural vegetation on hillsides
   (B) a checkerboard pattern created by agricultural use of land
   (C) the sizes of major oceans
   (D) the number of ships constructed in New England
   (E) flight patterns of birds in migration

4. All of the following are correct statements about time zones EXCEPT:

   (A) Time zones are geometrically subdivided by meridians each 15° of longitude apart.
   (B) The local time in neighboring zones is exactly one hour different.
   (C) The organization of the world into time zones requires that somewhere on the globe the date has
       to change.
   (D) Many areas have adopted daylight savings time during spring and summer months.
   (E) The People's Republic of China has more time zones than the United States does because China
       is a larger country.

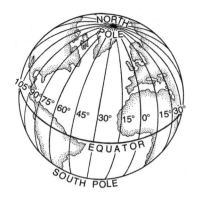

5. The meridians shown on the map above calculate the

(A) distance north and south of the equator
(B) relative location of bodies of water to land masses
(C) distance east and west of the prime meridian
(D) arrangement of objects on earth's surface in relationship to one another
(E) organization of earth's surface into distinct areas that are viewed as different from other areas

6. A special type of map designed to reveal the nature of local topography is called a

(A) Peters projection map
(B) Robinson projection map
(C) local-global continuum map
(D) reference map
(E) contour map

7. Which of the following is NOT a physical site characteristic?

(A) the location of a smaller street in relation to a main street
(B) amount of rainfall
(C) type of soil
(D) elevation
(E) type of vegetation

8. Mathematical calculations using latitude and longitude allow us to determine the

(A) relative location of a particular place
(B) physical site characteristics of all places on earth
(C) toponym of a particular place
(D) absolute location of a particular place
(E) arrangement of objects on earth's surface

9. The map above describes the countries and inhabitants of the world, as known to

(A) Europeans during the Middle Ages
(B) Ancient Greeks
(C) Muslim scholars in the Middle East
(D) German scholars during the 17th century
(E) Arab geographers during the 18th century

10. Which of the following is a type of region categorization that emphasizes the relationship between core and peripheral areas?

(A) formal regions
(B) uniform regions
(C) functional regions
(D) perceptual regions
(E) vernacular regions

11. Which of the following modern trends is most directly responsible for the phenomenon of space-time compression?

(A) regionalization
(B) globalization
(C) democratization
(D) fragmentation
(E) acculturation

12. Which of the following would be best illustrated by a large-scale map?

   (A) the arrangement of streets in a village
   (B) major road crossings in a town
   (C) connecting highways between towns in a region
   (D) major highways that connect regions in a large country
   (E) connections among major world cities

13. If it is midnight at the prime meridian, then at the International Date Line it is

   (A) midnight of the previous day
   (B) midnight of the following day
   (C) 6 P.M.
   (D) 6 A.M.
   (E) noon

14. If it is 9 A.M. in New York City, what time would it be in Los Angeles (assuming both are on standard time)?

   (A) noon
   (B) 10 A.M.
   (C) 6 A.M.
   (D) 1 P.M.
   (E) 7 A.M.

15. Which of the following characteristics of a place is most important in determining its centrality or isolation?

   (A) absolute location
   (B) physical site characteristics
   (C) toponym
   (D) relative location
   (E) pattern

16. The art and science of mapmaking is called

   (A) cartography
   (B) topography
   (C) physical geography
   (D) spatial analysis
   (E) territorial morphology

17. Which of the following is the most important function of a toponym?

(A) to define the mathematical relationship between the size of an area on a map and its actual size
(B) to define a location relative to other human and physical features on the landscape
(C) to distinguish a particular place from other places on earth
(D) to identify similarities of physical or cultural features within a region
(E) to determine precise absolute locations on earth

18. The U.S. government agency most directly responsible for counting and collecting information about the country's inhabitants is the

(A) Office of Administration
(B) Office of Management and Budget
(C) Department of Health and Human Services
(D) Census Bureau
(E) Federal Reserve Board

19. Linear, centralized, random, and grid patterns help to define the

(A) position of something on earth's surface
(B) arrangement of objects on earth's surface in relation to other objects
(C) distance between objects on a map and the distance between objects on earth's surface
(D) organization of earth's surface into distinct areas
(E) physical gap or distance between two objects

20. The geographer who first calculated the earth's circumference with relative accuracy was

(A) Ptolemy
(B) Idrisi
(C) George Perkins Marsh
(D) Carl Sauer
(E) Eratosthenes

UNIT ONE FREE-RESPONSE QUESTION

All map projections attempt to represent a three-dimensional object (the earth) on a two-dimensional surface (a flat map). Three common projections are the Mercator projection, the Robinson projection, and the Peters projection.

    a. Describe one advantage of using the Mercator projection. Describe one disadvantage of using the Mercator projection.

    b. Describe one advantage of using the Robinson projection. Describe one disadvantage of using the Robinson projection.

    c. Describe one advantage of using the Peters projection. Describe one disadvantage of using the Peters projection.

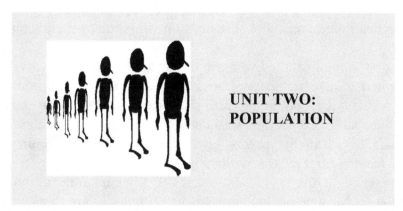

**UNIT TWO:
POPULATION**

By late 2011 or early 2012, the population of the world surpassed seven billion, with more people living on the planet than in any other time in history. The 20th century saw a "population explosion," with population increases so staggering that many scholars have warned of disastrous consequences in the near future. Although the consequences of this growth are controversial, we can be sure that the increases will continue, and that in the future the earth will be home to billions more human beings.

The study of population is called **demography,** a term derived from the ancient Greek words *demos*, meaning population or people, and *graphe*, meaning to describe. Demography is of interest to many social science disciplines including geography, with its special emphasis on spatial organization: the location of places, people, and events, and the connections among places and landscapes. **Population geography** focuses on the number, composition, and distribution of human beings on earth's surface. Population geographers are interested in population changes – both growth and movement – especially as they relate to the earth's environment and natural resources.

GEOGRAPHICAL ANALYSIS OF POPULATION

From the very beginning, people have been distributed unevenly over the planet's surface. Population geographers study *where* people are found, including the *places* where population is growing and how rapidly population growth is occurring. Geographers also explain *why* population rates are different in different places. It is important to view population on different scales: local, regional, and global. For example, the rapid overall increase in the world's population is much more meaningful if you analyze why some regions and localities are more threatened than others by overpopulation.

DISTRIBUTION, DENSITY, AND SCALE

The **distribution** of population refers to the arrangement of locations on the earth's surface where people live. The billions of people on earth are distributed very unevenly, with some land areas nearly uninhabited, others sparsely settled, and still others densely populated. About half of the world's people live in rural areas, and about half live in or near cities, although the definition of what constitutes a city varies from place to place. Population maps may be drawn at different scales, usually in the form of **dot maps**, with each dot representing a certain number of people. On the largest scale – for example, a rural county in the United States – such a map may actually show the location of every individual, with each dot representing one person. On a medium scale, such as a single country, a dot might represent 5,000 people. On the smallest scale – a map of the world – a dot often represents 100,000 people. These dots measure **population density**, or the number of people that live in a given area of land.

Looking at population distribution on a global scale, some important general conclusions include:

- Almost 90% of all people live north of the equator; only 10% live in the southern hemisphere. There are many reasons for this uneven distribution, but one important factor is that more land on the earth's surface lies north of the equator.
- More than half of all people live on about 5% of the land, and almost nine-tenths on less than 20%. Rapidly growing urban areas increasingly dominate the globe, with people leaving rural areas and clustering in cities and towns.
- Most people live in areas close to sea level. The higher the altitude, the fewer the inhabitants. Most arable land is at lower altitudes, as are areas closest to rivers and oceans, providing access to water and transportation.
- About two-thirds of world population is concentrated within 300 miles of the ocean. Many that live inland settle in river valleys. Since the beginning, humans have congregated around bodies of water, and that pattern is still evident in the world today.

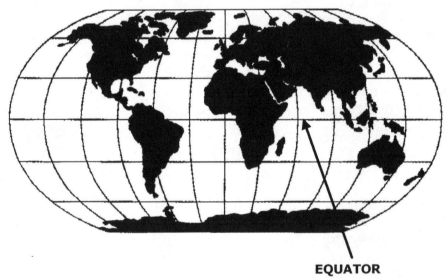

EQUATOR

Land and Population Distribution. Notice how much land mass is north of the equator, helping to explain the fact that 90% of all people live in the Northern Hemisphere.

ARITHMETIC AND PHYSIOLOGICAL POPULATION DENSITY

Population density may be computed in several ways, including the calculation of arithmetic density and physiological density. Both measures help geographers to describe the distribution of people in comparison to natural resources available.

Arithmetic (or crude) density, or the total number of people divided by total land area, is the measure most often used by geographers. For example, the United States has about 310 million people and about 9,600,000 square kilometers of land space. As a result, the U.S. has an arithmetic density of 32 people per square kilometer (310 million divided by 9,600,000). We may compare the arithmetic density of individual countries in order to get an idea about how population is distributed.

COMPARATIVE ARITHMETIC POPULATION DENSITY

Country	Arithmetic Density (per square kilometer)
Singapore	7197
South Korea	505
United Kingdom	253
Nigeria	171
Turkey	93
Nicaragua	45
United States	32
Argentina	15
Canada	3

Source: www.worldatlas.com, 2010 estimates

As useful as arithmetic density is, it does not tell us anything about population distribution within individual countries. Clearly, most countries include both urban and rural areas, with large variations in population distributions. Another limitation is that arithmetic density gives us only a broad idea about the strain the population might put on the land areas. In contrast, **physiological population density** measures the pressure that people may place on the land to produce enough food. It divides the number of people into square kilometers of **arable land**, or land that is suited for agriculture. So even though Egypt is comparatively sparsely population, with an arithmetic density of 78, its physiological density is more than 3500! Since so much of Egypt is desert, its people put a great deal of pressure on the arable land, giving the country a very high physiological density.

CARRYING CAPACITY AND SUSTAINABILITY

It is important to consider physiological population density when thinking about **overpopulation**, or the circumstance of too many people for the land to support. **Carrying capacity** (the number of people an area can support on a sustained basis) is not a consistent figure, and it depends largely on the area's level of technology. For example, a region where farmers make use of irrigation and fertilizers can support many more people than a region whose farmers do not. An industrial society is able to import raw materials from others areas, convert them into finished products, and export them into finished products. With the income brought in by these exports, the country may buy the food that it cannot produce at home. Japan is an example of an industrial country with a very high carrying capacity, despite its relatively small land space.

Carrying capacity is related to the larger issue of **sustainability**, which is based on the principle that everything that we need for our survival and well-being depends, either directly or indirectly, on our natural environment. Sustainability creates and maintains the conditions under which humans and nature exist in productive harmony, and when the carrying capacity of the land is not equal to its population, that harmony is disrupted and threatens the long-term sustainability of the area.

POPULATION PYRAMIDS

An important way to analyze population is to use a graphic device called a **population pyramid** that represents age and sex composition. The pyramids take different shapes, according to the distribution of males and females at each age level. For example, the first pyramid on page 34 is for Afghanistan. At the bottom of the pyramid are the statistics for 0-5 year olds: about 2.5 million males and about 2.5 million females. Notice how much the pyramid narrows as it goes up in age groups until finally there are very few males or females in the age groups 75 and up.

Contrast the population pyramid for France in the second figure on page 34. Notice that the base of the pyramid is narrower than it is in the middle. France has about 2 million males and 2 million females in the age groups from about 30 to 60. Also notice that in the older age groups, there are more women than men. Compared to the pyramid for Afghanistan, France has fewer in the lowest age group for 0-5 year olds.

The shape of a country's population pyramid is affected by many factors, including the level of health care available, the impact of war (that disproportionately kills men), availability of birth control, cultural values, and level of economic development. The population pyramid helps demographers to assess needs and issues of the present and future. For example, a country with many older people (like France) will have different health care needs than a country with younger people (like Afghanistan). Hospitals in France are more likely to specialize in treating diseases of middle and older age, such as heart disease and cancer, whereas hospitals in Afghanistan are more likely to encounter health issues among their young people, such as problems of women in childbirth.

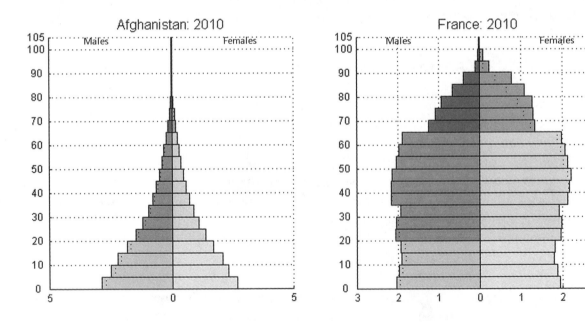

Contrasting Population Pyramids. The pyramids above show population (in millions) by age and sex in Afghanistan and France in 2010.

POPULATION CONCENTRATIONS

Two-thirds of the world's population is concentrated in four regions: East Asia, South Asia, Southeast Asia, and Western Europe. The regions are located in the Northern Hemisphere between 10° and 55° north latitude, except for the southernmost part of Southeast Asia.

EAST ASIA – about one-fifth of all humans live in East Asia, which consists of eastern China, the islands of Japan, the Korean Peninsula, and the island of Taiwan. The Chinese population is concentrated near the Pacific Coast and in several fertile river valleys, such as the Huang and the Yangtze. China is the world's most populous country, but much of the western part, mainly deserts and mountains, is sparsely inhabited. China has more than 150 growing cities with more than one million inhabitants, but two-thirds still live in rural areas. In contrast, about three-fourths of all Japanese and Koreans live in urban areas.

SOUTH ASIA – Another one-fifth of the world's people live in South Asia, which includes India, Pakistan, Bangladesh, and the island of Sri Lanka. Much of the population is concentrated in the Indus and Ganges River valleys and along India's two long coastlines. Like China, most regions in South Asia are rural. Although many large cities are located there, only about one-fourth of the people live in urban areas.

SOUTHEAST ASIA – About 500 million people live in Southeast Asia, mostly on a series of islands off the coast of Asia, including Java, Sumatra, Borneo, Papua New Guinea, and the Philippines. Thousands of islands make up the country of Indonesia, the world's fourth most populous country. Like the East and South Asians, most Southeast Asians live in rural areas.

EUROPE – The only non-Asian area of population concentration is Europe, a region that includes dozens of countries of varying sizes. In contrast to population in the three Asian regions, Europe's population is primarily concentrated in urban areas, and less than 20 percent of its inhabitants are farmers. European terrain and environment are not as closely related to population distribution as they are in Asia. An axis of dense population follows the location of Europe's coal-fields, reflecting the importance of industrialization to population growth.

POPULATION PATTERNS: RACE AND ETHNICITY

Distributions of population are very much affected by race and ethnicity. Both are socially constructed terms that are defined by beliefs and perceptions. **Race** is a category composed of people who share biologically transmitted traits that members of a society consider important. **Ethnicity** is less based on physical characteristics, and emphasizes a shared cultural heritage, such as language, religion, and customs. Because many people live in areas or neighborhoods with people of the same race and/or ethnicity, patterns of population distribution are often determined by these two characteristics. For example, on a national scale, Canada's two largest ethnic groups are those of British Isles origin (28%)

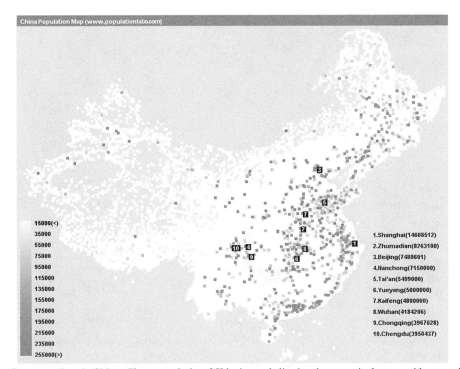

Population Concentrations in China. The vast majority of China's people live in urban areas in the east, with many cities located along rivers and in coastal areas. Large stretches of mountains and deserts make the western and northern parts of the country less habitable.

Language-based ethnicity in Canada. The population distribution of Canada is strongly affected by language-based ethnicity. Most of Canada's people speak English as a first language, but most of the inhabitants of Quebec speak French as a first language.

Minority share (%) of U.S. population growth, by decade, 1950s – 2000s

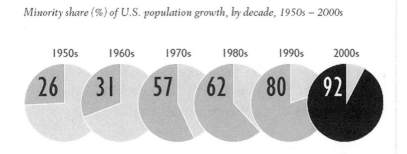

Population Change. The chart above shows the minority share (%) of U.S. population growth by decade, 1950s-2000s. Non-whites accounted for the overwhelming majority (92%) of U.S. population growth in the 2000s.

Source: "Five Things the Census Revealed about America in 2011," Brookings Institute, http://www.brookings.edu

\and those of French origin (23%). Although many Canadians speak both English and French, English-speakers dominate most of the country. However, Quebec is a predominantly French-speaking territory. A study of population distribution of Canada shows a significant division based on language-based ethnicity. One result has been an ongoing movement in Quebec to establish the province as a nation separate from the rest of Canada.

In the United States, the U.S. Census Bureau keeps elaborate population statistics based on race and ethnicity. When citizens register with the Bureau every ten years, they answer a questionnaire that asks them to self-identify as one race/ethnicity or a combination of races/ethnicities. The majority of people identify themselves as white, but significant minorities categorize themselves as black, Asian, and American Indian. Citizens are also asked to self-identify their national ancestry, with many people reporting multiple ancestries. Also, non-whites account for a large percentage of the population growth, so that the white "majority" is shrinking in proportion to minorities.

POPULATION GROWTH AND DECLINE

Until the mid-18th century, the population of the world showed very little overall growth. Populations increased or decreased according to various conditions. In times of war, disease, and famine, populations decreased; in times of peace, health, and plenty, populations increased. Until about 8,000 B.C.E., the **natural increase** (percentage by which the population grew) was close to zero. The **agricultural (or Neolithic) revolution** changed that, though, because the domestication of plants and animals meant that human beings created larger and more stable sources of food, so more people survived. For thousands of years the **doubling rate**, or the length of time needed to double the population, was very long. Until about 1750 **birth rates** (number of babies born per year per 1000 people alive) were high because there were few reliable methods of birth control. However, the **death rates** (number of deaths per year per 1000 people alive) were also high because disease and famine resulted in relatively short life spans.

A dramatic change occurred, though, about 1750, mainly as a result of the **Industrial Revolution**, which began in England in the latter half of the 18th century and spread to other parts of Europe and North America during the 19th century. The Industrial Revolution brought about major improvements in technology that created an unprecedented amount of wealth. Notice the change reflected in the chart below.

The chart illustrates the **population explosion,** the trend toward rapid population increase in place since 1750. Doubling time has dropped quickly since the mid-20th century, as world population grew to 6 ½ billion by the early 21st century. Notice that more sharp increases are predicted throughout the 21st century, with the largest boom in poor nations. In contrast, populations in rich nations are expected to level off, especially since many of them have aging populations, as is illustrated by the population pyramid for France on page 34.

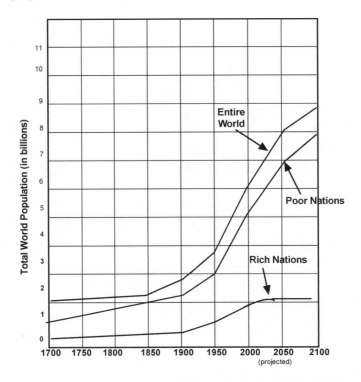

The Increase in World Population, 1700-2100

THEORIES OF POPULATION GROWTH

Before the end of the 18th century, some observers began to calculate future population growth and predict dire consequences for the planet should the growth continue. During the late 20th century, the **zero population growth** movement set as its goal the leveling off of the world's population in order to insure that the earth would be able to sustain its inhabitants. Over time, a number of important theories have analyzed patterns of growth in the past, assessed conditions of the present, and projected consequences for the future.

The First Alarm: Thomas Malthus

In 1798, a British economist named **Thomas Malthus** became the first critic to note that the world's population was increasing faster than the food supplies needed to sustain it. In *An Essay on the Principle of Population as It Affects the Future Improvement of Society,* Malthus used the principles of **exponential growth** v. **linear growth** to make his point. Population increases exponentially, or at what he called a "**geometric rate**," whereas food supplies grow at an **arithmetic rate**. Exponential growth is illustrated by the series of numbers 2, 4, 8, 16, 32 (geometric rate) because once children are born, they grow up to have children of their own. So once the population base gets so large, population will not immediately stabilize even if people begin having fewer children. Meanwhile, the linear growth of food is represented by the series 2, 3, 4, 5, 6 (arithmetic rate) because even with new agricultural technology, farmland is limited.

Malthus recognized that population growth could be stopped by birth control and/or abstinence, but he morally objected to the former and considered the latter to be highly unlikely. Therefore, the "gloomy parson" saw a future in which famine would surely prevail, accompanied by disease and wars fought for space on earth. These "negative checks" would be the forces that keep population growth contained.

In recent years, **neo-Malthusians** have continued to sound the alarm about population increase, with a best-selling book, *The Population Bomb*, written by Paul Ehrlich in 1968, popularizing the point of view. Since that time, Neo-Malthusianism has been the underpinning of international programs for population limitation by birth control and family planning. Many neo-Malthusians today are concerned that overpopulation may increase resource depletion or environmental degradation to a degree that is not sustainable with the potential of ecological collapse or other hazards. On the other hand, many critics say that Malthus was wrong on several counts. First, with increased colonization and immigration from Europe in the 19th century, much of the population pressure eased. Also, Malthus was not correct about the linear increase of food production. It too has grown exponentially through technological advancements (such as seed production and hybridization), advanced farming methods and equipment, and improved use of fertilizers. Many argue that food production is keeping up with population increase, and we will be able to maintain the balance as long as technological inventions continue.

The Vocabulary of Population Theory

All population theories rest on an understanding of these basic concepts:

- **Crude birth rate** is the number of live births in a given year for every thousand people in a population. To calculate it, divide the number of live births in a year by the society's total population and multiply the results by 1,000. For example, the crude birth rate in the U.S. is estimated to be about 14, somewhat higher than those in most European countries, but quite a bit lower than those in Asia, Latin America, and Africa. A number of African countries have crude birth rates that exceed 40. The birth rate is "crude" because it is based on the entire population, not just women in their childbearing years. Of course, if a country has a large number of young women, its overall birth rate may be high even if individual women are not having many children.

- **Total fertility rate** is the average number of children a woman will have throughout her childbearing years (from about age 15 to 49). To compute it, the assumption is made that a woman reaching a particular age in the future will be just as likely to have a child as is a woman of that age today. That of course is not always the case. However, the fertility rate gives us a better idea than the crude birth rate does about the size of families and the consequences for young women and men. Today fertility rates are falling almost everywhere, and in some countries they are declining dramatically. After China instituted its "one child policy" that restricted couples to having one child, its fertility rate dropped from more than 6 to less than 2. Despite a falling fertility rate, a country with a large percentage of young people(typical in a less developed country) will usually experience continued population growth. Once the large base of young people grows beyond child-bearing age, the overall population will gradually decline. This phenomenon is known as **demographic momentum.**

- **Crude death rate,** also called the **mortality rate**, is the number of deaths in a given year for every thousand people in a population. It is calculated like the crude birth rate, with the number of deaths in a year divided by the total population and multiplied by 1,000. Typically, in the past the highest rates were found in Africa, Asia, and Latin America (over 20); the lowest rates occurred in Europe, North America, and Australia (less than 10). In recent years, however, death rates in developing countries have dramatically declined as antibiotics, vaccinations, and pesticides have become available in all parts of the world. Also, since birth rates have declined significantly in Europe, death rates will increase since countries with a high proportion of elderly people naturally have higher death rates than those with a high proportion of young people.

- **Infant mortality rate** is the number of deaths among infants under one year of age for each thousand live births in a given year. To compute it, divide the number of deaths of children under one year of age by the number of live births during the same year and multiply by 1,000. Infant mortality rates are significant because it is at this young age that the greatest decline in mortality has occurred, largely as a result of improved health services. The drop in infant mortality accounts for a large part of the decline in the overall death rate in the last few decades because mortality in the first year of life is usually greater than in any other year.

- **Natural increase** of a population is the difference between the number of births and the number of deaths during a specific period. It is computed by subtracting the crude death rate from the crude birth rate, after first converting them to percentages. The term *natural* means that a country's growth rate excludes migration, or movement of people in and out of its borders.

- **Life expectancy** at birth measures the average number of years that a child can expect to live if the current mortality rates hold. According to the CIA Factbook, in 2012 Monaco had the highest life expectancy (89.68), and Chad had the lowest (48.69). Chad's low life expectancy is due to a combination of factors, including poverty and health and social conditions that compare unfavorably with those elsewhere. Political unrest has also led to low life expectancy rates in Chad, where violence between ethnic groups has led to many deaths. Life expectancy rates are different for men than for women, with women outliving men in almost all countries.

Demographic Transition Theory

All countries have experienced changes in natural increase, fertility, and mortality rates, but their patterns vary considerably. However, according to **demographic transition theory,** these variations follow an overall global pattern. The theory states that population patterns vary according to different levels of technological development, but all countries go through the same four stages. They are just at different points as they move through the "transition."

The four stages are:

- **Stage 1: Low Growth** – Preindustrial, agrarian societies have high birth rates because farm work is enhanced by larger families, so children are desirable. People in these societies also often have little access to birth control. Death rates are high because of low standards of living and little medical technology. As a result, natural increase was close to zero, and world population did not grow. Stage 1 characterized the earth's population until the mid-18th century, and some societies today are still in this initial phase.

- **Stage 2: High Growth** – Around 1750 industrialization brought about a **demographic transition** in Europe as death rates fell because of greater food supplies and scientific medicine. Yet birth rates remained high, so the natural increase exploded. The drop in the death rate became significant by the mid-19th century, and is known as the **"mortality revolution,"** or **epidemiological transition.** Another explanation for the drop in death rates is that fatal epidemic diseases became **endemic**, with the population developing partial immunities, so that deaths declined. New machines helped farmers increase agricultural production and feed the rapidly growing population, causing life expectancy to increase. According to demographic transition theory, many of the world's poorest countries today are in this high-growth stage with falling death rates but stable, high birth rates.

- **Stage 3: Moderate Growth** – This is the stage of a mature industrial economy, when the birth rate drops, curbing population growth once again. In Europe a rapid urbanization occurred as industrialization created more jobs in cities. According to demographic transition theory, fertility rates fall because more children survive to adulthood with improved health standards and access, and because high standards of living make raising children expensive. Children become economic liabilities rather than assets (as in Stages 1 and 2) because they require more years of schooling, and the nature of work changes so that child labor is restricted. Smaller families are made possible by birth control, and as birth rates follow death rates downward, the population growth slows further.

- **Stage 4: Low Growth** – In this stage a post-industrial economy completes the demographic transition. The birth rate keeps falling, partly because more women are working outside the home and partly because children become even more expensive. Higher education levels encourage women to delay marriage and children, and children need extensive education to fill post-industrial jobs. These trends are accompanied by steady death rates, so that population grows only very slowly or even decreases.

This cycle of growth stages has occurred in the United Kingdom and much of Europe, where countries have a population growth rate of close to zero. However, critics of demographic transition theory warn that it may be unwise to assume that all countries' demographic cycles will follow the sequence that occurred in industrializing Europe. The theory rests on the prediction that all countries will eventually industrialize, which is not necessarily true. Even if and when they do industrialize, population bases are much larger than they were when the population revolution began in Europe, so the effects may be different. For example, China is quickly industrializing now, but the population stands at about 1.4 billion, despite the fact that the one-child policy has been in effect for several decades. However, many demographers are predicting that most countries will stop growing at some time during the 21st century, and will reach **stationary population level (SLP).** However, these predictions are under constant revision, and no one knows for sure if and when the population explosion will end.

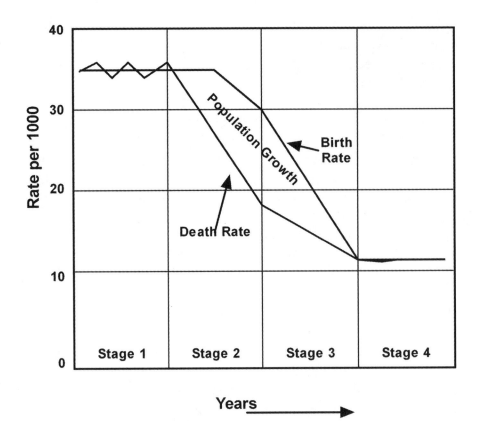

Stages in the Demographic Transition. According to demographic transition theory, all societies follow the same four demographic stages, causing population growth rates to vary considerably.

POPULATION AND NATURAL HAZARDS

Population levels have always fluctuated according to the natural environment. Historically when climate conditions have been favorable, population increases, partly because the food supply is sufficient when the climate is good. People adapt their life styles to climate conditions, so that predictable weather patterns are easily managed. However, should dramatic changes occur, the death rate would likely increase until adaptations, such as warmer housing and better methods of heating spaces, are made. For example, populations in many parts of Eurasia appear to have decreased significantly during the "Little Ice Age" of the 17th century. Likewise, population levels mat be negatively impacted by natural disasters, such as drought, hurricanes, typhoons, and tsunamis. Two of Malthus's "negative checks" – famine and disease – have often been the result of natural hazards that impact food production. In modern times in many areas, human endeavors have often lessened these negative checks through better health care and more control over food production. Many diseases have been either eradicated or controlled, and even though food distribution is still a problem that leads to famine, people in many countries now have access to nutritious foods. However, globalization has meant more contacts among peoples of the earth, and one result is the potential for rapid spread of communicable diseases. One example is **AIDS** (Acquired Immune Deficiency Syndrome), a disease that began in central Africa during the late 20th century, and spread to many countries around the world before the end of the century. Scientists warn of future outbreaks of Asian bird flu, a deadly virus that has been known to spread from birds to humans, and has the potential to become a major outbreak if not contained to localities. The fear of a **pandemic** (widespread epidemic) caused many areas in China and Southeast Asia to be strictly quarantined in 2003, with much international travel curtailed and many everyday activities highly restricted in the quarantined areas. Another threat – the swine flu – began in Mexico in 2009 and spread to other countries as international agencies kept a close eye on its progress.

EFFECTS OF POPULATION POLICIES

Over the past century many national governments have designed policies to influence the overall growth rate of their populations. Most governments today seek to reduce the rate of natural increase through various forms of **restrictive population policies.** These policies range from toleration of officially banned means of birth control to the actual prohibition of large families. Since the 1990s the United Nations and other international organizations have also taken an interest in controlling population growth.

China and India: National Population Policies

The two most populous countries of the world – China and India – have taken very different approaches to population growth. Their contrasting policies have resulted in different current population patterns and problems, as well as predictions for the future.

China

In 1965 Chinese leader Mao Zedong announced that an ever-expanding population is a "good thing," and in 1974 he denounced population policies as "imperialist tools" designed to weaken developing countries. At the time of Mao's death in 1976, China had about 850 million people with a birth rate of 25. His successors recognized that population growth was consuming more than half of the annual increase in the country's gross domestic product, so China introduced a campaign advocating the "two-child family." The government provided services – including abortions – that supported the program, resulting in a drop in China's birth rate to 19.5 by the late 1970s. In 1979, China's new leader, Deng Xiaoping, went even further by instituting the "one child policy." This program included both incentives and penalties to assure that couples produced only one child. Late marriages were encouraged, and free contraceptives, abortions, and sterilizations were provided to families that followed the policy. Penalties, including steep fines, were imposed on couples that had a second child. In 1984 the policy was relaxed in rural areas, where children's labor was still important, but it was reinstated in 2002 in reaction to reports that many rural births were not being reported to the government. In contrast, Chinese people in cities were generally more accepting of the one-child policy since it better suited urban life styles and needs. By 1986 the birth rate had fallen to 18, a figure far below those in other less developed countries.

However, the policy has had other consequences. One was a rise in female infanticide, or the killing of baby girls. Because traditional Chinese society has always valued males above females, many couples have wanted their one child to be a boy. If a girl is born instead, some choose to end the child's life so that they can try again to have a boy. The incidence of female infanticide is almost impossible to tally, but the practice has led to a disproportionate number of male to female children. In more recent years, as technology has allowed parents to know the gender of the child before birth, female infanticide has been replaced – at least in urban areas – with selective abortions. Over the years China's population pyramid has developed a lopsided number of young adult males to young adult females. The problem is so serious that many young men are unable to find women to marry. Some projections suggest that by the mid-21st century China's population numbers will start falling. If that occurs, it almost certainly will change the cultural tradition of sons taking care of their aging parents. There could be too few sons to carry out the responsibility, leaving China with a problem of what to do about a growing number of elderly people with no one to take care of them.

Census figures from 2010 indicate that demographics in China have changed rapidly in recent years. Not only is the ratio of baby boys to baby girls out of proportion, but China's population is dramatically aging. People above the age of 60 now represent 13.3% of the total, up from 10.3% in 2000, and those under the age of 14 declined from 23% to 17%. An increasingly vocal group of academic demographers has called for a relaxation of the one-child policy, and in 2011, one Chinese official in Guangdong – China's most populous province – joined in the criticism by advocating a "two-child" policy. Already, many exceptions exist, such as the allowance of two children for couples in which both partners are single children. Minorities – such as Tibetans and Uyghurs – are permitted a second child, whatever the sex of the first born, and the regulations are most relaxed in rural areas, where population pressures are minimal.

India

Unlike China, India has had a problem coordinating a centralized population policy. India is a federation of 28 states and 7 "union territories," all of which are culturally and politically diverse. The national government cannot force its will on the states and territories with their various problems and policies. Population growth is the greatest in the northeast in Assam, Nagaland, and Mizoram, where the rate of natural increase exceeded 4.5% during the 1970s. As a result, famine has plagued the area, even when there is adequate food in other parts of the country.

The Indian government started population planning in the 1950s by providing limited funds for family-planning clinics and programs, but they did little to stop population growth. In the 1960s the government invested heavily in a national program that it encouraged the states to join. However, rapid population growth continued, especially in the eastern states. Some of the state programs were controversial and unpopular. For example, in Maharashtra (the southwest) rioting broke out in opposition to a plan

Population Pressures in India. Population growth characterizes the entire country, but population pressures are greater in Assam, Nagaland, and Mizoram.

that required sterilization of anyone with three children or more. Today Indian state governments use advertising and persuasion to encourage families to have fewer children. A network of clinics has been established to aid women even in small villages.

Despite these coordination problems, India's birth rate has dropped by more than half in 35 years – from 5.7 children per woman in the mid-1960s to 2.7 in 2010. Nearly a third of India's people have lowered their fertility to replacement levels. However, most demographers predict that India will overtake China as the world's most populous country as early as 2030. So far, India's governments have been unable to come up with the coordination of resources necessary to curtail the continuing population growth.

International Policy Efforts

During the 1990s international organizations, especially the United Nation, began to coordinate efforts to control population growth on a global level. For the first time, population policy was officially tied to women's empowerment, especially in terms of their control over the number of children that they have. According to a statement issued by the International Conference on Population and Development, held in Cairo in 1994:

> "Improving the status of women also enhances their decision-making capacity at all levels in all spheres of life, especially in the area of sexuality and reproduction. This, in turn, is essential for the long-term success of population programmes. Experience shows that population and development programmes are most effective when steps have simultaneously been taken to improve the status of women."*

*Reference: "United Nations Population Information Network," www.un.org/popin/icpd/conference/offeng/poa.html

The Conference recommended that national governments pass laws that allow women to combine family roles with participation in the workforce. In 1995 the United National Fourth World Conference on Women was held in Beijing and attended by women from many countries, including less developed ones. The Conference affirmed the importance of women's ability to control their own fertility, especially in terms of allowing them to take advantage of educational and employment opportunities.

POPULATION MOVEMENT

People move from one place to another constantly, usually within a relatively small land space. For example, people move from home to work, shopping centers, school, or recreational and religious centers. This type of short-term, repetitive movement that occurs on a regular basis is called **circulation.** **Migration** is a different type of mobility because it involves a permanent move to a new location, either within a single country or from one country to another. **Spatial interaction** is the broad geographical term for the movement of peoples, ideas, and commodities within and between areas, whether it is circulation or migration. Geographers are generally more interested in migration than circulation because migration produces important changes for individuals and the regions that they move to and from. When relocations occur across political boundaries, they affect the population structures of both the areas of origin and destination. **The demographic equation** summarizes the population change over time in an area by combining natural change (death rate subtracted from birth rate) and **net migration**. **Emigration** is migration from a location, and **immigration** is migration to a location. Both types of migration usually occur at once; the difference is the net-migration rate for a region or country.

RAVENSTEIN'S LAWS OF MIGRATION

In 1885 British demographer Ernst Ravenstein wrote 11 migration laws, which he based on his study of **internal migration** (within the borders of a country) in England. Some of these laws still hold true today, including:

1) The majority of immigrants move only a short distance. **Distance decay** – the decline of an activity or function with increasing distance from its point of origin – describes this tendency for people to stay fairly close to home. Of course, since Ravenstein's time the scale of migration has increased, with modern transportation and communications systems making it possible for people to migrate to distant lands. However, **step migration,** or long-distance migration done in stages, is still the rule. For example, a person or family may move from a rural area to a small town. Later the move from small town to city may be made, resulting in long-distance migration, but only by short distances at a time. Another factor that reinforces this rule is **intervening opportunity,** or the fact that many who set out to move a long distance find good opportunities to settle before they reach their destinations. For example, migrants from a rural area bound for a big city may find employment in a town along the way, and decide to settle there instead.

2) Migrants who move longer distances tend to choose cities as their destinations. Most are leaving rural areas and moving to urban locations. In Ravenstein's day the city was London, but the principle may be applied to late 19th and early 20th century moves from Europe to cities on the eastern seaboard of the United States. In modern day, many internal migrations within developing nations are from rural to urban areas.

3) Each migration flow produces a counterflow. When one group moves into an area, another group often moves out. For example, when European immigrants moved into cities in the eastern United States, they usually settled in the most affordable areas. Once they prospered, they moved to better neighborhoods, while the newest immigrants took over their old neighborhoods. As one group moves in, the other is encouraged to move out. As a result of this back-and-forth flow, net migrations to an area are often small, disguising the large amount of movement actually going on.

4) Families are less likely to make international moves than young adults, and historically, most international migrants have been young males. Young adults have fewer restrictions on their movements, partly because they don't yet have family commitments of their own. Traditionally, women have been less free to travel by themselves, and since it is easier for one person to move than it is for many, until recently, single young males made most international moves. However, as women have gained more freedoms in many countries, the number of young women who immigrate to new countries has risen.

Ravenstein also noted an inverse relationship between the volume of migration and the distance between source and destination. Geographers came to call this proposal the **gravity model**, a measure of the interaction of places. This model states that spatial interaction – including migration – is directly related to the size of the populations and inversely related to the distance between them. Distance decay means that an individual's **critical distance** – the distance beyond which cost, effort, and means strongly influence willingness to travel – will eventually prevent a migration from occurring. So a large city has a greater gravitational pull than a small one, but it still tends to pull people that live closer rather than farther away.

REASONS FOR MIGRATING

Migration may be forced or voluntary. An example of involuntary migration is the forced transport of 10 million Africans to the Western Hemisphere as slaves beginning in the 16th century. In the 1990s, Serb soldiers forced ethnic Albanians to flee their homes in Kosovo. There are countless reasons why people voluntarily migrate, but most of them are economic. A **push factor** encourages people to move from the region that they live in, and a **pull factor** is one that attracts them to a new region. For any one person that migrates, usually a combination of push and pull factors explains the relocation.

Economic Push and Pull Factors

People often think about leaving places that have few job opportunities to immigrate to places where jobs are available. The opportunity is in the eye of the beholder – it may or may not exist in reality. Farmers may be pushed off their land because of drought, invasion, or landlords, and may decide to seek their fortunes in nearby cities. The pull of the cities may be enhanced by industrial growth and the jobs that accompany it. Even if there are not enough jobs to go around, the push factors may be so strong that the migrants have little incentive to return to the farms. Economic push and pull factors exist on all scales from local to global. People not only move from one continent or country to another. They also move between regions within countries, and even between neighborhoods in a city. Economic push and pull factors help to explain the overall worldwide movement of people from rural to urban areas during the 19th and 20th centuries.

Cultural Push and Pull Factors

Cultural push factors include many involuntary migrations. Millions of people have been shipped to other countries as slaves or as prisoners, as happened from Africa to the Americas during the 17th, 18th, and early 19th centuries. In more recent times **refugees** have been forced to migrate from their homes and cannot return for fear of persecution because of their religion, race, nationality, or political opinions. Examples are Palestinians and Afghans. Palestinians left Israel after the country was created in 1948, and also left areas taken over by Israel in 1967. Refugees from Afghanistan fled from the extended civil war that began when the Soviet Union invaded the country in 1979. Internal migrations have occurred on the Indian subcontinent since India gained independence in 1947. Most migration has been based on religion, with Muslims migrating to the newly created country of Pakistan and other Muslim areas of India, and Hindus migrating out of the Muslim areas. Today millions of people in Africa are refugees as a result of intense ethnic conflicts, such as those in Rwanda and Darfur. The Balkan area is another region of recent refugee migrations, as fighting among cultural groups caused many to flee their homes during conflicts of the 1990s.

Cultural push factors include changing politics and government control. In the early 19th century Germans who led a movement to democratize the government lost their bid and had to escape for fear of retribution from the authoritarian government. Many came to the United States, with its pull attraction of democratic government. During the 1990s Eastern European nations broke free from Soviet control, and even though they established democratic governments, the pull factor of better jobs in Western Europe was enough to start a migration from east to west.

Environmental Push and Pull Factors

As communications and transportation improved during the 20th and early 21st centuries, more people have moved to more pleasant environments than before. For example, people have moved to Colorado to be close to the recreational and aesthetic pull of the Rocky Mountains. Seashores also pull people to settle, as demonstrated by migrations to Florida, California, and lands along the Mediterranean Sea. For those with health problems related to damp, cold climates, moving to dry climates (such as Arizona) is appealing. People may be pushed from their homes by adverse environmental conditions, as seen in the wake of Hurricane Katrina that hit New Orleans and the Mississippi coastline in 2005. Homes and businesses were destroyed and city services disrupted to such an extent that many that thought they were only temporarily leaving their homes became permanent migrants to inland areas.

Major environmental factors include:

- **Climate** – Most of the sparsely populated areas of the world have unpleasant and uninhabitable climates for human beings, including extreme cold, heat, or drought. Although humans are remarkably adaptable in their ability to live in a wide variety of climates, they generally prefer the humid and subhumid tropics, subtropics, or midlatitudes.

- **Elevations** – Most regions of sparse populations in the middle and higher latitudes are high elevations where the climate tends to be colder. However, inhabitants of the tropics often prefer to live at higher elevations, where mountain valleys and basins provide havens from excessive heat.

- **Seacoasts** – The tendency for people to settle on or near the seacoast in most striking in Eurasia, Australia, and South America, where major cities cluster around the rim of each continent. In Australia, half the total population lives in just five port cities, and most everyone else lives in nearby coastal areas. Large parts of interior South America consist of jungle or sparsely settled dry plains, or pampas, and most of the cities are located along the coasts, partly because many were founded by the export-oriented Spanish and Portuguese during colonial days.

- **Disease** – Although modern medicine has altered this factor significantly, historically disease has affected migration choices for humans. For example, after the fall of the Ancient Roman Empire, Italy and other areas in the Mediterranean region were virtually depopulated by a malaria epidemic. Animal diseases may also affect human choices of settlement, such as sleeping sickness that attacks cows (but not humans) in East Africa. Since people there depend heavily on cattle for sustenance, entire tribes have migrated away from infested areas, leaving them unpopulated.

Environmental factors may also create **intervening obstacles**, or physical features that halt or slow migration from one place to another. For example, people moving to the West Coast of the United States in the 19th century encountered the intervening obstacles of wide plains, mountains, and deserts that discouraged many from making the trek. Intervening obstacles may also be cultural, as is the case when migrants encounter governmental regulations for when reaching their destinations. Most countries have laws that restrict overall numbers of immigrants, as well as numbers from specific countries of origin. Migrants encounter further obstacles when they face requirements for citizenship or long-term stays in their destination countries.

Major migrations impact both the region that people leave and the region that is their destination. For example, the major migration of Europeans to the Americas during the 16th, 17th, and 18th centuries relieved population growth pressures in Europe. However, European contacts in the New World exposed Native Americans to new diseases, decimating their populations in one of the most dramatic demographic shifts in world history.

MAJOR MIGRATIONS AT DIFFERENT SCALES

Migrations occur on many scales from global to local. They may be internal (within a country) or international. Internal migrations may be **interregional** (between regions) or **intraregional** (within one region). International migrations may be **forced** (involuntary) or **voluntary** (the migrant chooses to move).

Global Migration Patterns

On a global scale, Asia, Latin America, and Africa have net **out-migration**, which means that more people emigrate from them than immigrate to them. In contrast, North America, Europe, and Oceania (Australia, New Zealand, and South Sea islands) have net **in-migration**, which means that more people immigrate to them than emigrate from them. In other words, people are migrating from less developed to more developed countries. Migrants from countries with relatively few available jobs and high natural increase rates head for wealthier countries, where job prospects are better. The largest flows include:

- From Asia to Europe
- From Asia to North America
- From South America to North America

Major Global Migrations. The largest flows of people in the modern world are from Asia to North America, Asia to Europe, and South America to North America. In many cases people are leaving areas where jobs are less plentiful and lower paying, and migrating to areas where the job market is more promising.

U.S. Immigration Patterns

The United States is an important example for studying international migration since many of its citizens are direct descendents of immigrants. About 70 million people have migrated to the United States since 1820, including 30 million who are currently alive. Other countries, such as Canada and Australia, now have larger percentages of immigrants than the U.S. has. The Middle East has the largest overall percentage of immigrants, with about one-half of the region's total population migrated from other areas. However, the U.S. is the third most populous country in the world, so its patterns of immigration are a study in itself.

The U.S. has had three main eras of immigration:

1) **Initial settlement of colonies** – Prior to independence in 1776, about 1 million Europeans migrated to the American colonies, and another million came during the early days of the republic (before 1840). The overwhelming majority of these immigrants came from Great Britain, but some came from the Netherlands, Sweden, France, Germany, and the Iberian Peninsula (Spain and Portugal). Another large group from Africa was forced to migrate as slaves. About 400,000 Africans were shipped to the American colonies during the 18th century, and even though the slave trade was made illegal in 1808, another quarter million came between 1808 and 1861, when the Civil War began.

2) **Emigration from Europe** – The emigration from Europe to the Americas in the 19th and early 20th centuries is among the most significant human migrations in recent centuries. About 75 million departed for the Americas between 1835 and 1935. The largest number went to the United States, but they had many other destinations. The British went to North America, Australia, New Zealand, and South Africa. The Spanish and Portuguese settled in Central and South America. Although millions of Europeans eventually returned home, the net outflow from Europe was huge. Three waves came to the United States:

   - **1840s and 1850s** – The two largest groups of immigrants were the Irish, who were escaping desperate economic conditions, and the Germans, who were escaping difficult political conditions.
   - **Late 1800s** – After a decline in immigration during the Civil War of the 1860s, immigration rates rose again during the 1870s and continued until the early 1890s. More than ¾ of the immigrants came from Northern and Western Europe. Germans and Irish continued to arrive, and the number of Scandinavians increased significantly. An important pull factor was the Industrial Revolution in the United States, which created a demand for factory labor that resulted in plentiful jobs for immigrants.
   - **Early 1900s** – After an economic depression during the 1890s, the continuing industrial boom in the U.S. meant that immigration resumed its rapid increase after the turn of the century, reaching peak levels around 1910. The major difference was that more immigrants during this period came from Southern and Eastern Europe. Important feeder countries were Italy, Russia, and Austria-Hungary. The Industrial Revolution had spread to these countries, and populations were increasing, so many left to seek their fortunes in the U.S. For Russian Jews, political persecution was another motivation to leave.

3) **Immigration since 1945** – Immigration to the U.S. again slowed during the Great Depression of the 1930s and World War II in the early 1940s. It increased steadily during the 1950s and 1960s, when major changes in immigration laws brought a new mix of migrants. Previous laws had greatly restricted Asian immigration, but the laws were lifted in the 1960s. In the late 20th century, annual immigration from China, the Philippines, India, and Vietnam increased dramatically, with many Vietnamese seeking asylum as refugees from the communist takeover of their government. Asians also migrated to Canada in large numbers. Another major source of immigration in recent years has been Latin America, with Mexico topping a total of 8 million by the end of the 20th century. Like Asian immigration, Latin American immigration was encouraged by a change in U.S. law. The 1986 Immigration Reform and Control Act allowed the government to issue visas to several hundred thousand people who had previously entered the country illegally. Economic factors have been important to immigrants from both Asia and Latin America, as they moved from areas with fewer job opportunities to the more prosperous United States.

The composition of the U. S. population has greatly changed over time as a result of immigration. Before the 20th century, most immigrants were from Northern and Western Europe, resulting in a population with largely European roots. The early 20th century brought Eastern and Southern Europeans, adding to the cultural diversity of the country. The late 20th century brought even more widespread cultural influences from Asia and Latin America, and over time, as generations grow up in the U.S., the country will continue to change in the 21st century.

Intraregional Migrations

As Ravenstein pointed out, most migrations are to destinations that are close to home, either internal to a country or between neighboring countries. Within the United States, for example, African-Americans began migrating from the South to the North during World War I in response to growing labor demands and dwindling numbers of immigrants to fill jobs. The migration continued during the 1920s, dropped during the depression years of the 1930s, then resumed its upward climb in the 1940s. Most were moving from rural to urban areas, so the migration represented major life style changes. Starting in the 1970s, a countertrend began: some African Americans began moving back to the South. Some possible pull factors for this new movement are changing civil rights patterns and increasing job opportunities in the South. One current push factor may be deteriorating living conditions in the urban North.

Some intraregional migrations result from **dislocation** of people forced from their home due to ethnic strife, war, or natural disasters. Some examples include:

- **South Asia** – Millions of people from Afghanistan have fled the country, first when the Soviet Union invaded in 1979, and next during the 1990s when intertribal strife caused many to flee to neighboring Pakistan. The number of refugees increased after the events of September 11, 2001, when the United States retaliated against terrorist bases in Afghanistan. Another area of movement is Sri Lanka, where ethnic strife has sent refugees to different parts of the island, depending on their identity as minority Tamils or majority Sinhalese.

- **Southeast Asia** – The international emigration from Vietnam when the U.S. pulled its troops out in 1975 gave way to more regional displacement by the 1990s. Civil war in Cambodia produced such violence that refugees escaped to camps across the border to Thailand. Other refugee camps exist in Myanmar (Burma) as minorities have tried to escape from repressive military rule.

- **The Balkans** – When Yugoslavia collapsed during the early 1990s, ethnic conflicts created a huge refugee crisis in the Balkans. Serbs, Macedonians, Bosnians, and Albanians are just a few of the ethnicities that clashed for economic and religious reason. The area was broken up into many small countries in an effort to solve the problems, but many people are still dislocated from their homes today.

- **Sub-Saharan Africa** – In recent years some of the most serious refugee crises have occurred in Sub-Saharan Africa. The conflict between Hutus and Tutsis in Rwanda resulted in a million deaths in April 1994, and millions more moved to escape the violence. The refugees spilled into the Congo, Tanzania, and Uganda, creating crises in all of these neighboring areas. In Sudan, civil war has raged between the Arabs of the north and the Africans of the south, creating the worst refugee crisis of the early 21st century. Ethnic-based civil wars in Liberia and Sierra Leone have also sent refugees streaming into neighboring countries.

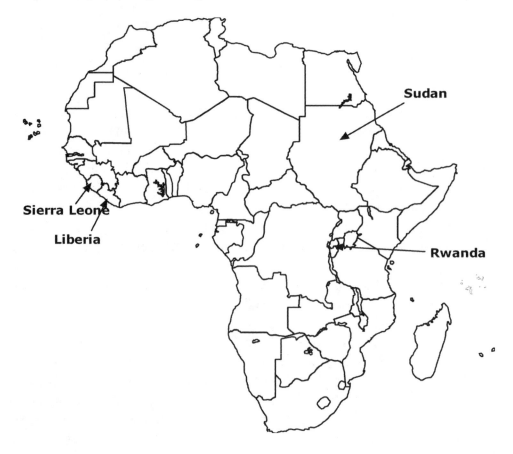

Out-Migration Areas of Africa. This map shows some areas of ethnic strife in Sub-Saharan Africa that have caused major movement of refugees both within each country and across the borders into neighboring countries.

Immigration Issues in Europe

Increased numbers of immigrants from eastern Europe, Turkey, the Middle East, and Africa have fed anti-foreign feelings in many countries, including Italy, Germany, Britain, and France. In Italy a new party, the Northern League, gained political support – particularly in the prosperous north – by its opposition to immigration. In Germany, immigrants from struggling eastern European countries inspired incidents in which gangs of **neo-Nazis,** who reiterated Adolf Hitler's racist doctrines, burned immigrant housing and demonstrated against foreigners. Since reunification in 1990, some 49 foreigners – almost all of them Turks, Africans, or Asians – have been killed by neo-Nazis in fire bombings, beatings, or stabbings. These movements have been denounced by many figures of authority, and when the anti-immigrant Freedom Party gained a share in the ruling coalition in Austria in 2000, the other EU nations refused to formally cooperate with the Austrian government.

In France, the division between native French and immigrants from northern and equatorial Africa is a major source of discord within the society and the political system. After Algeria received independence from the French in the 1950s, many Algerians associated with colonialism immigrated to France to escape the new Algerian government's wrath. Today, there are some 9 million foreigners living in France, about 16% of the entire population. Between 4 and 5 million are Muslims from northern and equatorial Africa, and this group's arrival in France has caused racial tensions. Many have not assimilated into French society, partly because of prejudice toward them, and partly because they don't want to abandon their customs. For example, some French people have been horrified by the polygamous practices of some Muslim families. Many French schools have required students to wear uniforms, and some Muslim girls have refused to abandon their head coverings as signs of their religion. The result has been the creation of immigrant ghettoes with high crime rates and accusations that the police harass Muslim men. Politically, the National Front – a political party on the far right – has focused on a policy of deporting Muslims, and not integrating them into French society.

Although far right parties have had less success in Britain, anti-immigrant feelings have concerned the government, especially after two minority men were arrested in connection with attacks on Glasgow Airport in 2007. According to the 2001 census, only about 7.1% of the British population is of non-European origin, with most coming from countries that were formerly British colonies. However, the minority ethnic population grew by 53% between 1991 and 2001, from 3 million in 1991 to 4.6 million in 2001. The main groups were Indian (23% of all non-European population), Pakistani (16%), Afro-Caribbean (12.2%), and Black African (10.5%). Because of tight immigration restrictions in the past, most ethnic minorities in Britain today are young, with about half of the population under the age of 25. The growth in percentages of minorities has grown despite the restrictions that were placed on further immigration during the Thatcher administration of the 1980s. Immigration restrictions are currently under debate, but the current government has allowed the restrictions to remain in place.

MIGRATION SELECTIVITY

Not everyone is equally likely to migrate, even if they are influenced by the same push and pull factors. For example, job prospects may be equally bleak for people in an area, but only some of them will make the decision to move. This tendency for certain types of people to move is called **migration selectivity**, and it is influenced by these characteristics:

1) **Age** – As Ravenstein observed in the late 19th century, young people are most likely to migrate. People are most likely to move during their early adult years between the ages of 18 and 30. During these years, people leave their parents' homes to attend school, take a job, join the military, marry, and begin families. These life-events are usually accompanied by changes in residence. Migration rates are also high among young children, whose parents generally fall within the young adult age range.

2) **Education** – People with higher levels of education are more likely to make long-distance moves than are less educated people. For young adults, going to college often means traveling some distance from home, and education exposes them to new ideas and knowledge about far away places. Also, as one becomes highly qualified for professional jobs, it may be necessary to change locations in order to follow one's career. Areas with net out-migrations are usually hardest hit by the loss of young, well-educated people, who are often attracted to net in-migration areas with better jobs and more appealing life styles.

3) **Kinship and friendship ties** – People who have relatives and/or friends who have migrated previously to other areas are more likely to migrate as well. This phenomenon is known as **chain migration** – a stream of people out of an area as first movers communicate with people back home and stimulate others to follow later. The first movers may encourage others with their stories of job opportunities or abundant land. All migrants within the chain are comforted by the fact that they will have support from family and friends as they settle closely together to help adjust to their new homes. Such selective migration helped to create ethnic neighborhoods – such as "Little Italies" or "Chinatowns" – in U.S. cities on both coasts during the 19th and 20th centuries.

SHORT TERM CIRCULATION AND ACTIVITY SPACE

Migration is a major area of interest in population geography, but another type of mobility is also the subject of a field of study. Short term circulation of individuals – or movement that does not involve relocation of residence – is confined to **activity space**, an area in which an individual moves about as he or she pursues regular, day-to-day activities. Although people do venture out from these spaces on occasion, activity space is the area that is reachable on a typical day. The types of trips that people take within their activity spaces are determined by several factors:

- **Age group** – School-age children are usually dependent on parents to take them long distances away from home, so when they venture out alone, it is usually by foot or bicycle. Teenagers have larger activity spaces as their ability to travel further away from home increases, especially as they begin to drive. Wage-earning adults often have to travel to work and back, so their activity space is generally quite different from that of children. Once they retire from work, older people may see their activity spaces shrink in size.

- **Ability to travel** – This factor is often related to age, but activity space is clearly limited by the means of travel. In countries where individuals do not have access to cars, their activity spaces are generally fairly small. Also, ability to travel is directly related to income levels, with poorer people in all countries generally having smaller activity spaces than wealthier people. People who live in suburbs may have larger spaces than those that live in cities, even if income levels are comparable. Suburbs are often spread out, and people have to travel further distances to take care of daily needs.

- **Opportunities to travel** – If a family is self-sufficient, taking care of their own needs, they may not have the desire to travel far away, especially if there are no schools, stores, or work places for them to visit. **Awareness space** may be limited as well so that their knowledge of opportunity locations beyond the normal activity space is minimal. Poverty and physical isolation may contribute to a lack of awareness space.

All people live within a **space-time prism** that sets the limits for their activities. They have only so much time to be mobile, and space is limited by their ability to move. For example, if people do not have cars, they cannot take jobs long distance away from home because by the time they walk to and from work, they practically do not have time for other activities. As a result, they must choose jobs that lie within their space-time prisms.

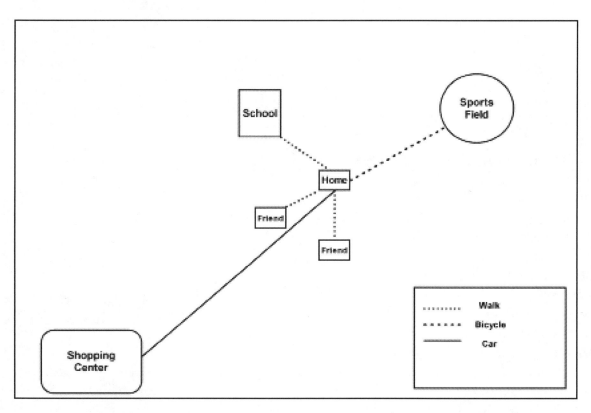

Activity space for an 8-year old boy that lives in suburban United States. For his trip to the shopping center, he would be dependent on an adult to get him there.

Population geography is a diverse field with interest in distributions, growth, and movement of human populations. In many ways, basic themes of human geography, such as scale, pattern, place, and interdependence (See Unit I) may all be illustrated with population topics. Just as importantly, population concepts and theories crosscut almost every other field of human geography, as we will see in Units III - VII.

TERMS AND CONCEPTS

activity space
agricultural revolution
AIDS
arable land
arithmetic growth
arithmetic population density
awareness space
carrying capacity
chain migration
circulation
critical distance
crude birth rate
crude death rate
demographic equation
demographic momentum
demographic transition theory
demography
density
dislocation
distance decay
dot maps
doubling rate
emigration
endemic
epidemiologic transition (mortality revolution)
ethnicity
exponential growth
female infanticide
forced migration
geometric rate
gravity model
immigration
Industrial Revolution
infant mortality rate
in-migration
internal migration
inter-regional migration
intervening obstacles
intervening opportunity
intra-regional migration
life expectancy
linear growth
Malthus, Thomas
migration
migration selectivity

natural increase
neo-Malthusians
net-migration rate
one child policy
out-migration
overpopulation
pandemic
physiological population density
population concentrations
population explosion
population geography
population pyramid
pull factors
push factors
race
Ravenstein, Ernst
refugees
restrictive population policies
space-time prism
spatial interaction
stationary population level
step migration
sustainability
total fertility rate
voluntary migration
zero population growth

MULTIPLE-CHOICE QUESTIONS
UNIT TWO

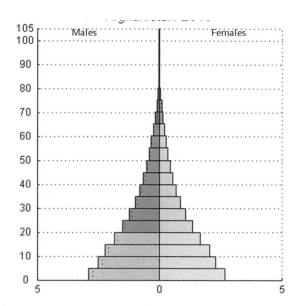

1. The country represented by the population pyramid above is most likely characterized by

   (A) adequate health care for the elderly
   (B) readily available birth control
   (C) high death rates for women in childbirth
   (D) persistent warfare
   (E) low rates of heart disease and cancer

2. Which of the following best describes the phenomenon of demographic momentum?

   (A) Despite a falling fertility rate, the population of a country with a large percentage of young people
       continues to grow.
   (B) In countries where birth rates have declined, the proportion of elderly people naturally increases.
   (C) The drop in infant mortality accounts for a large part of the decline in the overall death rate in
       recent years in many countries.
   (D) The difference between the number of births and the number of deaths during a specific period
       is explained by demographic momentum.
   (E) The average number of years that a child can expect to live increases as a country industrializes.

3. The pressure that people place on the land to produce enough food is measured by

   (A) arithmetic (or crude) density
   (B) physiological population density
   (C) population concentrations
   (D) the stationary population level
   (E) the demographic equation

4, According to demographic transition theory at which stages in a country's development is population most likely to increase?

(A) Stages 1 and 2
(B) Stages 3 and 4
(C) Stages 2 and 4
(D) Stages 1 and 4
(E) Stages 2 and 3

5. During the late 1800s, an important pull factor for immigrants to the United States was

(A) a potato famine in Ireland
(B) political unrest of Germany and Eastern Europe
(C) political persecution in Russia
(D) the Industrial Revolution in the U.S.
(E) forced migration of slaves from Africa

6. The gravity model describes an inverse relationship between the

(A) volume of migration and the distance between source and destination
(B) step migration and intervening opportunities
(C) flows and counterflows of migrations
(D) intervening obstacles and intervening opportunities
(E) environmental push and pull factors and cultural push and pull factors

7. Refugees fleeing from the Balkans during the 1990s were mostly reacting to

(A) economic push factors
(B) economic pull factors
(C) cultural pull factors
(D) cultural push factors
(E) environmental push factors

8. Which of the following is least likely to have a high population density?

(A) coastal areas of South America
(B) river valleys in Africa
(C) interior areas of Australia
(D) sea level altitudes in North America
(E) coastal areas of India

9. Which of the following is an accurate statement about the population of China?

(A) The population is spread out fairly evenly across the country.
(B) Population is more concentrated in the southern part of the country.
(C) The western part of the country is sparsely populated.
(D) Population hugs the coastlines with almost no large inland cities.
(E) Population is more concentrated in the northern part of the country.

10. The Chinese government's population policies since 1979 have resulted in

(A) an overall reduction in the country's population
(B) a disproportionately large number of young women in the population
(C) tighter restrictions for family sizes of ethnic minorities than for Han Chinese
(D) a rapidly aging population
(E) a strict one-child policy for almost all families

11. Which of the following areas of the world generally have net out-migrations?

(A) Asia and North America
(B) Africa and Europe
(C) Latin America and Oceania
(D) Europe and North America
(E) Africa and Asia

> "Improving the status of women also enhances their decision-making capacity at all levels in all spheres of life, especially in the area of sexuality and reproduction. This, in turn, is essential for the long-term success of population programmes. Experience shows that population and development programmes are most effective when steps have simultaneously been taken to improve the status of women."*
>
> *Reference: "United Nations Population Information Network," www.un.org/popin/icpd/conference/offeng/poa.html

12. Which of the following would the author of the statement above be most likely to support?

(A) Population rates should be controlled by the central government.
(B) Women should be able to control their own fertility.
(C) Population rates should be controlled by regional governments.
(D) Population increases should be encouraged, especially in less developed countries.
(E) Population control is not an international issue.

13. Population density is most often represented by

(A) population pyramids
(B) circle graphs
(C) contour maps
(D) toponyms
(E) dot maps

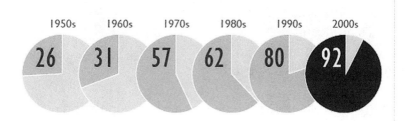

Minority share (%) of U.S. population growth, by decade, 1950s – 2000s

14. Which of the following statements is not supported by the graph above?

   (A) The minority share of U.S. population growth has grown significantly since the 1950s.
   (B) By the 2000s, the U.S. population was 92% minority.
   (C) The white majority share of U.S. population growth has decreased significantly since the 1950s.
   (D) The minority share of U.S. population growth has grown steadily during each decade since the 1950s.
   (E) Since the 1970s, the minority share of the overall U.S. population growth was more than 50%.

15. Which of the following was predicted by Thomas Malthus in the late 18th century?

   (A) Population growth in the future would be checked by famine, disease, and wars.
   (B) Population growth in the future would have no checks to slow it down.
   (C) Population growth in the future would by checked by industrial development.
   (D) Population growth in the future would be supported by increasing food supplies.
   (E) Population growth in Europe would be checked by increased colonization and immigration.

16. By the early 21st century, crude birth rates were highest in

   (A) Asia, Latin America, and Africa
   (B) Asia, Europe, and Africa
   (C) Europe, North America, and Latin America
   (D) North America, Africa, and Asia
   (E) Latin America, North America, and Asia

17. In recent years, death rates in developing countries have

   (A) stayed about the same
   (B) decreased slightly
   (C) increased slightly
   (D) increased significantly
   (E) decreased significantly

18. The "mortality revolution" occurred in Europe during the mid-19th century when

   (A) birth rates dropped significantly
   (B) pandemics lowered population levels dramatically
   (C) death rates dropped significantly
   (D) birth rates and death rates both rose significantly
   (E) a stationary population level was achieved

19. Which of the following is an accurate statement regarding population policies in India?

   (A) India's successful population policies have most likely prevented the country from becoming the most populous country in the world as early as 2030.
   (B) Despite policy coordination problems, India's birth rate has dropped by more than half in the last 35 years.
   (C) India's government has made few attempts to curtail population growth.
   (D) Like China, India has had a problem coordinating a centralized population policy.
   (E) India has followed China's lead in establishing a "one child policy" on the national level.

20. The demographic equation summarizes population change over time in an area by combining

   (A) immigration and emigration rates
   (B) spatial interactions and migrations
   (C) distance decay and step migration
   (D) natural change and net migration
   (E) push and pull factors for migration

21. Which of the following was the most significant human migration to occur during the 19th and early 20th centuries?

   (A) emigration from Asia to Europe
   (B) emigration from Europe to the Americas
   (C) emigration from Africa to Asia
   (D) emigration from Latin America to North America
   (E) emigration from Asia to North America

22. In recent years, a significant intraregional migration has occurred from Afghanistan to

   (A) India
   (B) the United States
   (C) Australia
   (D) Southeast Asia
   (E) Pakistan

23. The areas identified on the map above are areas that have experienced significant

   (A) in-migration
   (B) population increases
   (C) decreases in demographic momentum
   (D) internal migration
   (E) out-migration

24. Ernst Ravenstein's demographic studies focused mainly on

   (A) migration
   (B) natural increases in population
   (C) spatial interactions
   (D) fertility rates
   (E) population density

25. Canada's two largest language-based ethnic groups are

   (A) English and Spanish
   (B) Russian and Inuit
   (C) English and German
   (D) English and French
   (E) French and German

FREE-RESPONSE QUESTION
UNIT TWO

Thomas Malthus was one of the most influential theorists to write about population growth.

a. Explain Malthus's principle of exponential growth. Explain Malthus's principle of linear growth.

b. Identify two negative checks on population growth that Malthus described, and explain what effects these two checks would have on population growth in the future.

c. Explain two criticisms of Malthus's predictions for population growth.

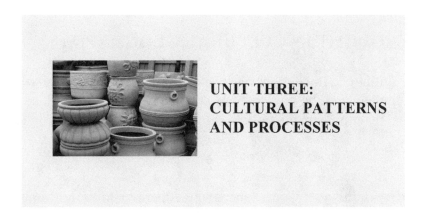

**UNIT THREE:
CULTURAL PATTERNS
AND PROCESSES**

If you have ever studied the earth's surface from an airplane thousands of feet in the air, you have observed the **cultural landscape**, the modification of the natural landscape by human activities. From the air, you get a whole new perspective on mountains, deserts, and rivers, but you also notice the many dramatic ways that people alter the land. For example, flying over the Midwestern United States you see the "checkerboards" created by intersections of crops, fields, and woods. Many times roads that lead to houses and barns mark borders. Cities, too, are impressive examples of the human imprint, with their large downtown buildings connected by road systems to the sprawling suburbs that surround them. The transformation of the land and the ways that humans interact with the environment are the special interests of **cultural geography**, an important component of the human geography course. **Cultural ecology** is the field that studies the relationship between the natural environment and culture. The cultural landscape provides ready evidence that humans transform and adapt to the land, and it offers clues about the cultural practices and priorities of its inhabitants, both present and past.

Cultural Landscape in Peru. This view of the Sacred Valley near Cuzco reflects cultural adaptation to the natural environment of mountain valleys. The human imprint is apparent not only in the town that is built in the flat part of the valley, but also in the surrounding agricultural fields, which are carved both into the valley and up the mountainsides as terraces.

SCHOOLS OF THOUGHT IN CULTURAL GEOGRAPHY

Through the years, cultural geographers have developed many different perspectives on the spatial interaction between humans and the land. These perspectives may be divided into four schools of thought: environmental determinism, possibilism, environmental perception, and humans as modifiers of the earth.

- **Environmental determinism** – Geographers who adhere to environmental determinism believe that the physical environment, especially the climate and terrain, actively shapes cultures, so that human responses are almost completely molded by the environment. Logically, then, similar physical environments produce similar cultures. Mountain cultures are simple, backward, and freedom-loving, and people who live near coasts center their activities on fishing and navigating the oceans or rivers. Temperate climates produce inventive, industrious, and democratic societies that are most likely to control others. Environmental determinism was popular during the early 20th century, especially among English-speaking geographers who used their perspective to explain why Britain came to dominate the globe.

- **Possibilism** – Possibilists recognize the importance of the physical environment, but they believe that cultural heritage is at least as important as the physical environment in shaping human behavior. People, then, are the primary architects of culture, and any physical environment offers many possibilities for a culture to develop. People make choices based on the opportunities and limitations of the physical environment, but their choices are also guided by cultural heritage. Most possibilists believe that technology increases the number of possibilities a people have, so that technologically advanced cultures have more control over their physical surroundings.

- **Environmental perception** – Whereas possibilism describes humans as making choices within the setting of their physical environment, environmental perception emphasizes the importance of human perception of the environment, rather than the actual character of the land. Perception, in turn, is shaped by the teachings of culture. For example, culture shapes our views of hazards and disasters, and human reactions will vary, depending on their cultural beliefs and values. For example, if people believe that a devastating flood was caused by the displeasure of the gods, they likely respond by building an alter, or by some other action intended to placate the gods. On the other hand, if people believe that the flood was a natural disaster, they most likely react by trying to prevent future floods, perhaps by building a dam.

- **Cultural determinism** – This perspective emphasizes human culture as ultimately more important than physical environment in shaping human actions. In contrast to environmental determinism, the humans-as-modifers approach views human culture as the molder of the physical environment. Some cultural determinists have seen humans in opposition to nature, and if nature is not controlled, humans are destined to die. Others have emphasized the negative impact that humans have had on the environment, and have urged people to take action to alter their impact. For example, modern movements to "take back the earth" encourage action to reverse global warming, air and water pollution, or the destruction of rain forests.

CONCEPTS OF CULTURE

Culture is the complex mix of values, beliefs, behaviors, and material objects that together form a people's way of life. Most social scientists are interested in the study of culture, but geographers specialize in the ways that culture affects the natural environment, as well as the spatial organization that culture stimulates. Culture may be divided into two types:

- **Non-material culture** – This type of culture consists of *abstract* concepts of values, beliefs, and behaviors. **Values** are culturally-defined standards that guide the way people assess desirability, goodness, and beauty, and that serve as guidelines for moral living. For example, one culture may consider body piercing to be an enhancement of human beauty. Other cultures may see it as a distortion of human appearance. On a broader level, one culture may emphasize the importance of abiding by the wishes of a supreme being, while another culture may extol the ability of human beings to set their own parameters. **Beliefs** are specific statements that people hold to be true, and they are almost always based on values. For example, the broad value that humans are able to guide their own lives may encourage a more specific belief in a democratic government that allows people to exercise their abilities. **Behaviors**, or actions that people take, are generally based on values and beliefs as reflected in **norms**, the rules and expectations by which a society guides the behavior of its members.

- **Material culture** – This type of culture includes a wide range of concrete human creations called **artifacts,** which reflect values, beliefs, and behaviors. You can readily see material culture as it relates to the environment from an airplane – the roads, houses, buildings, cars, farm equipment, and airport runways. But look beyond the objects themselves. Why do people build houses? Why are the houses arranged in the patterns that you see? Why are the checkerboards arranged as they are, and where do the roads lead? The answers to these questions lie in the values, beliefs, and behaviors (non-material culture) that humans use to guide the creation and maintenance of their artifacts (material culture).

CULTURE REGIONS, TRAITS, AND COMPLEXES

Separating culture into non-material and material types helps to sort out its complexities. Culture ties directly to geography's emphasis on space with the concept of a **culture region**, an area marked by culture that distinguishes it from other regions. Non-material culture, such as clothing and building style, reflect the values, beliefs, and behaviors of the people that live in the region. A single attribute of a culture is called a **culture trait**, and a culture region consists of countless numbers of traits. For example, a trait may be the practice of wearing colorful clothing with the group's own skillful weave and design. Another culture trait may be the building of roads and bridges across mountain ranges. Yet another trait may be the construction of buildings without mortar, and another the terracing of land for crop growth. Put all of these – and thousands of others – together, and you may study the culture region that survives today around the Andes Mountains in South America.

Culture traits are not necessarily confined to a single culture. For example, people in many cultures use brushes to clean their teeth and to make their hair more attractive, and they usually use different kinds of brushes for the two types of activities. However, the trait combines with others in a distinctive way,

Material culture, past and present. The adaptability of human material culture is evident in this photo of a modern-day French village. The narrow streets were built in an earlier time when people traveled by foot, animal, or wagon. The motorcycle parked by its owner's door is a reflection of modern technology's adaptation to material culture (winding streets, houses without garages) from the past.

so that a **culture complex** is formed. A culture complex consists of common values, beliefs, behaviors, and artifacts that make a group in an area distinct from others. For example, a large country such as China has many culture complexes. One complex that surrounds the modern city of Xi'an combines religions and beliefs, such as Buddhism, Islam, and Confucianism, in a way that makes it identifiable as a separate culture complex. However, particular traits, such as following Confucian principles, are shared by other complexes around them. Any area with strong cultural ties that binds its people together forms a **culture system,** a group of interconnected culture complexes. On the map, a culture region can represent an entire culture system that intertwines with its locational and environmental circumstances to form a **geographic region.**

CULTURAL HEARTHS

Historians specialize in the identification of **cultural hearths**, the areas where civilizations first began that radiated the customs, innovations, and ideologies that culturally transformed the world. Early cultural hearths developed in Southwest Asia, North Africa, South Asia, and East Asia in the valleys and basin of great river systems. Cultural hearths evolved later in Central and South America, and their geography shaped cultural development not around river valleys, but around mountain ranges and central highlands. Another cultural hearth with its own culture complex developed centuries later in West Africa, very much influenced by earlier hearths along the Nile River in Northeast Africa. Another unique cultural hearth developed in the islands of the Aegean Sea, where the inhabitants were joined by easy water access among islands and mainlands.

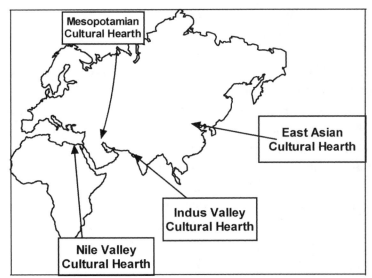

Earliest Cultural Hearths. The earliest cultural hearths were almost completely determined by their geographical locations. All were in river valleys where the soil was the most fertile and water most available for growing crops and transportation.

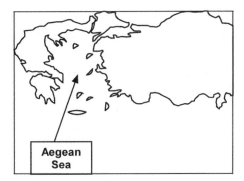

Early Aegean Cultural Hearth. This cultural hearth differed from earlier hearths in that it centered on the Aegean Sea, not on a river valley. The sea is calm and the islands numerous, allowing for easy transportation for Ancient Greeks to trade for goods that their natural environment did not provide.

From their centers, the hearths grew until they came into contact with one another, although their inhabitants' ability to travel to and contact other cultural hearths was limited by their levels of technology and by distance. Cultural hearths have shifted greatly over time. For example, the Industrial Revolution of the 18th and 19th century shifted cultural hearths to Europe and North America, with modern shifts in the 21st century continuing to occur.

CULTURAL DIFFUSION

The early cultural hearths were centers for innovation and invention, and their non-material and material culture spread to areas around them through a process called **cultural diffusion.** Over time, as cultural hearths have shifted, cultural diffusion has spread cultural traits to most parts of the globe. This long and complicated spread of culture often makes it difficult to trace the origin, spread, and timing of a particular trait. Whenever it is possible, developments that can be traced to a specific civilization are known as **independent inventions.** For example, the democratic process of gathering assemblies to discuss and vote on issues is often seen as an independent invention of the Ancient Greeks.

Diffusion occurs through the movement of people, goods, and ideas. **Carl Sauer** focused on this process in *Agricultural Origins and Dispersals*, written in 1952. Another famous geographer that wrote about cultural diffusion about the same time was **Torsten Hagerstrand.** Since the time of these pioneers, geographers have classified diffusion processes into two broad categories:

- **Expansion diffusion** – This type of diffusion is said to occur when an innovation or idea develops in a source area and remains strong there while also spreading outward. One form of expansion diffusion is **contagious diffusion**, when almost all individuals and areas outward from the source region are affected. The term implies the importance of direct contact between those in the source region and those in outlying areas, much as a contagious disease requires contact between those that have the disease and those that don't. The rate of diffusion is influenced by **time-distance decay,** so that the influence of the cultural traits weakens as time and distance increase. Another type of expansion diffusion is **hierarchical diffusion**, where ideas and artifacts spread first between larger places or prominent people and only later to smaller places or less prominent people. For example, as Islam spread to Sub-Saharan Africa by the 9th century C.E., its first converts were the elites, so that for centuries the kings and nobility were Muslim, but their subjects usually retained native religions, and only later converted to Islam. A third form of expansion diffusion is **stimulus diffusion** in which a basic idea, though not the specific trait itself, stimulates imitative behavior within a population. The idea may be too vague, different, or unattainable to be readily adopted by the new area. However, this does not mean that the idea has no impact at all. For example, as Buddhism spread from the main continent of Asia to Japan, the Japanese imitated designs for Buddhist temples, but interpretations of colors were often transmitted by verbal or written descriptions, not by someone who had actually seen a temple on the mainland. As a result, even today many Japanese temples are trimmed in bright orange, not the more traditional red seen in China.

- **Relocation diffusion** – In this process of diffusion, individuals or populations migrating from the source areas physically carry the innovation or idea to new areas. For example, Christian Europeans carried their faith to the Americas, where they often actively set about converting natives to Christianity, especially in Latin America. As a result, Christianity spread rapidly throughout the Western Hemisphere, ensuring its status as a major world religion. On a smaller scale, later immigrants to the United States carried their customs along to contained areas of settlement. A particular form of relocation diffusion is **migrant diffusion**, where the spread of cultural traits is slow enough that they weaken in the area of origin by the time they reach other areas. Examples are the contagious diseases that spread rapidly through the Native American populations that came into contact with Europeans in the New World during the 15th and 16th centuries. Immunities were built up so that the diseases faded in Europe at the same time they were raging in the Americas.

ACCULTURATION

When cultures come into contact, one culture often dominates the other. In the process called **acculturation,** the less dominant culture adopts some of the traits of the more influential one. Acculturation typically takes place when immigrants take on the values, attitudes, customs, and language of their new country. The dominant country is usually changed by this process as well. For example, in the United States today, years of migration from Latin America have led to the custom of adding Spanish to signs, phone recordings, and even government forms that had previously only appeared in English. If over time, the immigrants lose their native customs, including religion and language, **assimilation** occurs, meaning that the dominant culture completely absorbs the less dominant one. Assimilation sometimes occurs over the course of several generations, so that those that immigrate do not become fully assimilated, but their children or grandchildren do.

Sometimes two-way flows of culture reflect a more equal exchange of cultural traits, a process called **transculturation.** For example, as Buddhism spread from its origins in India throughout Asia, many of those that came in contact with the new religion already were steeped in the philosophical beliefs of Confucianism. Both forces were strong, and they clashed fiercely, but eventually transculturation occurred, and both Buddhism and Confucianism remained in place to influence large populations throughout the broad expanse of East Asia.

ETHNOCENTRISM AND CULTURAL RELATIVISM

Because culture interacts with the physical environment to shape human values and actions, almost all people exhibit **ethnocentrism,** the practice of judging another culture by the standards of one's own culture. Some ethnocentrism is necessary for people to be emotionally attached to their way of life, but ethnocentrism also generates misunderstanding and sometimes conflict. If one culture considers itself to be superior to others, the basis is laid for taking over other lands or for killing people or destroying property. Ethnocentrism takes many less harmful forms, and it is reflected even in our language. For example, people in Europe and North America have often referred to China as the "Far East" (a term that is unknown to the Chinese) because China is far east of Europeans and North Americans. On the other hand, the Chinese historically have referred to their land as the "Middle Kingdom" because it is in the center of the world.

In contrast to ethnocentrism, **cultural relativism** is the practice of evaluating a culture by its own standards. To practice cultural relativism, a person would have to put aside his or her own cultural preferences and consider another culture based on its own people's needs and values. Cultural relativists argue that in the modern world where people come into increased contact with one another, the importance of understanding other cultures becomes ever greater. Critics of cultural relativism point out problems that come with accepting all actions and values as equal, leading an individual to ignore or dismiss those that are clearly harmful or unjust.

CULTURAL DIFFERENCES

When cultural traits diffuse from society to society, they commonly go through various alterations. Rarely do they arrive completely intact, largely because the new group will adapt them to meet their needs, or interpret them according to their beliefs and values. The process of the fusion of old and new is called **syncretism**, a major explanation for how and why cultural changes occur. These changes inevitably lead to wide cultural differences in many areas, including languages and religions. Broad cultural differences between culture complexes and regions lead to varying ethnic identities, as well as to contrasting expectations for the roles that men and women play in society.

LANGUAGE

Language is the key to the world of culture. No other single culture trait more commonly binds people together because language is a set of symbols that allow people to communicate with one another. Over time, humans have devised hundreds of alphabets. Even the basic rules for writing differ. For example, most people in Western societies write from left to right, but people in Northern Africa and Western Asia write right to left, and people in Eastern Asia write from top to bottom.

Language is a systematic means of communicating ideas and feelings through the use of signs, gestures, marks, or vocal sounds. Language not only allows for communication, but it ensures the continuity of culture, or **cultural transmission**, the process by which one generation passes culture to the next. Without language, the accumulated wisdom of previous generations would be much more difficult to pass on to children. Every society transmits culture through speech, and most today also pass it along through writing as well. The preservation of culture is much more likely if at least some of a society's members can read and write because written records often last long after they are created. Writing was invented some 5,000 years ago, although until the 20th century most ordinary people were illiterate. Today high-income nations are nearly universally literate, and literacy rates are increasing in most other countries of the world.

Linguists estimate that between 5,000 and 6,000 languages are in use in the world today, with some much more widely used than others. Only ten languages are spoken by at least 100 million people: Spanish, Portuguese, Russian, German, Mandarin and Wu Chinese, English, Hindi, Bengali, Arabic, and Japanese. These most commonly spoken languages have diffused from their origins in many ways, including through trade, conquests, and/or migrations. Some areas of the world are characterized by **linguistic fragmentation,** a condition in which many languages are spoken, each by a relatively small number of people. This condition may result in an area where many major languages have diffused or where people have existed in relative isolation from others. An example is the Caucasus region of Eastern Europe, where many different cultural groups have settled and retained their languages. Today several thousand languages are spoken by fewer than 2 million people.

THE TEN MOST COMMONLY SPOKEN LANGUAGES
(Percentages for first language speakers only)

Mandarin Chinese	**12.44 %**
Spanish	**4.85%**
English	**4.83%**
Arabic	**3.25%**
Hindi	**2.68%**
Bengali	**2.66%**
Portuguese	**2.62%**
Russian	**2.12%**
Japanese	**1.8%**
Standard German	**1.33%**

Source: The CIA Factbook, 2009 estimates

Sources of Ten Major World Languages. Although there are thousands of languages spoken today, the majority of people in the world speak one of the languages indicated on the map. The map shows the origins of these languages before they diffused to many other areas of the world.

Language Families, Languages, and Dialects

How we define language depends on society's view of what makes up a cultural community, so the distinctions between language families, languages, and dialects are far from clear. However, each category represents a difference of scale, with language families having the broadest global perspective and dialects representing local variations of a language. **Linguistic geography** is the study of speech areas and their local variations by mapping word choices, pronunciations, or grammatical constructions.

- **Language families** – Languages are usually grouped into families with a shared, but fairly distant origin. The most commonly cited is the **Indo-European family**, since languages in this family are spoken by about half the world's people, with English as the most widely used. Other Indo-European languages include Spanish, English, Hindi, Portuguese, Bengali, Russian, German, Marathi, French, Italian, Punjabi, and Urdu, accounting for over 1.7 billion native speakers. Romance languages form a **sub-family**, with origins in Latin, including Spanish, French, and Italian. The distant origins of the Indo-European family are thought to be in the vicinity of the Black Sea where speakers of a root language dispersed all over Europe and Central Asia, spreading their language that changed as it diffused, eventually evolving into distinct languages. Some analysts suggest that these inhabitants swept westward on horseback and conquered earlier inhabitants. Others believe that it was the spread of agriculture, not conquest, that was responsible for diffusing the Indo-European root language throughout Europe and Central Asia. Other language families include Afro-Asiatic, Niger-Congo, Dravidian, and American Indian, and scholars propose that they too diffused from cultural hearths long ago.

- **Languages** – Languages are culturally defined, with **standard languages** those that are recognized by the government and the intellectual elite as the norm for use in schools, government, media, and other aspects of public life. Standard languages are often the dialects identified with countries' capital cities or centers of power at the time the nations developed. For example, standard French is based on the dialect of Paris, which in the late 12th century began to dominate the land space that eventually became France. In China, standard Chinese is Mandarin Chinese heard in and around the capital, Beijing. However, many other versions of the language are spoken, including Wu Chinese, which is spoken in Shanghai and many other major cities south of Beijing. Sometimes, especially in multilingual states, a standard language may be designated as an **official language,** or the language endorsed and recognized by the government as the one that everyone should know and use. Countries may designate more than one official language, especially if linguistically distinct groups lobby the government for recognition of their languages.

- **Dialects** – On the sub-national scale, dialects may be thought of as regional variants of a standard language. Although most people in the country may understand the standard language, they speak with differences in vocabulary, and they put words together in phrases in different ways. Also, pronunciations vary, and people in some areas speak more quickly or slowly than people in other areas. An accent reveals almost anyone's regional home. Linguistic geographers map the area in which particular words are used, marking their limits as **isoglosses,** boundaries within which the words are spoken. An isogloss in not a clear line of demarcation, however, with the use of particular words fading as the boundary is approached. Major languages that have diffused widely from their origins often have hundreds of dialects. For example, on the world level British, American, Indian, and Australian English are all distinctive dialects. Regionally, in Britain alone, dialects may be grouped in three ways: Southern British English, Northern British English, and Scottish English, each containing several more localized variations. Dialect regions in the eastern United States may be divided into the North (New England and adjacent Canada extending to a secondary dialect area centered in New York City), the Midland (central New Jersey to central Delaware, spreading extensively across the interior of the United States and Canada), and the South (East Coast from Chesapeake Bay south). Dozens of other dialects exist in the mid-section and along the West Coast.

Coping with Language Barriers

People from different language groups are often quite creative in trying to communicate, even though their native tongues are mutually incomprehensible. **Bilingualism** (the ability to communicate in two languages) and **multilingualism** (the ability to communicate in more than two languages) may permit one person to speak the common language, or both to switch to a jointly understood third language. However, long-term contact between less skilled people sometimes results in the creation of a **pidgin**, an amalgamation of languages that borrows words from several. A pidgin is a hybrid that serves as a second language for everyone who uses it. For example, Lingala is a hybrid of Congolese dialects that the French invented to aid in communication among some 270 ethnic groups. If a pidgin becomes the first language of a group of speakers – who may have lost their former native tongue through disuse – a **creole** has evolved. An example is Haitian Creole, the language of Haiti, derived from pidginized French used in the slave trade.

An established language that comes to be spoken and understood over a large area is sometimes called a **lingua franca**, named after a medieval dialect of France spoken by Crusaders from various European

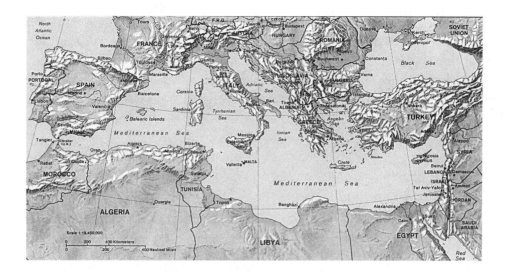

The modern area around the Mediterranean Sea. Most of the area around the Mediterranean Sea was dominated by the Roman Empire by the early 2nd century C.E. As political power spread, Latin became the **lingua franca** of the area. Once the empire fell, the area reverted to cultural practices of its various ethnicities, as reflected in the country and city names on the modern map. However, Latin blended with native tongues to create modern languages of Spanish, French, Italian, Romanian, and Portuguese.

countries as they pursued their quest to recapture the Holy Lands from the Turks. After the Crusades were over the language remained useful in the regions around the eastern Mediterranean Sea to facilitate trade and travel. Many years earlier, between 300 B.C.E. and 500 C.E., the lingua franca of the Mediterranean was Greek, which was later replaced by Latin, the Roman language. Latin became the standard language of the entire Roman Empire, which stretched from Britain in the Northwest to lands far east of the Mediterranean. After the fall of the empire, people became isolated from one another and reverted to speaking their individual dialects that had never disappeared entirely, and Latin became a "dead" language. However, even though it did not survive as a major language, its influence is still seen in the development of the "Romance languages" that combined local dialects with Latin to create major modern languages such as French, Italian, and Spanish.

Today an important example of a lingua franca is English, which has become a language of international communication. The rapid growth in importance of English is reflected in the large number of students learning English as a second language in schools in many countries around the world. Some 200 million people speak English fluently as a second language, and countless others have some working knowledge of the language. Other than English, modern lingua franca languages include Swahili in East Africa, Hindustani in South Asia, and Russian in the former Soviet Union.

Toponymy

Toponymy is the study of place names, a special interest of linguistic geography. Place names become a part of the cultural landscape that remains long after the name givers have disappeared from the scene. In the United States, a classic study of toponymy is George Stewart's *Names on the Land: A Historical Account of Place-Naming in the United States*. A careful study of a map can reveal cultural identities and histories by simply noticing names of geographical and political features. For example, many names honor kings, queens, or heroes, such as "Maryland" for Queen Mary, "Virginia" for the Virgin Queen Elizabeth, "Carolina" and "Georgia" for English kings Charles and George. Other names reflect geographical origins: "York" (New York), the "Jersey Isles" (New Jersey), and "Hampshire"

(New Hampshire). Localized or temporary settlements, such as the Dutch around New York Harbor, live on in their place names, "Breukelyn" (Brooklyn) and "Haarlem" (Harlem). Some place names are simply descriptive ("Rocky Mountains," "Salt Lake City"), and others denote incidents or events ("Battle Creek," Michigan) or commemorate religious figures ("San Francisco," "St. Louis"). In Canada, French ethnicity is reflected in place names in Quebec: "Trois-Rivieres," "Grand Mère," "Chateau-Richer," "Montreal," and "Quebec."

Many place names have two or more parts. For example, names often contain the word "town," "ton," "burgh," or "ville" (all references to a town) and a person ("Johnstown," "Pottstown," "Youngstown," "Charleston," "Princeton," "Pittsburgh," "Knoxville," "Nashville"). Other two part names use prefixes, such as "new," "big," or "little," that appear in many languages. An example is "Big River" in English, which is found as "Rio Grande" in Spanish, and "Mississippi" in Algonquin.

Language Extinction

Extinct languages were once in use, but are no longer spoken or read in daily activities by anyone in the world. The process of extinction no doubt has been going on throughout history and prehistory, but it seems to be accelerating as communication and transportation improvements bring world languages to most parts of the globe. An example of an extinct language is Gothic, widely spoken by people in Eastern and Northern Europe during the 3rd century C.E. The entire language family that Gothic originated from has disappeared, with the latest speakers of Gothic dying out in the Crimean area of Russia during the 16th century.

Some organizations are trying to preserve endangered languages, as evidenced by the European Union's European Bureau of Lesser Used Languages, which provides financial support, especially to Celtic languages. Ethnic groups have also pushed for measures to preserve their languages, such as the movement in Wales to continue to teach Welsh, not just English, in their schools. In modern day Peru about 3 to 4 million people speak the native language Quechua, with a few others in Bolivia and Ecuador. Spanish has been the dominant language of these countries since the Spanish conquest in the 16th century, and Quechua has been in slow decline, spoken mainly in rural areas. However, in recent days two members of Peru's Congress have insisted on delivering their speeches in Quechua, so that the legislature has been forced to hire translators. On an international level, Google has launched a version of its search engine in Quechua, and Microsoft has provided Quechua translations of its Windows and Office programs.   In 2006 Peru's president signed a law making discrimination on the basis of language a criminal offence.

RELIGION

Unlike language, which is important in all cultures, religion varies in its cultural influence. Historically, almost all cultures have centered on religion, and today many still do. However, in recent years other ideologies have replaced religion as key cultural components in some societies. One such ideology is **humanism**, with roots in Ancient Greece and Rome (and more recently the European Renaissance), which emphasizes the ability of human beings to guide their own lives. Another is **Marxism**, which transformed communism into a central ideology in many areas during the 20th century. However, even in societies that are largely non-religious, people are strongly influenced by religious values from earlier days.

Religion distinguishes itself from other belief systems by its emphasis on the sacred and divine. According to French sociologist Emile Durkheim, religion is important in explaining anything that surpasses the limits of our knowledge. As human beings, we define most objects, events, and experiences as **profane**, or ordinary, but we define some things as **sacred**, or extraordinary, inspiring a sense of awe and reverence. Religions usually explain the relationship of the individual to the world, as well as the meaning of life and death, and what happens to people after they die. These beliefs become intertwined with other values, beliefs, and customs of the society so that they become basic to a people's way of life. For example, almost since its founding Islam has been the basis for *shari'a* law that defines the political systems of many Muslim countries.

Geographers are interested in religion because it shapes the cultural landscape, with predominant religions varying among regions of the world. Geographers document the places where various religions are located and offer explanations as to why some religions have diffused globally, whereas others have remained highly localized.

Universalizing Religions

The three main **universalizing religions** are Christianity, Islam, and Buddhism. Each attempts to be global in its appeal to all people, wherever they may live in the world, not just to those in one location. They contrast to **ethnic religions** that appeal primarily to one group of people living in one place. About 60% of the world's population identifies with a universalizing religion, 24% to an ethnic religion, and about 16% to no religion. Each of the three universalizing religions is divided into subgroups:

- **Branches** are large and basic divisions within a religion.
- **Denominations** are divisions of branches that unite local groups in a single administrative body.
- **Sects** are relatively small groups that do not affiliate with the more mainstream denominations.

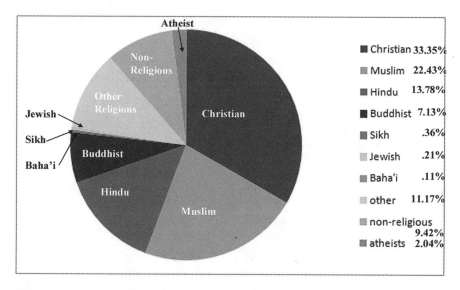

Christian	33.35%
Muslim	22.43%
Hindu	13.78%
Buddhist	7.13%
Sikh	.36%
Jewish	.21%
Baha'i	.11%
other	11.17%
non-religious	9.42%
atheists	2.04%

Major Religions of the World as a Percentage of World Population. Although there are many different religions in the world, most people that call themselves religious adhere to the few religions identified on the chart. More than 60% of the world's population identifies with one of the three universalizing religions: Christianity, Islam, or Buddhism. The largest single ethnic religion is Hinduism, with nearly 14% of the world's population, mostly located on the Indian subcontinent.

Christianity

Christianity has by far the most followers, with about 2.3 billion people worldwide calling themselves Christians. It also has the most widespread distribution, and it is the predominant religion in North America, South America, Europe, and Australia. Christianity has three major branches:

- **Roman Catholic** – About 50% of the world's Christians are Roman Catholic, with concentrations in Latin America, French Canada (Quebec), Central Africa, and Southern and Eastern Europe.

- **Protestant** – About 18% of the world's Christians are Protestants. This branch first split from the Catholic Church in the 16th century, and it later divided into hundreds of denominations. Protestantism is strong in North America, Northern Europe, Britain, South Africa, and Australia.

- **Eastern Orthodox** – About 12% of all Christians are Eastern Orthodox, a branch that officially split from Roman Catholicism in the 11th century C.E. It is strong in Eastern Europe and Russia.

Other Christians affiliate with a variety of African, Asian, and Latin American churches that cannot be categorized with the three major branches. Many communities were isolated from others at an early point in the development of the religion, but have remained Christian over the centuries. Examples are the Ethiopian Church, with about 10 million followers, and the Coptic Church of Egypt, Ethiopia, and Eritrea with about 50 million adherents.

More than one-half of U.S. adults consider themselves Protestants and one-fourth identify as Catholics. Only about 4% – according to an ABC news poll in 2011 – identify as adherents to a non-Christian religion - Jews, Muslims, Buddhists, and a smattering of others. Although the diversity of Protestant denominations is great, regional differences mean that most people live in communities where one denomination predominates. For example, Baptists prevail in the southern states from Texas east to Virginia and Georgia. Many Methodists live in the Northeast and the Southwest, and Lutherans concentrate in Minnesota and North Dakota. Members of the Church of Jesus Christ of Latter Day Saints (Mormons) live mainly in the state

PROTESTANTISM IN THE UNITED STATES
(as a percentage of total population)

Baptist Church	16%
Methodist Church	7%
Pentecostal Church	6%
Lutheran Church	3%
Presbyterian Church	2%
Episcopalian Church	1%

Christianity in the United States. About 50% of the U.S. population is Protestant, but they belong to hundreds of different denominations and sects. Even the major denominations above are divided into different churches. For example, Baptists are divided into Southern Baptists, Northern Baptists, National Baptists, National Missionary Baptists, and Progressive National Baptists. Many Protestants belong to independent denominations that do not affiliate with the major groups listed above.

of Utah and its surrounding areas. These patterns are determined partly by movements of people in history. For example, Mormons traveled to Utah to escape religious persecution in the east, and immigrants from Scandinavia brought their Lutheran religion with them to the northern part of the Midwest.

Islam

The second largest world religion is Islam, with about 1.6 billion adherents. It is the predominant religion of the Middle East from North Africa to Central Asia, but about half of the world's Muslims live in four countries outside the Middle East: Indonesia, Pakistan, Bangladesh, and India. The religion is spreading rapidly to other areas, including North America and Europe, and overall it is growing more quickly than Christianity is. For example, there are about 2.6 million Muslims in the United States, making Islam a significant part of religious life in that country. It is also the youngest of the world religions, with a founding date in the 7th century C.E. on the Arabian Peninsula.

Islam is divided into two main branches:

- **Sunni** comprise 83% of all Muslims and is the largest branch in the Middle East and Asia. Although many live in the Middle East, the country with the largest concentration of Sunni Muslims is Indonesia.

- **Shiites** make up about 16% of all Muslims, and most are located in only a few countries of the Middle East. Nearly 40% of all Shiites live in Iran, 15% in Pakistan, 10% in Iraq, and 10% in Turkey, Azerbaijan, Afghanistan, and Yemen.

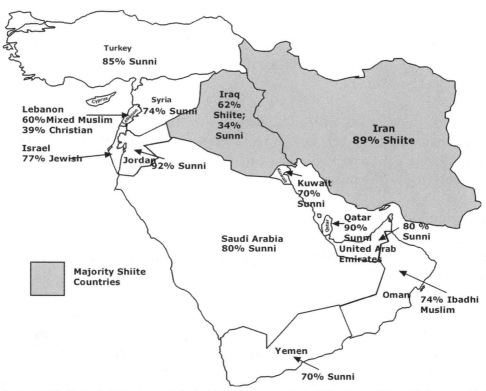

Sunnis and Shiites in the Middle East. Only two countries in the Middle East are majority Shiite: Iran and Iraq. All the rest, with the exceptions of Lebanon and Israel, are majority Sunni. A great deal of ethnic identity is based on Sunni or Shiite affiliation, and the two branches historically have experienced many tensions. The religious split is part of the reason the Middle East is one of the political and religious "hot spots" of our age.

The split between Sunni and Shiite branches occurred very early in the history of the religion, when an argument erupted over the rightful successor to Muhammad, the religion's 7th century founder. The Sunni believed that the successor should be chosen by agreement among the religious leaders, but the Shiites believed that the successor should be a member of Muhammad's family. The Sunni won the argument, but the Shiites refused to accept the decision, and the two branches have maintained their separate identities ever since, creating major divisions among and within Muslim countries that have often led to conflict.

Buddhism

Although Buddhism is the world's third major universalizing religion, it has only 365 million followers, considerably fewer than Christianity and Islam have. The religion began on the Indian subcontinent, where its founder, Siddhartha (the Buddha) lived. The religion diffused along the Silk Road and water routes across the Indian Ocean, mainly to East and Southeast Asia, where it remains a strong religion today. Today India is overwhelmingly Hindu and Islam, with only a small fraction of its citizens identifying as Buddhists.

Buddhism has three main branches:

- **Mahayana** – 56% of Buddhists are Mahayana, or "Big Wheel," characterized by broad incorporation of ideas and gods from other religions as it spread into East Asia.

- **Theraveda** – About 38% of Buddhists are Theraveda, characterized by a stricter adherence to the original teachings of the Buddha. This branch is strong in Southeast Asia.

- **Tantrayana** – Only about 6% of Buddhists are Tantrayana, the "Vehicle of the Text," with its emphasis on magic as well as different meditation techniques. It is found primarily in Tibet and Mongolia.

An accurate count of Buddhists is difficult because eastern religions don't require their followers to identify with only one religion. In contrast to most Westerners, many Asians combine their religious beliefs so that they claim to be adherents to more than one belief system. For example, in Japan, many Buddhists also subscribe to Shintoism, a native Japanese religion.

Other Universalizing Religions

Two other religions – **Sikhism** and **Baha'i** – qualify as universalizing religions because they actively seek converts to their broad views and beliefs. About 21 million Sikhs live in the Punjab region of India, with about 3 million more living elsewhere. Sikhs stress continual improvement and movement toward perfection by taking individual responsibility for their actions, a universal message that appeals to many. Sikhism combines beliefs from Hinduism and Islam – the two largest religions on the Indian subcontinent – but centers on the teachings of its founder, Guru Nanak. Baha'i is a relatively new faith, founded in Iran in 1844 by Siyyid 'Ali Muhammad, known as the Bab (Persian for "gateway"). Most followers live in Iran, where they are viewed by some Shiite Muslims as heretics to the faith, since they believe that Husayn 'Ali Nuri (Known as Baha'u'llah, or "Glory of God") was the prophet and messenger of God, not Muhammad, the founder of the Islamic faith.

Ethnic Religions

Ethnic religions differ from universalizing religions in that they generally do not seek converts outside the group that gave rise to the religion. As a result, they tend to be spatially concentrated. The main exception is Judaism, whose adherents are widely scattered.

Hinduism

Although Hinduism is the world's third largest religion, most of its 800 million adherents live in India. A few live in the neighboring country of Nepal, and only about 1% are dispersed around the world. Hindus make up 80% of the population of India, 90% of Nepal, and a small minority in every other country. Hinduism is generally regarded as the world's oldest organized religion still in practice, but it is not tightly organized into branches or denominations. It has no central god or a single holy book, so each individual decides the best way to worship. There is a belief in the existence of a universal spirit (Brahman) that manifests itself in many shapes and forms, including the gods Vishnu and Shiva, but Hindus show allegiance to different gods.

The Chinese Religions

Because eastern religions do not require their followers to adhere to only one faith, Buddhism often blends with local belief systems, including **Confucianism** and **Daoism.** Neither religion involves concepts of supernatural omnipotence, so they are often viewed as philosophies, not religions. Confucianism provides a code of moral conduct based on humaneness and family loyalty. Daoism holds that human happiness lies in maintaining proper harmony with nature. These faiths survive in China today, and are also influential in Korea and Japan. There is no reliable data on the number of adherents, but the collective influence of the Chinese religious complex is huge, particularly since the religions have diffused not only to Korea and Japan, but to almost all other parts of East and Southeast Asia.

Shintoism

Shintoism is a native ethnic religion of Japan that focuses particularly on nature and reverence of ancestors. Ancient Shintoists considered forces of nature to be sacred, especially the sun and the moon, but also rivers, trees, rocks, and mountains. In the late 19th century Shintoism became the official state religion as part of an effort by the government to increase Japanese nationalism. Shintoism still thrives in Japan, although it is no longer the official state religion. Prayers are offered to ancestors, and shrines mark reverence for house deities.

Judaism

Judaism is one of the world's oldest religions, with a founding around 2000 B.C.E. by Abraham in the lands bordering the eastern Mediterranean Sea. Throughout its long existence, it has remained fundamentally an ethnic religion, a fact reflected in its relatively low numbers – about 15 million adherents. Unlike most other ethnic religions, its members are spread widely across the earth, mainly because of **diaspora**, or forced exodus from their lands of origin. About 6 millions Jews live in the United States, 4 million in Israel, and 2 million in the former Soviet Union. Within the United States,

Jews are heavily concentrated in the urban Northeast, with about one-third living in the New York area alone. The only country where Jews constitute a majority is Israel, a country created in 1948 as the Jewish homeland, the area where the religion began.

The influence of Judaism expands far beyond its numbers. It was the first recorded **monotheistic religion**, centered on the belief in one God. Christianity and Islam also have their roots in Judaism. Jesus was born a Jew, and Muhammad traced his ancestry to Abraham.

Shamanism and Traditional Religions

Shamanism is an ethnic religion in which people follow their shaman, a religious leader and teacher who is believed to be in contact with the supernatural. The religion takes different forms, largely because its followers are isolated from one another. Shamanism is reflected in the "totem poles" of North American natives, and shamans in East Asia are believed to be in contact with the ancestors, an important value in China, Korea, and Japan. Shamanism in Africa often takes the form of **animism**, the belief that inanimate objects (rocks, mountain, rivers, plants) have spirits and conscious life. Shamanism is a **traditional religion**, an integral part of a local culture and society, but not all traditional religions are shamanist. Traditional African religions involve beliefs in a god as creator and protector, in spirits, and in a life hereafter, opening the way for Christianity and Islam to convert some Africans to their beliefs. However, most Africans still adhere to their native religions, especially among ordinary, non-elite people.

The Spatial Impact of Religions

Geographers study the impact of universalizing and ethnic religions on the landscape. In large cities around the world, the tallest, most centralized, and elaborate buildings are often religious structures. Places of worship vary with the religion – churches, mosques, temples, synagogues, pagodas – but many other structures are arranged around the religious buildings. For example, the Hindu cultural landscape – urban as well as rural – is dotted with shrines that impose minimal disruption to the natural landscape. Shrines and temples are located near water, because water is part of sacred rituals, and it is believed that gods will not venture far from water. Buddhism also has affected the natural landscape through its respect for the Bodhi tree, where the Buddha first received his enlightenment in the Ganges River Valley. Bodhi trees are protected in Buddhist lands, with the religion diffused as far as China and Japan, marking the cultural landscapes of many villages and towns.

An important religious land use that impacts the cultural landscape has to do with disposing of the dead. In several religions – Christianity, Islam, and Judaism – the dead are buried in specially designated areas called cemeteries. Early Christians buried their dead in the yard around the church, but as these areas became overcrowded, separate burial grounds were established outside the city walls. Cemeteries may take up significant space in a community. Before the widespread development of public parks in the 19th century, cemeteries were often the only green space in cities. Cemeteries are still used as parks in Muslim countries. Because cemeteries take up land space, the government in China has ordered that the practice of burial be discontinued in order to preserve land for agriculture. Cremation is increasingly practiced instead.

The Cultural Imprint of the Gothic Cathedral. Gothic cathedrals were built at great expense and effort all over Europe during the Middle Ages. Today they still dominate the cultural landscapes of many cities, towns, and villages.

POPULAR AND FOLK CULTURE

Culture may be categorized according to spatial distribution into two basic types: folk culture and popular culture. **Folk culture** is traditionally practiced by small, homogeneous groups living in isolated rural areas. **Popular culture** is found in large heterogeneous societies that are bonded by a common culture despite the many differences among the people that share it.

Folk Culture

Folk culture is controlled by tradition, and resistance to change is strong. Most groups are self-sufficient, and their tools, food, and music tend to be homemade. Buildings are constructed with local materials without architects or blueprints, but with clear purposes and plans in mind. **Folk life** is the composite culture, both material and non-material, that shapes the lives of folk societies, such as those in rural areas in the early settlement of the United States. Today true folk societies no longer exist in the U.S., although the Amish, with their rejection of electricity, cars, and modern dress, are one of the least altered folk groups in the country. When many people who live in a land space share at least some of the same folk customs, a **folk culture region** may be recognized. For example, in the area around Lancaster, Pennsylvania, the Amish have settled into farmhouses that are readily identifiable by the lack of electrical lines, buggies and horses outside, and people who dress in traditional styles. Although other people live in the area, the unique cultural landscape created by the Amish make the area a distinct folk culture region. Although only about 70,000 Amish people live in the U.S. today, their folk culture remains visible on the landscape in at least 17 states, with the largest concentrations today in Pennsylvania, Ohio, and Indiana.

Cultural Diversity

Folk cultures usually contribute to cultural diversity because they are relatively isolated. They may diffuse to other locations, but generally the diffusion is slow because people often don't leave the areas where they grow up. A group's unique folk customs develop through centuries of relative isolation from customs practiced by other cultural groups. Geographers P. Karan and Cotton Mather found good examples of cultural diversity among isolated folk societies that live in the Himalayan Mountains in Central Asia. Despite the fact that spatial distances are small, the groups' cultures are very different from one another. For example, only Tibetan Buddhists in the northern regions paint divine figures, such as monks and saints. In contrast, Hindus in the south prefer to paint scenes from everyday life. Some groups concentrate their art on plants and flowers, while others paint symbols and designs that reflect their religious animism.

The Physical Environment

Environmental conditions limit the variety of human life anywhere, but since folk societies are usually agricultural with limited technology, they are particularly responsive to the environment. However, their methods for dealing with the environment differ greatly. For example, the custom of wearing wooden shoes in the Netherlands comes from an adaptation to working in fields that are very wet because much of the land is below sea level. Other folk cultures that work in wet fields have adapted to the environment in other ways, making the Dutch custom unique.

Food habits derive from the environment according to the climate and growing season. Rice will not grow in the cold, drier climates that wheat prefers, so the environment limits food production. However, folk societies prepare and cook foods in various ways, and they even differ in what they consider to be edible. For example, Hindu taboos against eating cows deprive some of a readily available food source. However, the taboo makes environmental sense because oxen (castrated male cows) are necessary for pulling plows that must prepare the fields when the monsoon rains arrive every year. Other food taboos have no environmental basis, such as American avoidance of eating insects, which are a readily available source of nutrition.

Housing Styles

Housing structures reflect both cultural and environmental influences. Folk societies are limited in their building materials by the resources available in the environment. So if trees are available, wooden houses will be built, but if not, they will be constructed of stone, grass, sod, skins, or whatever else is available. Similarly, construction techniques also reflect the environment, such as building a steep roof in cold climates to reduce the accumulation of snow. Variations, though, are not always explained by environment. Cultural influences are reflected in housing styles, such as sacred walls or corners built in houses in China, Fiji, the Middle East, India, and Africa. In parts of Java, the front door always faces south, the direction of the all-important South Sea Goddess. People in similar climates choose different styles for their buildings. Some may organize everything around a central courtyard, others may build balconies on the front of their houses, and still others may build decks or patios on the back. Cultures define zones of privacy differently within a home's property, with many in East Asia building doors and walls for entrance into a garden area, a zone of privacy not usually found in homes in the West.

Housing styles may diffuse to other areas, particularly as folk cultures break up and are replaced by larger popular cultures. Traditional styles come from folk culture centers, and diffuse wherever the houses are practical or appealing to build. An example is the New England saltbox house, a practical adaptation to cold weather climate that is now widely found throughout the Great Lakes area, New York, and Pennsylvania. A Middle Atlantic style originated as a one-room log cabin with a stone chimney and

New England Houses. On the left is the saltbox house style originating in New England around 1650 and commonly built by the early 18th century. On the right is the "Cape Cod" style , also a New England style, that originated in the late 17th century. Both styles diffused west and south through New York, Pennsylvania, New Jersey, Ohio, and Michigan by the early 19th century.

Traditional House in Peru. The thatched-roof house in the modern-day photo above provides evidence that housing styles still may reflect folk cultures. Thatched roofs appear in other cultures, but this style is particular to the Andes Mountain valleys in South America.

fireplace at one end. The houses were built on to with time, often with additional rooms, a porch, and a second floor. The style spread westward throughout the mid-section of the country to the Mississippi River. In the South, houses were often built on raised platforms or stilts to allow for cool air to circulate under the floors. A similar style of house diffused from its source in the Lower Chesapeake Bay area southward along the coast as far as Georgia.

Folk Music

North American folk music began as immigrants carried their songs to the New World, but the imported songs became Americanized, and new songs were added by American experiences. The songs developed from several folk culture regions:

- The Northern song area – This region includes the Maritime Provinces of Canada, New England, and the Middle Atlantic states. Its ballads are close to English originals, a characteristic reinforced by new immigrants. The fiddle is featured at dances, and fife-and-drum bands were popular in the early years of the Republic.

- The Southern and Appalachian song area – This region extends westward to Texas, and the music is characterized by unaccompanied, high-pitched, nasal solo singing. The words speak of hard lives, and the backwoods style that emerged forms the roots of "country" music.

- The Western song area – West of the Mississippi River this regional music reflects the experiences of cowboys, plains farmers, river people, and gold seekers. Some are reworked lumberjack ballads of the North.

- The Black Song Style Family – This style grew out of the slave experience in the rural South, and features both choral and instrumental music, a strong beat, and deep-pitched mellow voices.

Popular Culture

In the United States folk cultures broke down during the 20th century as automobiles, radios, motion pictures, and a national press began to homogenize America. Mechanization, mass production, and mass distribution through stores and mail order diminished self-sufficiency and household crafts. Popular culture began to replace traditional culture in everyday life throughout the United States, Canada, and most other industrialized countries. **Popular culture** is primarily but not exclusively urban-based, with a general mass of people conforming to and then abandoning ever-changing cultural trends. Popular culture is pervasive, and involves the vast majority of a population, exposing them to similar consumer and recreational choices, and leads them to behave in similar ways. Folk culture encourages cultural diversity among groups; popular culture breeds homogeneity.

In reality, folk cultures don't go away entirely, but they blend with popular culture, and differences between local and universal become less apparent.

National Uniformities and Globalization

Landscapes of uniformity through popular culture tend to take on a national character, so that the American or Canadian way of life is different from the English or the Japanese way of life. National chain stores, gas stations, restaurants, and motels appear, all with identical outside and inside architecture and style. In recent years many of these chain stores have globalized, so that they may be seen in many countries. In particular, American popular culture has diffused to many areas of the world through global communication and transportation networks. The globalization of popular culture is seen in clothing styles, television shows, movies, and acceptance of western business conduct and institutions. Of course, standardization is not complete, and national and regional cultural contrasts still remain.

Many people resent the globalization of popular culture, and some governments officially oppose or control it. Iran restricts Western radio and television programs and enforces traditional dress for women, including head coverings. China, Saudi Arabia, and many other countries impose internet surveillance and censorship and demand that U.S.-based search engines filter offensive content. In recent years the globalization of popular culture has come to be seen as a type of dominance by the West, and resisting it is thought to preserve non-Western ways of life.

Environmental Impact of Popular Culture

Popular culture is less likely than folk culture to be distributed with consideration for physical features, partly because it often significantly modifies or controls the environment. Technologies can reproduce natural features, yet place them in unnatural settings. For example, the "strip" in Las Vegas is lined with hotels and casinos that reproduce the cultures of ancient Egypt, New York City, Venice, Paris, the Middle East, and ancient Rome – all set within the natural desert landscape.

Some environmental consequences of popular culture include:

- **Uniform landscapes** – Not only do buildings look alike, but they are arranged on streets that look the same no matter where they are. Fast food restaurants are next door to chain motels, which in turn border gas stations and convenience stores. These structures are designed so that both local residents and visitors immediately recognize the purpose of the building, or perhaps even the name of the company.

- **Increased demand for natural resources** – Fads may increase demands for animal skins, such as mink, jaguar, leopard, or kangaroo for fashionable clothing. Eating habits may demand consumption of food that is not efficient to produce. For example, to produce 1 pound of beef, the animal needs to consume about 10 pounds of grain. For chicken, the ratio is 1 to 3. This grain could be fed to people directly, bypassing the inefficiency of producing the meat.

- **Pollution** – One of the most significant problems of modern mass society is the pollution created by a high volume of wastes – solids, liquids, and gases – that must be absorbed into the environment. Solid products – cans, bottles, old cars, paper, and plastics – are discarded rather than recycled. Folk cultures have sometimes been hard on the environment, too. For example, during the Middle Ages, many of the forests of Europe were cut down to provide fuel for warmth and cooking. However, the level of waste that folk cultures generate is usually far less than that created by people in the era of popular culture.

CULTURAL LANDSCAPES AND CULTURAL IDENTITY

Each culture region develops a distinctive cultural landscape as people modify the environment to their specific needs, technologies, and lifestyles. For example, terraced fields of crops up the mountainsides represent a distinctive feature of the cultural landscape of the Andes Mountain region in South America. The cultural landscape of the Rocky Mountain region in North America looks very different because the U.S. and Canadian cultures formed at different times, with a different mix of population, money, diets, technology, and trade patterns.

Landscapes and Values

The value systems of cultures affect the ways people use the natural environment, and so, the appearance of the cultural landscape. Native Americans of the Central Plains were basically hunters and gatherers who viewed the land space not as property but as the source of their sustenance, whereas Europeans coming into the area looked for areas to grow their crops and animals to trade back east. In many ways the buffalo symbolized the contrasting value systems. Native Americans used every part of animals that they killed because they were necessary for survival. Europeans saw buffalo as a source of hides to sell or trade, and left the carcasses to rot, leaving Native Americans without the necessities of life. Farmers who moved into the area valued soil, and so changed the cultural landscape from one that characterized hunting and gathering to one dotted with farmhouses, fences, roads, and rows of crops. In areas where industry has displaced agriculture, energy is more valuable than soil, and so the cultural landscape changes to one marked with factories, cities, and centers of distribution. Today unaltered wilderness has again become valued as an end in itself, as a place that inspires and comforts the human spirit. Those with this value want factories dissembled, mines reclaimed, and deforested areas reseeded.

Landscapes and Identity

Culture is evident everywhere throughout the landscape in adaptations of the natural landscape as well as in toponyms, types of architecture, and designs of towns and cities. People express cultural beliefs through transforming elements of the world into **symbols** that carry a particular meaning recognized by people who share a culture. Examples are monuments, flags, slogans, or religious icons, and through landscaping and house types. Symbols express personal identity in many different ways. A national flag represents an affiliation with a country, and a cross is a religious symbol to many Christians. Landscaping a piece of property may express a need for order, beauty, and creativity. Geographers who study the cultural landscape recognize that the concept of **regional identity** can be problematic as symbols clash with values of people in other regions. For example, the Muslim practice of never depicting Allah or Muhammad in paintings or drawings clashed with the western value of freedom of the press when a Danish cartoonist broke the ban in 2005. Religious structures and figures, languages, political leaders, and sports teams may all serve as sources of regional identity.

Cultural Identity through Mascots. The above drawings of a bear, a blue jay, and a bobcat represent some common mascots for sports teams. The symbol represents more than the team, but the cultural identity of a school that often draws from a culture region. The cultural landscape around the school often makes common use of the symbols, and students even wear them on their clothing and book bags.

Symbols. The three symbols above represent various cultural landscapes and help to form cultural identities. The Buddha statue on the left is a complex symbol central to many Buddhist beliefs; in many western countries, the hand gesture in the middle symbolizes victory; and the hand gesture on the right symbolizes prayer.

Symbolic Landscapes

All landscapes can be seen as symbolic, since they have accumulated various meanings over time. The signs and images found in the landscape convey to us messages that demand interpretation. At the simplest level, traffic signs tell us to "stop," "slow down," or travel at a certain speed. Public monuments and statues are symbols deliberately inserted into the landscape as messages to be read. They often commemorate bravery, feats performed in battle, or political allegiance. Although many symbols today are international, others reflect regional cultures that give people a sense of place.

Universal Symbols. This photo taken in Xi'an, China, of three Americans and three Muslim Chinese illustrates the point that symbols may cross cultures and have international meaning.

TERMS AND CONCEPTS

acculturation
animism
artifacts
assimilation
Baha'i
behaviors
beliefs
bilingualism
Buddhism
Confucianism
contagious diffusion
creole
cultural determinism
cultural diffusion
cultural ecology
cultural geography
cultural hearths
cultural landscape
cultural relativism
cultural transmission
culture complex
culture region
culture system
culture trait
Daoism
dialect
diasporas
Durkheim's sacred and profane
Eastern Orthodox
environmental determinism
ethnic religion
ethnocentrism
extinct language
folk culture
folk culture region
folk life
geographic region
Hagerstrand, Torste
hierarchical diffusion
Hinduism
humanism
independent inventions
Indo-European language family
Islam
isogloss

Judaism
language
language families
language sub-family
lingua franca
linguistic fragmentation
linguistic geography
Mahayana
Marxism
material culture
migrant diffusion
monotheistic religion
multilingualism
non-material culture
norms
official language
pidgin
popular culture
Protestants
regional identity
religion: branches, denominations, sects
relocation diffusion
Roman Catholics
Sauer, Carl
shamanism
Shiite
Sikhism
standard language
stimulus diffusion
Sunni
symbolic landscape
symbols
syncretism
Tantrayana
Theraveda
time-distance decay
toponymy
traditional religion
transculturation
universalizing religion

MULTIPLE-CHOICE QUESTIONS
UNIT THREE

1. The Indo-European language family has its distant origins in the area around the

  (A) Baltic Sea
  (B) Iberian Peninsula
  (C) Black Sea
  (D) Italian Peninsula
  (E) Arabian Peninsula

2. Which of the following is an example of a cultural landscape?

  (A) a coral reef
  (B) a stand of pine trees
  (C) tropical jungle
  (D) terraced fields of crops up a mountainside
  (E) a glacier

3. Which of the following was not one of the earliest ancient cultural hearths?

  (A) Nile Valley
  (B) Indus Valley
  (C) Mesopotamia
  (D) East Asia
  (E) Mississippi Valley

4. Mahayana, Theraveda, and Tantrayana are three branches of

  (A) Islam
  (B) Buddhism
  (C) Sikhism
  (D) Hinduism
  (E) Daoism

5. Globalization has encouraged the diffusion of

  (A) popular culture
  (B) ethnic religions
  (C) linguistic fragmentation
  (D) folk culture
  (E) ethnocentrism

6. A European who refers to China as the "Far East" is reflecting a form of

(A) cultural relativism
(B) ethnocentricism
(C) assimilation
(D) animism
(E) humanism

7. Which of the following countries has the largest percentage of Roman Catholics?

(A) the United States
(B) Great Britain
(C) Indonesia
(D) Brazil
(E) India

8. Toponymy is the study of

(A) place names
(B) extinct languages
(C) religious affiliations
(D) dialects
(E) linguistic fragmentation

9. Which of the following is a particular form of relocation diffusion in which the spread of culture traits is slow enough that they weaken in the area of origin by the time they reach other areas?

(A) contagious diffusion
(B) hierarchical diffusion
(C) migrant diffusion
(D) stimulus diffusion
(E) expansion diffusion

10. A condition in which many languages are spoken, each by a relatively small number of people, is called

(A) syncretism
(B) linguistic relativism
(C) bilingualism
(D) diasporas
(E) linguistic fragmentation

11. The field that studies the relationship between the natural environment and culture is called

   (A) environmental determinism
   (B) cultural diffusion
   (C) syncretism
   (D) linguistic geography
   (E) cultural ecology

12. In contrast to societies that are strongly influenced by popular culture, folk societies are

   (A) more limited in their building materials by the resources available in the environment
   (B) less likely to promote religious values
   (C) less resistant to cultural change
   (D) more inclined to tolerate a variety of social customs and behaviors
   (E) more likely to place a strain on natural resources

13. The type of culture that includes a wide range of artifacts is called

   (A) popular culture
   (B) material culture
   (C) folk culture
   (D) a culture region
   (E) non-material culture

14. Which of the following is a dialect?

   (A) Indo-European
   (B) Romance
   (C) southern United States
   (D) Latin
   (E) Dravidian

15. Which of the following is NOT a place name in the United States that reflects geographical origins?

   (A) New York
   (B) New Jersey
   (C) Germantown, Pennsylvania
   (D) Pottstown
   (E) New Hampshire

16. Of the languages illustrated on the map above, which has the highest percentage of first language speakers?

   (A) Spanish
   (B) English
   (C) Hindi
   (D) Arabic
   (E) Mandarin Chinese

17. Which of the following schools of thought puts most emphasis on the importance of the physical environment in shaping cultures?

   (A) possibilism
   (B) cultural ecology
   (C) environmental determinism
   (D) environmental perception
   (E) cultural determinism

18. Culture complexes are made up of many culture

   (A) traits
   (B) regions
   (C) systems
   (D) hearths
   (E) dialects

19. As Islam spread to Sub Saharan Africa by the 9th century, its first converts were the elites, but most ordinary people retained their native religions. This phenomenon illustrates the process of

    (A) contagious diffusion
    (B) hierarchical diffusion
    (C) stimulation diffusion
    (D) relocation diffusion
    (E) migrant diffusion

20. Acculturation is a process whereby

    (A) the more dominant culture adopts most of the traits of the less dominant culture
    (B) the dominant culture completely absorbs the less dominant one
    (C) cultural traits are equally exchanged between two cultures
    (D) the less dominant culture adopts some of the traits of the more influential one
    (E) non-material and material culture spread to areas around them

21. The process by which one generation passes culture to the next is called

    (A) cultural transmission
    (B) assimilation
    (C) cultural relativism
    (D) syncretism
    (E) cultural diffusion

22. Linguistic geographers use isoglosses to mark

    (A) the creation of pidgins
    (B) the extent to which a lingua franca is used in a particular area
    (C) the limits for an area in which particular words are used
    (D) the area in which an official language is used
    (E) the area in which an extinct language is used

23. The branch of Christianity that has the largest number of adherents is

    (A) Eastern Orthodoxy
    (B) Protestantism
    (C) Lutheranism
    (D) Roman Catholicism
    (E) the Baptist Church

24. Which of the following is NOT an ethnic religion?

(A) Hinduism
(B) Sikhism
(C) Shintoism
(D) Judaism
(E) Shamanism

25. The statue above is an important symbol for adherents of

(A) Hinduism
(B) Eastern Orthodoxy
(C) Islam
(D) Confucianism
(E) Buddhism

FREE-RESPONSE QUESTION
UNIT THREE

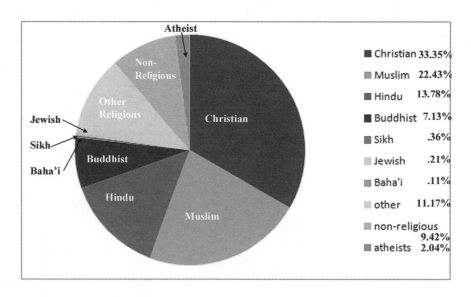

The chart above shows major religions of the world as a percentage of world population.

a. Define universalizing religion. Define ethnic religion.

b. Identify one universalizing religion, and explain one specific reason why it is a universalizing religion.

c. Identify one ethnic religion, and explain one specific reason why it is an ethnic religion.

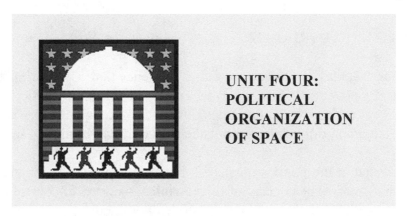

**UNIT FOUR:
POLITICAL
ORGANIZATION
OF SPACE**

Have you ever looked through a historical atlas of the world to study changes in civilizations and their borders? If you have, you know that change is the rule rather than the exception. The world in 4,000 C.E. looks very similar physically to our world today. If you study familiar land and water shapes you realize that geological history moves at a much slower pace than political history. On the other hand, try to trace any nation in existence today, and while some are older than others, you don't have to go very far back in history to find its origins. Yet no matter what time period you choose over the past 6000 years or so, the political imprint of human beings is there. **Political geography** is the study of the political organization of the planet, a constantly changing collage of countries that once were kingdoms or parts of empires, or perhaps scatterings of independent tribes. Through all the changes, however, one truth emerges: almost from the beginning of history, humans have divided their living space into political units or territories.

TERRITORIAL DIMENSIONS OF POLITICS

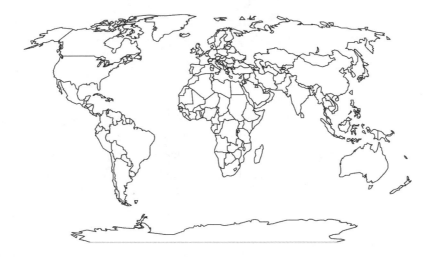

No doubt you have seen maps like the one above many times. But take a look at it with a fresh eye. You see land shapes and a few lakes and seas, but most physical features of the earth's surface are not apparent. Instead, the emphasis is on political organization, the nearly 200 nation states that the world is divided into. Notice the inequality of countries in terms of territory (some are much larger than others), and differences in terms of location. Some countries are landlocked, without coasts on the open seas, but most have direct access to a global ocean. The borders that separate them have resulted from countless negotiations, some violent but others not. This modern state system that the map reflects is the product of a political-territory order with European roots. At the core of the system are the concepts of territoriality, sovereignty, and the "nation-state.."

THE CONCEPT OF TERRITORIALITY

Most people understand that the term **government** is a reference to the leadership and institutions that make policy decisions for a country. However, what exactly is **politics?** Politics is basically all about power. Who has the power to make the decisions? How did they get the power? What challenges do leaders face from others – both inside and outside the country's borders – in keeping the power?

Geographers are interested in the politics of place – how land space is organized according to who asserts power over what areas. The concept of **territoriality** – efforts to control pieces of the earth's surface for political and social ends – is basic to the study of political geography. According to Robert Sack, human territoriality differs from the instinctual territoriality of animals in that it takes many different forms, depending on the social and geographical context. For example, a political leader in a democratic nation would not be able to claim control of the land simply because his father had that control. Instead, he would have to operate within the rules of his society (like winning an election) to gain political power. The rules reflect attitudes toward land and territory as defined by the **political culture** – the collection of political beliefs, values, practices, and institutions that the government is based on.

THE NATURE AND MEANING OF BOUNDARIES

A state is separated from its neighbors by **boundaries**, invisible lines that mark the extent of a state's territory and the control that its leaders have. Sometimes boundaries are set by physical features, like rivers, shores, or mountains, and other times they are drawn to separate ethnic groups from one another. Boundaries may be set by negotiation or war with neighbors, which often leaves states open to changes in the future. Boundaries completely surround an individual state to mark its outer limits, giving it a distinctive shape. Because boundary lines mark the place where two or more states come into direct contact, they have the potential to create conflict.

Types of boundaries

Historically, **frontiers** rather than boundaries separated states. A frontier is a geographic zone where no state exercises power, whereas a boundary is a thin, imaginary line. Frontiers provide buffers between states, although states may fight for control of the frontier. For example, France and England fought over frontier areas in North America in the French and Indian (Seven Years') War in the mid-18th century. However, boundaries put states right next to one another, increasing the potential for conflict. Frontier land has all but disappeared from the earth, with only Antarctica and the Arabian Peninsula left with significant neutral zone areas.

Boundaries may be categorized into two types:

- **Physical boundaries** – Physical features are easy to see, both in reality and on maps, so they often make good boundaries. Mountains limit contact between nationalities living on opposite sides, and they are usually sparsely populated. Desert boundaries are common in Africa and Asia, although their exact locations are often are not easily spotted in reality. However, they generally prove to be reliable and relatively permanent. Rivers, lakes, and oceans are the physical features most commonly used as boundaries.

Water boundaries are visible and relatively unchanging, and they are typically set in the middle of the water, a practice that follows the **median-line principle**. Ocean boundaries cause problems because states generally claim that the boundary lies not at the coastline but out at sea. Today rights to off-shore drilling of oil and fishing can sometimes be disputed, so international treaties have addressed the problem. The Law of the Sea (1983) standardized territorial limits for most countries at 12 nautical miles (14 land miles), and gave rights to fish and other marine life within 200 miles.

- **Cultural boundaries** – The boundaries between some states are set by ethnic differences, especially those based on language and/or religion. Cultural boundaries are also called **consequent boundaries.** One example of a boundary based on religion was the one that partitioned Pakistan from India in 1947. The borders for the new state of Pakistan were drawn around Muslim portions of the subcontinent, in an effort to separate Muslims from Hindus. The partition did little to solve the problems between the two religions, and in some ways made them worse, as people caught on the "wrong side" of the line struggled to reposition themselves. Language boundaries have been very important in Europe, since cultural identities have often been based on language. Again, the lines are not always easy to set, with the boundary between France and Germany shifting back and forth within a population area with mixed heritages. After World War I the Allied leaders tried to redraw the map of Europe based on ethnic lines. For example, they carved from the large empire of Austria-Hungary several small ethnically-based states, including Bulgaria, Hungary, Poland, and Romania. The Balkans were united under the new country of Yugoslavia, which fell apart during the 1990s into several smaller ethnically based countries, a process referred to as **"Balkanization."** The Balkans illustrate the tendency for mountain ranges (such as the Caucasus) to form **shatter belts,** or zones of great cultural complexity containing many small cultural groups who find refuge in the isolation created by rough terrain. Shatter belts are often areas of cultural tension that may spread to other areas.

The Balkans. This area between the Adriatic and Black Seas has historically diverse ethnicities that were combined into one country called "Yugoslavia" after World War I. The union lasted until the 1990s when ethnic tensions exploded, leading to the creation of new ethnically-based small states, a process called **"Balkanization".**

Sometimes **geometric boundaries** are set between countries. These are straight, imaginary lines that generally have good reasons behind their creation. For example, when North and South Korea were divided during the early Cold War, the 38th parallel was chosen to demark communist vs. U.S. control. The method was also used in Vietnam, when the country was split in two at the 17th parallel to separate the North, controlled by Hanoi, from the South, controlled by Saigon.

SHAPES, SIZE, AND RELATIVE LOCATIONS OF STATES

Territorial morphology is a term that describes the shapes, sizes, and relative locations of states. All of these characteristics help to determine the opportunities available to and challenges faced by the country collectively and its citizens individually.

Shape

The shapes of states control the length of their boundaries with other states, and in turn the potential for communication and conflict with neighbors. A state's shape affects cultural identity, social unity, and the ease or difficulty that the government has in ruling its subjects. Countries may be categorized into five basic shapes:

1) **compact states** – In a compact state, the distance from the center to any boundary is about the same, giving it a shape similar to a circle. If the capital is in the center, then the geographical location eases its ability to rule. Compactness also promotes good communications among all regions.

2) **prorupted states** – An otherwise compact state with a large projecting extension is a prorupted state. Often proruptions exist in order to reach a natural resource, such as a river or the ocean, and occasionally they actually cut another country in two to do that. An example is the Democratic Republic of Congo, which split a small fragment (called Cabinda) of Angola from the main country.

3) **elongated states** – These states have a long and narrow shape, sometimes because of physical geography and other times for political or economic reasons. The South American country of Chile is located on a long, narrow strip of coastline between the Pacific Ocean and the Andes Mountains. Gambia in West Africa follows the Atlantic Ocean coastline, but it was carved out of the larger country of Senegal for political reasons during colonial times. Elongated states often have communication and transportation problems, since a city at one end is a long way from a city at the other end. This is especially problematic if the capital is not centralized.

4) **fragmented states** – These states have several discontinuous pieces of territory. Any state that is composed of islands is a fragmented state. This can be problematic if some of the islands are remote, as they are in Indonesia. Although the majority of its population live on two of the islands – Java and Sumatra – those on remote islands may be difficult to control. For example, the island of East Timor received its independence from Indonesia after resisting an invasion by the Indonesian army. Once East Timor gained independence, other remote islands (such as Ambon and Aceh) have tried unsuccessfully to secede, causing a great deal of tension within the territories claimed by Indonesia. A different kind of fragmentation occurs if a piece of the territory is separated by another state, as occurs in eastern India, where the country of Bangladesh separates the state of West Bengal from the rest of India.

5) **perforated states** – A state that completely surrounds another one is a **perforated state.** The best example is South Africa, where the apartheid (segregationist) government separated primarily black Lesotho from the rest of the country, leaving it completely surrounded by South Africa.

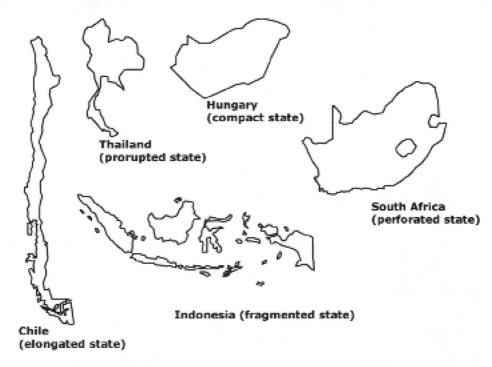

Shapes of states created by their boundaries can sometimes create **exclaves** and **enclaves.** Exclaves are small bits of territory that lie on coasts separated from the state by the territory of another state. An example is Cabinda, a part of the African state of Angola that is separated by the Democratic Republic of the Congo. Enclaves are landlocked within another country, so that the country totally surrounds it. The enclave of Nagorno-Karabakh is an exclave of Armenian Christians who are surrounded by Muslim Azerbaijan. Armenia has demanded that the enclave be included in its territory, with a 10-mile corridor linking it to the country. The situation has caused major tension between Armenia and Azerbaijan.

Size

States vary in size from the largest (Russia) at over 6.5 million square miles, or over 11% of the earth's surface, to **microstates**, such as Liechtenstein, Andorra, and San Morino, with land spaces of just a few square miles. An advantage to size is that it increases the chances of having important natural resources, such as mineral ores and fertile soil, but much of that falls to its location. For example, both Russia and Canada are large countries, but a great deal of their land is so far north that it is frozen, making it impossible to farm and difficult to mine in many areas. Small states are more likely to hold homogeneous populations, which decreases potential conflicts within the country, although there are many other bases for conflict than ethnicity. Small countries may also wield power beyond their size, such as Britain, although countries with large amounts of land space often have advantages of human and natural resources. Size alone is not critical in determining a country's power and stability, but it is a contributing factor.

Relative Location

The significance of size and shape as factors in national well-being can be modified by a state's location, both absolute and relative. For example, Iceland has a reasonably compact shape, but its absolute

Liechtenstein is one of the world's smallest states, called a "microstate." It only encompasses a few square miles, and is tucked in between two relatively small states, Switzerland and Austria.

location at 65° N. latitude means that most of the country is uninhabited, with settlement confined to the coastlines. A state's relative location is also important. **Landlocked states**, those lacking ocean frontage and surrounded by other states, are at a disadvantage for trade, sea resources (such as fish), transportation, and communication. Often a landlocked country tries to arrange the use of a foreign port. There are about 40 landlocked countries in the world, a number that was much smaller before the break up of the Soviet Union, when Kazakhstan, Uzbekistan, Kyrgyzstan, Tajikistan, Turkmenistan, Moldova, Azerbaijan, Belarus, and Armenia became independent. Examples of landlocked countries in Asia are Nepal, Bhutan, Laos, and Mongolia. A number of countries in Africa are landlocked, including Botswana, Zimbabwe, Zambia, Rwanda, Central African Republic, Chad, Niger, and Burundi. In South America, Paraguay and Bolivia are landlocked, and disputes over water access have often erupted. For example, Chile and land-locked Bolivia have not had diplomatic ties for three decades, and the conflict stems from a late 19th-century war in which Bolivia lost its access to the ocean.

Sometimes a good relative location is an important asset for a state. For example, Singapore is a very small state located in Southeast Asia, at a crossroads of international travel that links East Asia to South Asia. It has used its good relative location to build industry and communication links, so that today Singapore is one of the most prosperous states in the world.

The Great Wall. The Great Wall as we see it today was built during the Ming Dynasty that ruled from the 13th to 17th centuries C.E. A much earlier wall was built starting in the 3rd century B.C.E., but little of that older wall remains today. For centuries, the wall served as the northern boundary of the Empire of China.

Functions of Boundaries

Historically states and empires have built walls to mark the limits of their governmental control. For example, the Romans built Hadrian's Wall in northern England to keep out the "barbarians" and leave a clear boundary that marked what they would protect and what they wouldn't. Perhaps most famous of all is the Great Wall, built and rebuilt over centuries to keep "barbarians" from the north out of Chinese lands. In much more recent days the Berlin Wall was built to keep East Berliners from crossing into West Berlin, and walls and fences have been built along the border between Mexico and the United States. In all cases, walls and fences have served the function of keeping people *in* the areas where they live, and *out of* areas that they want to enter.

Today, boundaries still mark the limits of state jurisdiction, and serve as symbols of **sovereignty,** or the ability of the state to carry out actions or policies within its borders independently from interference either from the inside or the outside. The shape of the country's territory comes to represent a national consciousness, or **nationalism.** Modern nationalism is a sense of unity with fellow citizens and loyalty to the state to promote its culture and interests over those of other nations.

Internal Boundaries

Many modern countries divide their interiors into sections marked by internal boundaries. The United States consists of 50 states that are each divided into counties. Canada is divided into 10 provinces, two federal territories, and one self-governing homeland. Internal boundaries, like boundaries between countries, may be physical, cultural, or geometric. Canada's Quebec is primarily populated by French-speaking Canadians, although the boundaries don't exactly follow cultural lines. India's 28 states and six union territories are drawn along cultural lines. People in different states often speak different languages, reflecting the cultural diversity of the Indian subcontinent.

Boundary Disputes

Since World War II, almost half of the world's sovereign states have been involved in border disputes with their neighbors. The more neighbors that a state has, the greater the likelihood of conflict. Boundary disputes may be categorized in four ways:

1) **Positional (or definitional) disputes** occur when states argue about where the border actually is. The United States and Mexico feuded for years over their mutual border, even after it was officially set by treaty in 1848. The boundary between Argentina and Chile has been controversial because it follows the crests of the Andes Mountains and the watershed, which do not always coincide.

2) **Territorial disputes** arise over the ownership of a region, usually around mutual borders. Conflicts arise if the people of one state want to annex a territory whose population is ethnically related to them. War between Mexico and the United States broke out in areas (such as Texas and California) where many U.S. citizens had settled, and yet the Mexican government controlled the land space. This type of expansionism is called **irredentism**. A 20th century example is the German invasion of Czechoslovakia and Poland, areas with German minorities.

3) **Resource (or allocational) disputes** involve natural resources – such as mineral deposits, fertile farmland, or rich fishing groups – that lie in border areas. For example, the United States and Canada have feuded over fishing grounds in the Atlantic Ocean. The spark for the Persian Gulf War of 1990-91 was a dispute between Iraq and Kuwait regarding rights to oil.

4) **Functional (or operational) disputes** arise when neighboring states cannot agree on policies that apply in a border area. An example is the ongoing debate between the U.S. and Mexico regarding transport of people and goods across their long mutual border. The U.S. has generally wanted stricter controls put on immigration from Mexico, and also has pressured the Mexican government to control drug trafficking across the border.

EVOLUTION OF THE CONTEMPORARY POLITICAL PATTERN

The world has not always been divided into nation-states. In fact, the current pattern is a relatively new one, with the appearance of nation-states in Europe during the early 19th century. Many other configurations have been seen in the past. In ancient times, Egyptians were ruled by pharaohs, who were believed to be descendents of the gods. In contrast, ancient Mesopotamia was organized into city-states, with competing cities dominating the countryside around them. Ancient Greece also was configured into city-states. Another early organization was the "empire," with a military ruler who conquered and ruled large amounts of territory. Examples include Persia, the empire of Alexander the Great, the Roman Empire, and the Han Dynasty of China. In the Middle East, the founder of Islam, Muhammad, established a religious state called a "caliphate" that existed in different forms for about six centuries. Medieval Europe developed "kingdoms," relatively small areas dominated by kings supported by loyalty ties to the nobles in a political and economic configuration called "feudalism." The largest political organization of all times – the Mongol Empire of the 13th century – was ruled by a "Khan" (universal ruler), a military leader supported by a web of kinship ties. In Central America smaller civilizations eventually came to be controlled by the large Aztec Empire, and in South America the Inca formed a short-lived but powerful empire.

THE NATION-STATE CONCEPT

We commonly speak about individuals being powerful, but in today's world, power is territorially organized into **states**, or countries, that control what happens within their borders. What exactly is a state? German scholar Max Weber defined state as the organization that maintains a monopoly of violence over a territory. In other words, the state defines who can and cannot use weapons and force, and it sets the rules as to how violence is used. States often sponsor armies, navies, and/or air forces that legitimately use power and sometimes violence, but individual citizens are very restricted in their use of force. States also include **institutions**, stable, long lasting organizations that help to turn political ideas into policy. Common examples of institutions are bureaucracies, legislatures, judicial systems, and political parties. These institutions make states themselves long lasting, and often help them to endure even when leaders change. States by their very nature exercise **sovereignty,** the ability to carry out actions or policies within their borders independently from interference either from the inside or the outside.

States today do much more than keep order in society. Many have important institutions that promote general welfare – such as health, safe transportation, and effective communication systems – and economic stability. The concept of state is closely related to a **nation,** a group of people that is bound together by a common political identity. The term **nation-state** refers to a state whose territorial extent coincides with that occupied by a distinct nation or people, or at least, whose population shares a general sense of unity and allegiance to a set of common values. Nationalism is the sense of belonging and identity that distinguishes one nation from another. Nationalism is often translated as patriotism, or the resulting pride and loyalty that individuals may feel toward their nations. For more than 200 years now, national borders ideally have been drawn along the lines of group identity. For example, people within one area think of themselves as "French," and people in another area think of themselves as "English." Even though individual differences exist within nations, the nation provides the overriding identity for most of its citizens. However, the concept has always been problematic – as when "Armenians" live inside the borders of a country called "Azerbaijan." Especially now that globalization and fragmentation provide counter trends, the nature of nationalism and its impact on policy-making are clearly changing.

VARIATIONS OF THE NATION-STATE

A **binational** or **multinational state** is one that contains more than one nation. The former Soviet Union is a good example of a multinational state. It was divided into "soviet republics" that were based on nationality, such as the Ukraine, Kazakhstan, Estonia, Latvia, and Lithuania. When the country fell apart in 1991, it fell along ethnic boundaries into independent nation-states. Today Russia (one of the former soviet republics) remains a large multinational state that governs many ethnic groups. Just as ethnic pressures challenged the sovereignty of the Soviet government, the Russian government has faced "breakaway movements" – such as in Chechnya – that have threatened Russian stability. Minority ethnic groups may feel so strongly about their separate identities that they demand their independence. **Stateless nations** are a people without a state. In the Middle East the Kurds are a nation of some 20 million people divided among six states and dominant in none. Kurdish nationalism has survived over the centuries, and has played an important role in the politics that followed the reconfiguration of Iraq after the Iraqi War that began in 2003.

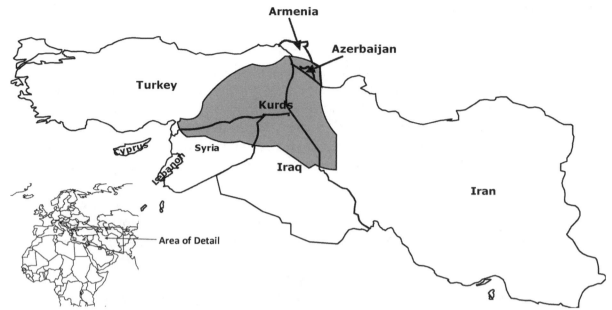

A Stateless Nation. The Kurds have had a national identity for many centuries, but they have never had a state. Instead, 20 million Kurds are spread in an area that crosses the formal borders of six countries: Turkey, Syria, Iraq, Iran, Armenia, and Azerbaijan.

THE ORGANIZATION OF STATES

Two important geographical clues to understanding how states are organized are its core area(s) and the size and functions of its capital city.

Core Areas

Most of the early nation-states grew over time from **core areas**, expanding outward along their frontiers. Their growth generally stopped when they bumped up against other nation-states, causing them to define boundaries. Today most European countries still have these same core areas, and many countries in other parts of the world also have well defined core areas. They may be identified on a map by examining population distributions and transport networks. As you travel away from the core area, into the state's **periphery** (outlying areas), towns get smaller, factories fewer, and open land more common. Clear examples of core areas are the Paris Basin in France and Japan's Kanto Plain, centered on the city of Tokyo. States with more than one core area – **multicore states** – may be problematic, especially if the areas are ethnically diverse, such as in Nigeria. Nigeria's northern core is primarily Muslim and its southern core is Christian, and the areas pull the country in different directions. To compensate for this tendency for the country to separate, the capital city was moved from Lagos (in the South) to Abuja, near the geographic center of the state.

A multicore character is not always problematic for a country. For example, the United States still has a primary core area that runs along its northeastern coastline from Washington D.C. to Boston. A secondary core area exists on the West Coast that runs from San Diego in the south to San Francisco in the north. Arguably, other core areas have developed around Chicago and other Midwestern cities, and Atlanta in the South. Despite the multiple core areas, regional differences do not threaten the existence of the state, as they do in Nigeria.

Nigeria's Core Areas. Nigeria was a British colony in West Africa until its independence in 1960, but its borders encompass numerous ethnic groups with clear cultural differences. The biggest split, however, is between the Muslim north and the Christian south. In an effort to strengthen the political unity of the country, the capital was moved from Lagos on the southern coast to Abuja, near the geographic center of the state. Despite the move, Lagos continues to be the center of the Christian south, and tensions still threaten the sovereignty of Nigeria's government.

The Capital City

In most states the capital city not only houses the government, but serves as the economic and cultural center as well. If no other city comes even close to rivaling the capital city in terms of size or influence, the capital city is a **primate city.** In some countries – such as the United States – other cities are as large or larger than the capital city, Washington, D.C. The U.S. capital is not a primate city because it is less of an economic center than cities such as Chicago and New York. However, the political heart is clearly in Washington, and it serves as a unifying symbol for the country.

If the capital city serves as a model for national objectives, especially for economic development and future hopes, it is sometimes called a **forward capital**. Japan's relocation of its capital from Kyoto to Tokyo expressed such a sentiment. A more modern example is Brasília, the present capital of Brazil. Traditionally, Brazil's population stretched along the country's coastline, and its capital had been the great port city of Rio de Janeiro. In an effort to refocus Brazil on its vast interior wealth, its leaders decided to build Brasília from scratch in a location far from the coast. Brasília was meant to symbolize the nation's new continental attitude, and no expense was spared in creating it as a showplace for the new Brazil. Capital cities symbolize their states through architecture, national landmarks, and historic buildings and monuments. Despite their efforts, most people still live close to the coast, and Rio de Janeiro retains its status as the largest city in Brazil.

ELECTORAL GEOGRAPHY

Citizens' commitment to their state may be affected by the types of contacts that they have with their government. In democracies an important connection between citizen and state is the **electoral process,** the methods used in a country for selecting leaders. For example, people may vote directly for a president and representatives to their legislatures (as in the United States), or they may vote only for legislators who in turn select the prime minister (as in Britain.) Elections may also take place for local officials, so electoral politics may be examined according to geographic scale – national, regional, and local. **Electoral geography** is the study of how the spatial configuration of electoral districts and voting patterns reflect and influence social and political affairs.

In the United States, boundaries separate 435 legislative districts, with each electing one representative to the lower house of the legislature – the House of Representatives. Boundaries are redrawn when the census is taken every ten years to ensure that representation is fair. In most European countries boundaries are redrawn by independent commissions, but in the United States, the job usually goes to the state legislatures. There the political party in control – either Democrats or Republicans – usually attempts to redraw boundaries to improve the chances of its supporters to win seats, a process called **gerrymandering.** District boundaries are drawn in strange ways in order to make it easy for the candidate of one party to win election in that district. The term is derived from the original gerrymanderer, Eldrige Gerry, who in the early 19th century had a Massachusetts district drawn in the shape of a salamander, to ensure the election of a Republican. Over the years both parties have been accused of manipulating districts in order to gain an advantage in membership in the House of Representatives.

Gerrymandering continues to be an issue in the U.S. today. A more recent form that appeared shortly after the 1990 census is **minority/majority districting**, or rearranging districts to allow a minority representative to be elected, and it is just as controversial as the old-style party gerrymandering. The Justice Department ordered North Carolina's 12th district to redraw proposed boundaries in order to allow for the election of one more black representative. This action resulted in a Supreme Court case in which the plaintiffs charged the Justice Department with reverse discrimination, or discrimination against the majority whites. The Court ruled narrowly, but allowed the district lines to be redrawn according to Justice Department standards.

During the 1990s several cases were brought to the Supreme Court regarding racial gerrymandering. The Court ruled in 2001 that race may be a factor in redistricting, but not the "dominant and controlling" one. An important result of the various decisions has been a substantial increase in the number of black and Latino representatives in the House of Representatives. For geographers, the important point is that voting patterns often reinforce a sense of regionalism and shape a government's response to issues in the future.

COLONIALISM AND IMPERIALISM

18th century European political philosophers developed the idea of the modern state, with the basic concept that people owe allegiance to a state and the people it represents rather than to its leader, such as a king or feudal lord. The new concept was accelerated by the French Revolution in 1789 and spread over Western Europe during the 19th century. European expansion during the 17th, 18th, and 19th centuries spread the new type of organization to the Americas, Asia, and Africa. Usually **colonies**, or dependent areas, were created first, and they were given fixed and recorded boundaries where none had formally existed before. In some cases Europeans took over empires with recognized outer limits, such as the Mughal in India, the Aztecs in Central America, and the Manchu in China. Other areas were loosely organized by tribes. In most cases, the new divisions were not based on meaningful cultural or physical lines, but on the limits of the colonizing empire's power.

The European colonization of Africa and Asia is often termed **imperialism**, or empire building, and it characterized the political landscape during the 19th and early 20th centuries. The phrase "The sun never sets on the British Empire" captures the reach that Britain had to most parts of the globe, as the tiny country transformed itself into the most powerful country in the world. A major source of tension before World War I (1914-1918) was the rise of Germany as an imperialist power, and after Germany was defeated in 1918, the country was stripped of its colonies. Most African and Asian colonies became independent after World War II, partly because the war greatly weakened the ability of European countries to maintain their overseas possessions.

EUROPEAN IMPRINTS ON AFRICA IN THE 19TH CENTURY

By the late 19th century European countries claimed almost all of Africa. A close study of a map of the day revealed these names of land spaces in Africa:

French West Africa	Anglo-Egyptian Sudan
Italian East Africa	British Somaliland
French Somaliland	Belgian Congo
French Equatorial Africa	Spanish Morocco
Spanish Guinea	Rhodesia
German Southwest Africa	German East Africa
Italian Somaliland	Portuguese Guinea
British East Africa	

Other areas, such as the Union of South Africa, Angola, Nigeria, and Algeria, were also European possessions, even if the names are less revealing. Only Ethiopia and Liberia were independent states. By the 1960s almost all colonies had received their independence.

As former colonies gained independence, they kept the idea of the state to organize their new political systems. They often retained the borders established by their former European rulers, and as a consequence, states' borders many times ignored cultural differences among populations. The idea of nation-states grew slowly at first, but expanded rapidly, particularly after the middle of the 20th century. At the time that the United States declared independence from Britain in 1776 there were only about 35 empires, kingdoms, and countries in the entire world. By the beginning of World War II in 1939, the number had only increased to about 70. Since 1945, the number has increased to about 200 nations as a result of a series of independence movements. The first "wave" occurred during the late 1940s, 1950s, and early 1960s, when many new nations were created out of former European colonies. Included were India, Pakistan, Bangladesh, Malaysia, Burma (now Myanmar), and Singapore in Asia, and Ghana, Nigeria, Kenya, Uganda, Tanzania, Malawi, Botswana, Zimbabwe, and Zambia in Africa. Another "wave" occurred when the Soviet Union dissolved in 1991, creating independent nations in Eastern Europe and Central Asia. Later in the 1990s several new states were created in the Balkans from Yugoslavia. Most remaining dependencies today are remnants of empires, located in relatively isolated areas with small populations, such as remote islands.

Former Soviet States in Central Asia. Until 1991 states like Kazakhstan, Azerbaijan, Armenia, Georgia, Turkmenistan, Uzbekistan, Tajikistan, and Kyrgyzstan were part of the Soviet Union. When the Soviet Union fell apart, 15 independent nation-states were created.

Today many of the world's countries have relatively small populations, with about 90 countries having populations under 5 million, and 33 with fewer than a half-million people.

FEDERAL AND UNITARY STATES

A well-integrated state consists of a stable, clearly bounded territory, served by well-developed institutions, an effective administrative framework, a productive core area, and an influential capital city. All states, however, face challenges, and their internal organizations often determine how successfully they deal with their problems.

Every state has multiple levels of authority, though the geographic distribution of power varies widely. States may be categorized into three types according to their internal geographic distribution of power:

1) A **unitary system** is one that concentrates all policy-making powers in one central geographic place. When the nation-state evolved in Europe, democracy had not yet developed, and governments ruled by force. Most European governments were highly centralized; the capital city represented authority that stretched to the limits of the state. Even though local governments developed, they had no separate powers, and most of the states were and still are relatively small in land space. As a result, most European governments today remain unitary states.

2) A **confederal system** spreads the power among many sub-units (such as states), and has a weak central government. Most attempts at confederal systems have not been long-lasting, although the modern government of Switzerland has very strong sub-governments, and comes as close to a modern confederation as exists. Examples of failed confederations are the United States government under the Articles of Confederation (1781-1789) and the Confederate States of America that consisted of the southern states of the United States during the Civil War (1861-1865).

3) A **federal system** divides the power between the central government and the sub-units. These developed in several colonial areas, including the United States, Canada, and Australia. Federal

systems were possible because the cultures were new, no single cities dominated the new countries, and in all three examples the land space is large, setting the stage for the development of regional governments. Federalism accommodates regional interests by allowing for diverse needs and preferences, but also features a central government that is strong enough to keep the countries from falling apart.

All political systems today fall on a continuum from the most concentrated amount of power to the least. Unitary governments may be placed on the left side, according to the degree of concentration; confederal governments are placed to the right; and federal governments fall in between. Most countries have unitary systems, although some are experimenting with **devolution**, or the transfer of some important powers from central governments to sub-governments.

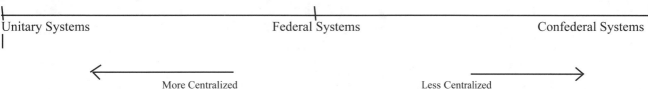

MODERN CHALLENGES TO THE NATION-STATE CONFIGURATION

Nation-states have always had their challenges, both internal and external, but today new supranational forces are at work that have led some to believe that the nation-state political configuration itself may be changing. Is it possible that large regional organizations, such as the European Union, will replace the smaller state units as basic organizational models? Or will international organizations, such as the United Nations, come to have true governing power over the nation-states? If so, then the very nature of sovereignty may be changing, especially if nation-states of the future have to abide by the rules of **supranational organizations** (cooperating groups of nations that operate on either a regional or international level) for all major decisions and rules.

CENTRIPETAL V. CENTRIFUGAL FORCES

A recurring set of forces affects all nation-states: **centripetal forces** that unify them, and **centrifugal forces** that tend to fragment them.

- **Centripetal forces** bind together the people of a state, giving it strength. One of the most powerful centripetal forces is **nationalism**, or identities based on nationhood. It encourages allegiance to a single country, and it promotes loyalty and commitment. Such emotions encourage people to obey the law and accept the country's overall ideologies. States promote nationalism in a number of ways, including the use of symbols, such as flags, rituals, and holidays that remind citizens of what the country stands for. Even when a society is highly heterogeneous, symbols are powerful tools for creating national unity. Institutions, such as schools, the armed forces, and religion, may also serve as centripetal forces. Schools are expected to instill the society's beliefs, values, and behaviors in the young, teach the nation's language, and encourage students to identify with the nation. Fast and efficient transportation and communication systems also tend to unify nations. National broadcasting companies usually take on the point of view of the nation, even if they broadcast internationally. Transportation systems make it easier for people to travel to other parts of the country, and give the government the ability to reach all of its citizens.

- **Centrifugal forces** oppose centripetal forces. They destabilize the government and encourage the country to fall apart. A country that is not well-organized or governed stands to lose the loyalty of its citizens, and weak institutions fail to provide the cohesive support that the government needs. Strong institutions may also challenge the government for the loyalty of the people. For example, when the U.S.S.R. was created in 1917, its leaders grounded the new country in the ideology of communism. To strengthen the state, they forbid the practice of the traditional religion, Russian Orthodoxy. Although church membership dropped dramatically, the religious institution never disappeared, and when the U.S.S.R. dissolved, the church reappeared and is regaining its strength today. The church was a centrifugal force in creating and maintaining loyalty to the communist state. Nationalism, too, can be a destabilizing force, especially if different ethnic groups within the country have more loyalty to their ethnicity than to the state and its government. These loyalties often lead to **separatist movements** in which nationalities within a country demand independence. Such movements served as centrifugal forces for the Soviet Union as various nationalities – Lithuanians, Ukrainians, Latvians, Georgians, and Armenians – challenged the government for their independence. Other examples are the Basques of Northern Spain, who have different customs (including language) from others in the country, and the Tamils in Sri Lanka, who have waged years of guerrilla warfare to defend what they see as majority threats to their culture, rights, and property. Characteristics that encourage separatist movements are a peripheral location and social and economic inequality. One reaction states have had to centrifugal force is **devolution**, or the decentralization of decision-making to regional governments. Britain has devolved power to the Scottish and Welsh parliaments in an effort to keep peace with Scotland and Wales. As a result, Britain's unitary government has taken some significant strides toward decentralization, although London is still the geographic center of decision-making for the country.

DEVOLUTION: ETHNIC, ECONOMIC AND SPATIAL FORCES

Devolution of government powers to sub-governments is usually a reaction to centrifugal forces – those that divide and destabilize. Devolutionary forces emerge in all kinds of states, old and new, mature and newly created. We may divide these forces into three basic types:

1) **Ethnic forces** – An **ethnic group** shares a well-developed sense of belonging to the same culture. That identity is based on a unique mixture of language, religion, and customs. If a state contains strong ethnic groups with identities that differ from those of the majority, it can threaten the territorial integrity of the state itself. **Ethnonationalism** – the tendency for an ethnic group to see itself as a distinct nation with a right to autonomy or independence – is a fundamental centrifugal force promoting devolution. The threat is usually stronger if the group is clustered in particular geographic spaces within the nation-state. For example, most French Canadians live in the province of Quebec, creating a large base for an independence movement. If ethnically French people were scattered evenly over the country, their sense of identity would be diluted, and the devolutionary force would most likely be weaker. Devolutionary forces in Britain – centered in Wales, Scotland, and Northern Ireland – have not been strong enough to destabilize the country, although violence in Northern Ireland has certainly destabilized the region. Political boundaries were rearranged on the Indian subcontinent to separate Hindus

and Muslims, resulting in the creation of the country of Pakistan. Ethnic forces broke up the nation-state of Yugoslavia during the 1990s, devolving it into the separate states of Slovenia, Croatia, Bosnia, Macedonia, and Serbia-Montenegro. Canada responded to pressures for a homeland for native Inuit by the 1999 creation of Nunavut as a separate territory, redrawing Canada's political borders for the first time since 1925.

2) **Economic forces** – Economic inequalities may also destabilize a nation-state, particularly if the inequalities are regional. For example, Italy is split between north and south by the "Ancona Line", an invisible line extending from Rome to the Adriatic coast at Ancona. The north is far more prosperous than the south, with the north clearly part of the European core area, and the south a part of the periphery. The north is industrialized, and the south is rural. These economic differences inspired the formation of the Northern League, which advocated an independent state called Padania that would shed the north of the "economic drag" they considered the south to be. The movement failed, but it did encourage the Italian government to devolve power to regional governments, moving it toward a more federal system. A similar economic force is at work in Catalonia in northern Spain, with Catalonians only about 17% of Spain's population, but accountable for 40% of all Spanish industrial exports.

3) **Spatial forces** – Spatially, devolutionary events most often occur on the margins of the state. Distance, remoteness, and peripheral location promote devolution, especially if water, desert,

Economic Devolutionary Forces in Italy and Spain. Geographically, southern Italy and most of Spain lie outside the European core, creating economic devolutionary forces within the two nation-states. In Spain, the Catalonians in the north are connected to the core, but the bulk of Spain is not. In Italy the core extends its reach over the northern half of the country, creating centrifugal tensions between north and south.

or mountains separate the areas from the center of power, and neighbor nations that may support separatist objectives. For example, the United States claims Puerto Rico as a territory, and has offered it recognition as a state. However, Puerto Ricans have consistently voted down the offer of statehood, and a small but vocal pro-independence movement has advocated complete separation from the U.S. The movement is encouraged by spatial forces; Puerto Rico is an island in the Caribbean, close to other islands that have their independence.

CHANGING GEOPOLITICAL CONCERNS

Geopolitics is the study of the spatial and territorial dimensions of power relationships within the global political-territorial order. This approach was taken by geographer **Friedrich Ratzel** in the 19th century, when he theorized that a state compares to a biological organism with a life cycle from birth to death, with a predictable rise and fall of power. The field became controversial after Adolf Hitler used this principle to justify the growth of the German state through attacking weaker states around him and aggressively promoting German nationalism. Meanwhile, a British geographer, Sir Halford Mackinder, concerned himself with power relationships surrounding Britain's global empire. Naval power was responsible for British power, but Mackinder believed that a land-based power, not a sea power, would ultimately rule the world. His **heartland theory** stated that the "pivot area" of the earth – Eurasia – holds the resources, both natural and human, to dominate the globe. When the Soviet Union emerged as a super power after World War II, the heartland theory attracted a great deal of support.

The rimland theory challenged the heartland theory in Nicholas Spykman's book *The Geography of Peace*, written in 1944. Spykman argued that the Eurasian rim, not its heart, held the key to global power. What is the rimland? It is a large swath of land that encircles the heartland, roughly touching oceans and seas. It includes China, Korea, Japan, Southeast Asia, India, the Arabian Peninsula, and Europe. This area is unlikely to fall under any one superpower's control, an important key to keeping a global, geopolitical balance of power.

In recent years, with ever-increasing globalization, geopolitics have reinvigorated, especially as they were dominated from 1945 to 1991 by the **Cold War**, the competition between two superpowers – the United States and the Soviet Union – for control of land spaces all over the world. With the fall of the Soviet Union in 1991, the U.S. was left as the only superpower, but in a world rapidly being redefined. Not only does Russia remain a force to contend with today, China is becoming an economic powerhouse that increasingly seeks participation in world trade and politics. Europe has united in an economic union that is developing more political bonds that may well foresee a new world order of supranational organizations that will challenge the sovereignty of the nation-state.

SUPRANATIONAL ORGANIZATIONS: CHANGING THE MEANING OF SOVEREIGNTY

Supranational organizations have been around for some time now, but their nature is changing, with some real implications for the sovereignty of individual nation-states. Several countries formed the Concert of Europe in the early 19th century in an effort to restore balance of power after the fall of Napoleon Bonaparte. It was a voluntary agreement, and it did not prevent the outbreak of several limited wars. However, many scholars believe that the effort to balance power that the agreement sparked was at least partly responsible for the relative peace among quarrelsome European neighbors until the outbreak of World War I in 1914. That war stimulated another more global effort to form a lasting international organization, and resulted in the creation of the League of Nations, whose fate was doomed with the outbreak of World War II in 1939. Even before the United States joined the war, U.S. President Franklin Roosevelt and British Prime Minister Winston Churchill agreed to try again when the war ended. In this spirit the United Nations was formed in 1945.

The United Nations

Only 49 nation-states signed the original charter of the United Nations in 1945, but because many new nations have been created since then, the membership of the U.N. has grown to 193 members by 2012. It has lasted for more than 65 years, and its membership makes it a truly global organization. Membership in the U.N. is voluntary, but it has some limited powers to force its members to abide by the organization's peacekeeping principles. As a result, it plays an important role in geopolitics, and changes the dynamics of international relationships from the previous almost exclusive focus on nation-states as individual actors on the world stage. The U.N. changes the nature of sovereignty by applying the concept to an organization with collective membership, not just to individual nation-states.

An important power of the U.N. is that its members can vote to establish a peacekeeping force in a "hotspot" and request states to contribute military forces. The body responsible for making this decision is the **Security Council**, and any one of its five permanent members (the U.S., Britain, France, China, and Russia) may veto a proposed peacekeeping action. During the era of the Cold War, the Security Council was often in gridlock because the U.S. and Russia almost always disagreed. Today that gridlock is broken, but it is still difficult for all five countries to agree on a single course of action. Peacekeeping forces have been sent to separate warring forces in Eastern Europe, the Middle East, and Sub-Saharan Africa. The U.N. forces are supposed to remain neutral, and they usually have restrictions on their rights to use weapons against either side in a dispute. Despite its limitations, the United Nations is a forum where most of the states of the world meet and vote on issues without resorting to war.

The U.N. is an umbrella organization that includes many sub-organizations that promote the general welfare of the world's citizens and monitor and aid world trade and other economic contacts. These efforts are funded by membership dues, and represent an extension of international cooperation into areas other than peacekeeping. Examples of such organizations are the World Bank, the International Court of Justice, and UNESCO (an economic and social council).

Regional Organizations

During the Cold War era, regional military alliances appeared, and countries joined them based on their affiliation either with the United States or Russia. The North Atlantic Treaty Organization (NATO) formed in the late 1940s with 14 European members, the United States, and Canada. An opposing alliance – the Warsaw Pact – began in 1955 that was composed of the Soviet Union and six Eastern European countries. Together the two organizations were designed to maintain a bipolar balance of power in Europe. The Warsaw Pact disbanded with the breakup of the Soviet Union, and NATO expanded to include many of its former members. Other regional organizations include the Organization of American States (OAS) created to promote social, cultural, political, and economic links among member states; the Arab League founded to promote the interests and sovereignty of countries in the Middle East; and the Organization for African Unity (OAU) that has promoted the elimination of minority white-ruled governments in southern Africa.

The European Union

A regional organization that promises to redefine the meaning of sovereignty is the **European Union.** All the countries of Europe are deeply affected by a trend toward **integration.** Integration is a process that encourages states to pool their sovereignty in order to gain political, economic, and social clout. Integration binds states together with common policies and shared rules. The organization began in an effort to revitalize a war-torn Europe after World War II ended. The most immediate need was to repair the nations' broken economies, so the initial goals were almost completely economic in intent. In 1949 the Council of Europe, which had little power, formed to provide an opportunity for national leaders to meet. The following year a supranational authority was formed to coordinate the coal and steel industries, both damaged heavily during the war.

The organization went through several name changes, but until 1993 its goals were exclusively economic. The Maastricht Treaty created the modern organization, and gave it authority in new areas, including monetary policy, foreign affairs, national security, transportation, the environment, justice, and tourism. The treaty established the **three pillars,** or spheres of authority:

1. Trade and other economic matters, including economic and monetary union into a single currency, and the creation of the European Central Bank
2. Justice and home affairs, including policy governing asylum, border crossing, immigration, and judicial cooperation on crime and terrorism
3. Common foreign and security policy, including joint positions and actions, and common defense policy

The EU has made remarkable strides in its ability to set European **monetary policy,** or control of the money supply. Today the euro has replaced the old national currencies, which are well on their way to being phased out. Also, the power to set basic interest rates and other fiscal policies is being passed from national banks and governments to the **European Monetary Union** and its central bank. Today, in 12 of the member countries, the euro is accepted as a common currency both in banking and for everyday business transactions. Two exceptions to the rule are Britain and Sweden, which as of 2012 still refuse to give up their national currencies in favor of a common European currency.

Even though the political and economic muscle of so many countries united is considerable, this rapid integration presents many difficult issues for the EU. First, organizational issues abound. Structures that work for six countries do not necessarily operate smoothly for 27. Second, the expansion brings in many former communist countries whose economies were relatively weak by the end of the 20th century. Older member states worry that immigrants from the east will flood their labor markets and strain their economies. EU supporters believe that these problems will be overshadowed by the benefits of common markets, currencies, political policies, and defense.

The European Union has long been defined by a tension between economic liberalism that favors open, free markets and an economic nationalism that seeks to protect national economic interests from the uncertainty of free markets. The older, more established EU members tend to reflect the latter policy orientation, while the newer, less economically-stable members often favor economic liberalism. Supranationalism encourages economic integration but the proper balance with national interests is often a controversial topic. The sovereign debt crisis that began with the near-collapse of the Greek economy in 2010 illustrates this tough issue, and the arguments that have erupted since then strike at the heart of this old tension.

It was no surprise that the debt crisis began in Greece, which failed to join the euro area when it was set up in 1999 because it did not meet the economic or fiscal criteria for membership. Revisions to its budget figures showed that it probably shouldn't have been allowed in when it did join in 2001. After the international banking crisis of 2008, concern for "sovereign debts" (debts of individual EU countries) increased, especially for those with high debt-to-GNP ratios. Attention focused first on Greece, and in May 2010, the eurozone countries and International Monetary Fund agreed to a large loan to Greece, conditional on the implementation of harsh austerity measures. The Greek bailout was followed by a rescue package for Ireland in November and another for Portugal in May 2111.

These bailouts have been controversial, with some arguing that they are essential for keeping the economic health of the entire EU region, but others complaining that it is unfair to expect taxpayers in healthier countries to pay for the economic woes of less stable members. The bailouts are particularly unpopular in Germany, where one poll showed that a majority of the public thinks that the rescue of Greece was a mistake. As talk of a second bailout for Greece materialized in mid-2011, there was strong resistance in Germany to further assistance to the Greek economy. At summit meetings in 2011, European political leaders discussed the possibility of "restructuring" the economies of Greece, Ireland, and Portugal. Economic structural adjustment would mean that at least part of the debt would be forgiven. Supporters of restructuring claim that it is the only way to allow the weakened countries to recover; critics believe that restructuring makes the stronger countries pay for the weaker ones, a process that they claim weakens the entire continent. The crisis seriously questions the economic stability of the euro and the European banking system, and so the solutions that European leaders find will almost certainly influence the future development of the EU.

The European Union. Ongoing expansion is a major characteristic of the European Union, with a total membership of 27 countries as of 2012. The European Union began with six members in 1957: Belgium, France, Germany, Italy, Luxembourg, and the Netherlands. Denmark, Great Britain, and Ireland joined in the early 1970s; Greece in 1981; Portugal and Spain in 1986; and Austria, Finland, and Sweden in 1995. Ten countries joined on May 2, 2004: Cyprus (Greek part), the Czech Republic, Estonia, Hungary, Latvia, Lithuania, Malta, Poland, Slovakia and Slovenia. Bulgaria and Romania joined on January 1, 2007.

FORCES OF CHANGE: GLOBALIZATION, DEMOCRATIZATION, AND RELIGIOUS POLITICS

In considering the changing political imprint on the earth's surface, it is important to take notice of overall patterns of development that affect everyone in the contemporary world. Two of these trends – democratization and the move toward market economies – indicate growing commonalities among nations, or the forces of **globalization.** The third represents fragmentation – the revival of ethnic or cultural politics.

1) Democratization

Even though democracy takes many different forms, more and more nations are turning toward some form of popular government. One broad, essential requirement for democracy is the existence of competitive elections that are regular, free, and fair. In other words, the election offers a real possibility that the incumbent government may be defeated. By this standard, a number of modern states that call themselves "democracies" fall into a gray area that is neither clearly democratic nor clearly undemocratic. Examples are Russia, Nigeria, and Indonesia. In contrast, liberal democracies display other democratic characteristics beyond having competitive elections:

- Civil liberties, such as freedom of belief, speech, and assembly
- Rule of law that provides for equal treatment of citizens and due process
- Neutrality of the judiciary and other checks on the abuse of power
- Open civil society that allows citizens to lead private lives and mass media to operate independently from government
- Civilian control of the military that restricts the likelihood of the military seizing control of the government

Countries that have regular, free, and fair competitive elections, but are missing these other qualities (civil liberties, rule of law, neutrality of the judiciary, open civil society, and civilian control of the military) are referred to as illiberal democracies.

According to political scientist Samuel Huntington, the modern world is now in a **"third wave" of democratization** that began during the 1970s. The "first wave" developed gradually over time; the "second wave" occurred after the Allied victory in World War II, and continued until the early 1960s. This second wave was characterized by de-colonization around the globe. The third wave is characterized by the defeat of dictatorial or totalitarian rulers from South America to Eastern Europe to some parts of Africa. The recent political turnover in Mexico may be interpreted as part of this "third wave" of democratization.

Why has democratization occurred? According to Huntington, some factors are:

- The loss of legitimacy by both right and left wing authoritarian regimes
- The expansion of an urban middle class in developing countries
- A new emphasis on "human rights" by the United States and the European Union
- The "snowball" effect has been important: when one country in a region becomes democratic, it influences others to do so. An example is Poland's influence on other nations of Eastern Europe during the 1980s.

One of the greatest obstacles to democratization is poverty because it blocks citizen participation in government. Huntington gauges democratic stability by this standard: democracy may be declared when a country has had at least two successive peaceful turnovers of power.

2) Movement Toward Market Economies

Many political economists today declare that the economic competition between capitalism and socialism that dominated the 20th century is now a part of the past. The old **command economies**, with socialist principles of centralized planning and state ownership are fading from existence, except in combination with market economies. The issue now is what type of **market economy** will be most successful: one that allows for significant control from the central government – a "**mixed economy**" – or one that does not – a pure market economy. For example, modern Germany has a "social market economy" that is team-oriented and emphasizes cooperation between management and organized labor. In contrast, the United States economy tends to be more individualistic and anti-government control.

Marketization is the term that describes the state's re-creation of a market in which property, labor, goods, and services can all function in a competitive environment to determine their value. **Privatization** is the transfer of state-owned property to private ownership. Because central political control of economies waned during the 20th century, some have speculated that market economies promote the move toward democratization of political institutions. However, both China and Russia have developed capitalist economies in recent years, but their governments have remained highly authoritarian in nature.

3) Revival of Ethnic or Cultural Politics

Until recently, few political scientists predicted that **fragmentation** – divisions based on ethnic or cultural identity – would become increasingly important in world politics. A few years ago **nationalism** – identities based on nationhood – seemed to be declining in favor of increasing globalization. However, nationality questions almost certainly blocked Mikhail Gorbachev's attempts to resuscitate the Soviet Union, and national identities remain strong in most parts of the world. Perhaps most dramatically, the **politicization of religion** (the use of religious principles to promote political ends and vice versa) has dominated world politics during the early 21st century. Most Westerners have been caught off guard by this turn of events, especially in the United States, where separation of church and state has been a basic political principle since the founding of the country.

Samuel Huntington argues that our most important and dangerous future conflicts will be based on clashes of civilizations, not on socioeconomic or even ideological differences. He divides the world into several different cultural areas that may already be poised to threaten world peace: the West, the Orthodox world (Russia), Islamic countries, Latin American, Africa, the Hindu world, the Confucian world, the Buddhist world, and Japan. Some political scientists criticize Huntington by saying that he distorts cultural divisions and that he underestimates the importance of cultural conflicts within nations. In either case – a world divided into cultural regions or a world organized into multicultural nations – the revival of ethnic or cultural politics tends to emphasize differences among nations rather than commonalities.

TERMS AND CONCEPTS

Balkanization
binational or multinational state
boundary
centripetal force, centrifugal force
Cold War
colonies
command economy
compact states
confederal system
consequent boundaries
core area
core-periphery
cultural boundary
democratization
devolution
disputes: positional, territorial, resource, functional
economic force
electoral geography
elongated states
enclaves, exclaves
ethnic force
ethnonationalism
European Constitution
European Monetary Union
European Union
federal system
forward capital
fragmentation
fragmented states
frontiers
geometric boundary
gerrymandering
geopolitics
globalization
government
heartland theory
imperialism
institutions
integration
internal boundaries
irredentism
landlocked states
market economy

marketization
median-line principle
microstates
minority/majority districting
mixed economy
monetary policy
multicore state
nation
nation-state
nationalism
perforated states
physical boundary
political geography
political culture
politicization of religion
politics
primate city
privatization
Ratzel, Friedrich
relative location
rimland theory
Security Council
separatist movement
shatter belts
sovereignty
spatial force
stateless nation
states
supranational organization
territorial morphology
territoriality
"third wave" of democratization
three pillars
unitary state

UNIT FOUR
MULTIPLE-CHOICE QUESTIONS

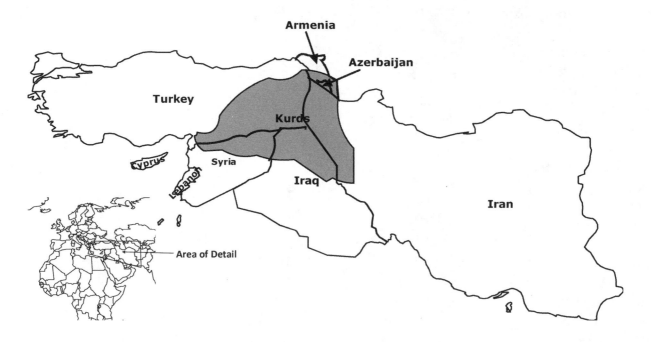

1. The shaded area on the map above is an example of a(n)

(A) stateless nation
(B) exclave
(C) fragmented state
(D) unitary state
(E) microstate

2. The practice of adjusting voting district boundaries in order to benefit the interest of one political party or group is called

(A) devolving
(B) territorializing
(C) gerrymandering
(D) minority-majority districting
(E) red lining

3. Which of the following is the best example of a fragmented state?

(A) Chile
(B) China
(C) Germany
(D) Indonesia
(E) Nigeria

4. All of the following are characteristics of most of the world's remaining dependencies EXCEPT:

(A) Most are remnants of empires.
(B) Most are located in relatively isolated areas.
(C) Most have small populations.
(D) Most are islands.
(E) Most are located in the southern hemisphere.

5. A unitary political system is one that

(A) concentrates policymaking power in the hands of one individual
(B) concentrates policymaking power in one geographic place
(C) has only one branch of government – the executive
(D) does not allow direct elections of public officials
(E) has only one house in the legislature

6. Which of the following types of political organizations most directly reflects the current trend toward integration?

(A) linkage institutions
(B) nongovernmental organizations
(C) national legislatures
(D) supranational organizations
(E) national judiciaries

7. A countertrend to fragmentation in global interactions today is

(A) corporatism
(B) democratic consolidation
(C) globalization
(D) radicalism
(E) privatization

8. Which of the following is an example of a centrifugal force within a nation-state?

(A) ethnic homogeneity
(B) a strong national economy
(C) a strong sense of nationalism
(D) economic equality among regions
(E) a separatist movement that demands independence

9. States with the ability to carry out actions or policies within their borders independently from interference are said to have

  (A) sovereignty
  (B) nationalism
  (C) traditional legitimacy
  (D) integration
  (E) a consensual political culture

10. A group of people bound together by a common identity is a(n)

  (A) state
  (B) nation
  (C) regime
  (D) institution
  (E) political system

11. The sovereign debt crisis in the EU reflects a tension between

  (A) communist and capitalist economies
  (B) the Commission and the European Parliament
  (C) those who favor open free markets and those who seek to protect national economic interests
  (D) those who support enlargement of the EU and those that do not
  (E) EU member-states and non-EU countries in Europe

12. Italy is split between north and south by the "Ancona Line," which illustrates a(n)

  (A) economic devolutionary force
  (B) economic centripetal force
  (C) ethnic devolutionary force
  (D) devolutionary spatial force
  (E) centripetal spatial force

13. Washington D.C. is not a good example of a primate city because it is

  (A) not a forward capital
  (B) not a capital city
  (C) close to the geographical center of the U.S.
  (D) not disproportionately large in relation to some other U.S. cities
  (E) not located in a core area of the U.S.

14. "Shatter belts" are geographical zones where tensions often explode based on

(A) economic boundaries
(B) cultural boundaries
(C) physical boundaries
(D) geometric boundaries
(E) functional boundaries

15. Which of the following is NOT a land-locked state?

(A) Czech Republic
(B) Switzerland
(C) Afghanistan
(D) Kazakhstan
(E) South Africa

16. During the late 1930s, Germany invaded Czechoslovakia and Poland, areas with large numbers of German minorities. This type of expansionism is called

(A) irredentism
(B) territoriality
(C) economic imperialism
(D) devolution
(E) integration

17. According to Halford Mackinder's heartland theory, which of the following countries would be most likely to dominate the globe?

(A) Japan
(B) the United States
(C) Britain
(D) Soviet Union
(E) India

18. Which of the following is the best example of a multicore state?

(A) France
(B) Japan
(C) Mexico
(D) Iceland
(E) Nigeria

19. The median-line principle is often used to define a

(A) desert boundary
(B) water boundary
(C) frontier
(D) mountain boundary
(E) consequent boundary

Thailand

20. Thailand is an example of a state with a shape that is

(A) perforated
(B) compact
(C) prorupted
(D) elongated
(E) fragmented

21. Which of the following is the best example of a state with a good relative location?

(A) Belarus
(B) Mongolia
(C) Bolivia
(D) Laos
(E) Singapore

22. A functional boundary dispute arises when neighboring states cannot agree on

(A) natural resources that lie in border areas
(B) policies that apply in a border area
(C) the ownership of a region around mutual borders
(D) where the border actually is
(E) where citizens from one or both states may settle

23. An example of a state with a federal system is (was)

(A) Britain
(B) France
(C) Confederate States of America
(D) the United States
(E) Germany

24. People of French heritage who live in the province of Quebec have created devolutionary forces in

(A) Australia
(B) Spain
(C) Canada
(D) Switzerland
(E) Germany

25. Which of the following is NOT a supranational organization?

(A) the U.S. Republican Party
(B) the European Union
(C) the United Nations
(D) NATO
(E) Organization of American States

UNIT FOUR
FREE-RESPONSE QUESTION

Most nation-states have grown over time from core areas.

a. Define a core area, and describe one way to identify a core area on a map.

b. Identify one multicore state and explain one reason why having more than one core area has been problematic for that state.

c. Identify a second multicore state and explain one reason why having more than one core area has not been problematic for that state.

**UNIT FIVE:
AGRICULTURE:
PRIMARY ECONOMIC
ACTIVITIES**

As we have seen in the previous units, the human imprint on the geographical landscape includes cultural activities, such as religion and language, as well as political configurations of the land. Another crucial influence on the organization of the earth's surface is the way that people make a living. Economic activities range from the simple to the complex and encompass human life from ancient to modern times. We may organize economic activities by dividing them into three types:

- **The primary sector (agriculture)** is the part of the economy that draws raw materials from the natural environment. The primary sector – agriculture, raising animals, fishing, forestry, and mining – is largest in low-income, pre-industrial nations.

- **The secondary sector (industry)** is the part of the economy that transforms raw materials into manufactured goods. This sector grows quickly as societies industrialize, and includes such operations as refining petroleum into gasoline and turning metals into tools and automobiles.

- **The tertiary sector (services)** is the part of the economy that involves services rather than goods. The tertiary sector grows with industrialization and comes to dominate **post-industrial societies,** or countries where most people are no longer employed in industry. Examples of tertiary jobs include construction, trade, finance, real estate, private services, government, and transportation. **The quaternary sector** is often seen as a subset of the tertiary sector. It includes service jobs concerned with research and development, management and administration, and processing and disseminating information.

Because the sectors represent necessary economic activities, most countries today have some people employed in all three. However, the percentages vary widely. Consider the examples on the chart on the next page.

COMPARATIVE ECONOMIC SECTORS
(as percentage of labor force by occupation)

Country	Primary (Agriculture)	Secondary (Industry)	Tertiary (Services)
China	38%	46.9%	43%
Iran	25%	31%	45%
Mexico	13.7%	23.4%	62.9%
Nigeria	70%	10%	20%
Russia	10%	31.9%	58.1%
United Kingdom	1.4%	18.2%	80.4%
United States	.7%	20.3%	79%

Source: *CIA World Factbook,* 2005-2010 (except Nigeria, 1999)

By comparing economic sectors, the United Kingdom is one example of a post-industrial society, with only 1.4% of its population engaged in agriculture, and 80.4% in services. The United States is another post-industrial country, with .7% in agriculture, and 79% in services. Russia appears to have moved into post-industrialism as well. Likewise, Mexico has moved away from agriculture (13.7%) toward services (62.9%), as has Iran to a lesser extent. Despite its recent economic boom, 38% of China's population is still employed in agriculture, and Nigeria has the largest percentage of its people (70%) employed in the primary sector.

In this unit we will explore agricultural activities, which belong to the primary sector. For thousands of years agriculture was the main economic activity of most people on earth, until the Industrial Revolution transformed economies first in Europe and North America, and eventually influenced most countries in the world.

THE ORIGIN AND SPREAD OF AGRICULTURE

Agriculture is the deliberate tending of crops and livestock in order to produce food and fiber. As is evident in the chart on the previous page, many countries today have relatively smaller percentages of their populations in agriculture. Yet total agricultural production in the world is at an all-time high, mainly because the nature of farming has changed with mechanization and farm consolidation, particularly in industrial and post-industrial countries. In all countries, the processes that produce, distribute, and determine the consumption of food play crucial roles. The ways that land is distributed to individuals and used for food production are determined by culture, as are the functions of livestock, and the consumption of food from crops and animals. For example, Hindus do not eat beef, and Muslims do not eat pork, and so the two religions greatly impact the nature of agriculture in lands where they have many adherents.

HUNTERS AND GATHERERS

The first humans probably emerged in eastern Africa, due to a happy confluence of availability of food, domesticable animals, and favorable climate. For thousands of years humans sustained themselves as **hunters and gatherers**, and as a result they were quite dependent on the abundance of food. Hunters gained skills in capturing and killing animals, and gatherers learned which plants and fruits were edible and nutritious. Technological inventions generally supported the fulfillment of these basic activities. Stones (and eventually metals) were shaped as tools and weapons, and techniques were developed for efficient gathering and storage of food.

The groups traveled frequently, establishing new home bases or camps. Their migrations depended on the movement of game and the seasonal growth of plants. Often they moved in a pattern over the same extent of land year after year, but as environments changed, sometimes the migrations were permanent. By 8000 B.C.E., humans had migrated to many other areas, probably following the herds and other available food sources. In general, hunters and gatherers left little imprint on the land. Major migrations include:

- Eastern Africa to Australia, the Middle East, Europe, and Asia

- Asia across the land bridge to the Americas

THE NEOLITHIC REVOLUTION

When, how, and why did people give up their wandering and settle to live in one place? First of all, it happened in different parts of the world at different times, but settled communities had developed in many places by 8000 B.C.E. The ability to settle was based almost entirely on successful cultivation of crops and domestication of animals. These drastic changes in human life are known collectively as the **Neolithic Revolution** that almost certainly happened independently in different places over a large span of time (independent invention). From these **agricultural hearths** farming practices diffused across the surface of the earth. For example, the people settling along the major rivers in China did not learn to farm because they were in contact with the people in the Indus River area. Instead, people in both areas probably figured out the advantages of settled life on their own, and both served as agricultural hearths. Although the Neolithic Revolution was one of the most significant marker events in world history, it occurred gradually and probably by trial and error.

The changes that resulted include:

- **Increase in reliable food supplies** – Agricultural skills allowed people to control food production, and domesticate animals. Both helped to make agricultural production more efficient and increased the availability of food.

- **Rapid increase in total human population** – Reliable food supplies meant that people were less likely to starve to death. Once people settled down, they were able to store their food for times of scarcity. With increasing life spans came increasing reproduction, and more children meant that there were more people to tend the land and animals.

- **Job specialization** – Other occupations than farming developed, since fewer people were needed to produce food. Some early specialized jobs include priests, traders, and builders.

- **Widening of gender differences** – Status distinctions between men and women increased, as men took over most agricultural cultivation and domestication of animals. Women were responsible for raising children, cooking food, and keeping the house, but in virtually all of the early civilizations men became dominant. Since men controlled agricultural production, **patriarchal systems** commonly developed, with men holding power in the family, the economy, and the government.

- **Development of distinction between settled people and nomads** (people who continued to move from place to place) – Many people did not settle into communities but remained as hunters and gatherers. As more settled communities developed, the distinction between agriculturalists and hunters and gatherers grew, with settled people generally considering their way of life to be superior.

According to cultural geographer Carl Sauer, the earliest form of plant cultivation was **vegetative planting,** in which new plants are produced by direct cloning from existing plants, such as cutting stems and dividing roots. People first learned to farm by deliberately dividing and transplanting plants already growing wild. **Seed agriculture**, or the production of plants through annual planting of seeds, came later. Most farmers today practice seed agriculture.

Vegetative Planting

Carl Sauer believes that vegetative planting probably originated in the diverse climates and topography of Southeast Asia, where a wide variety of plants existed that were suitable for dividing and transplanting. Also, the people did more fishing than hunting, so they were probably more settled, and so more likely to experiment with plants. The first plants domesticated in Southeast Asia included roots such as the taro and yam, and tree crops such as the banana and palm. Vegetative planting diffused from the Southeast Asian hearth northward and eastward to China and Japan, and westward through India, Southwest Asia, tropical Africa, and the area around the Mediterranean Sea. The first domesticated animals were probably dogs, pigs, and chickens.

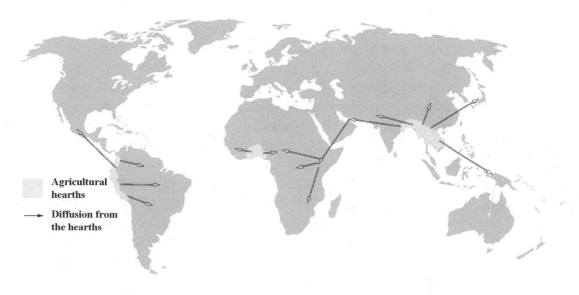

Agricultural hearths

→ **Diffusion from the hearths**

Origin and diffusion of vegetative planting. The earliest hearth was probably Southeast Asia, with other early hearths in West Africa and South America.

Other early hearths were probably in West Africa and northwestern South America. In West Africa plantings were possibly palm trees and yams, and in South America, manioc, sweet potatoes, and arrowroot. The practice diffused from South America to Central America and eastern areas of South America.

Seed Agriculture

Carl Sauer identified three hearths for seed agriculture in the Eastern Hemisphere: western India, northern China, and Ethiopia. From western India it diffused to Southwest Asia, where people first domesticated wheat and barley, two grains that later fed Europeans and Americans. In Southwest Asia the inhabitants also domesticated herd animals such as cattle, sheep, and goats. Cattle were used to plow the land before planting seeds, and were fed part of the harvested crop. Animals also provided milk, meat, and skins.

Seed agriculture diffused from Southwest Asia across Europe and through North Africa, with barley and cattle becoming more important farther north, as they thrived in cooler and moister climates. Seed agriculture also diffused eastward to northwestern India and the Indus River valley. From the northern China hearth, millet diffused to South Asia and Southeast Asia. The cultural hearth of rice is unknown, but it probably was Southeast Asia. Millet and sorghum were domesticated in the third independent hearth in Ethiopia, which today is ironically an area with widespread starvation.

Two independent seed agriculture hearths originated in the Western Hemisphere: southern Mexico and northern Peru. Southern Mexico was the point of origin for squash and maize (corn), with beans, cotton, and squash domesticated in Peru. Agriculture diffused to other areas, although it was not widespread over the hemisphere until the arrival of Europeans in the late 15th century. Only then were wheat, oats, and barley introduced to the Western Hemisphere, and maize and beans to the Eastern Hemisphere.

Over the years many innovations increased the chances of success for seed agricultural practices. Some early innovations were **irrigation** (the channeling of water to fields), plowing to loosen and turn the soil, fencing to keep animals out of fields, building terraces to provide level fields on hillsides, fertilizing with plant and animal waste, and weeding to support desirable crops..

The diffusion of both vegetative planting and seed agriculture from their multiple hearths created a wide variety of food raised and consumed around the world. For example, rice became the mainstay of diets in southern China and much of Southeast Asia, while grains were basic to farming in northern China. Through increased trade and other types of interactions, people in both areas were able to share diets, but variations in climate and topography continued to reinforce the original crops and diets. Food in the Western and Eastern Hemispheres was almost completely different until the **Columbian Exchange** began in the late 15th and 16th centuries, when products were carried both ways across the Atlantic and Pacific Oceans. In some cases a crop grown in one area, like the potato that originated in the Andes Mountain areas of South America, became a mainstay in another area (Ireland). However, beans, squash, and corn are still more commonly consumed in the Americas, and rice is still more basic to Asian cultures than to other areas of the world.

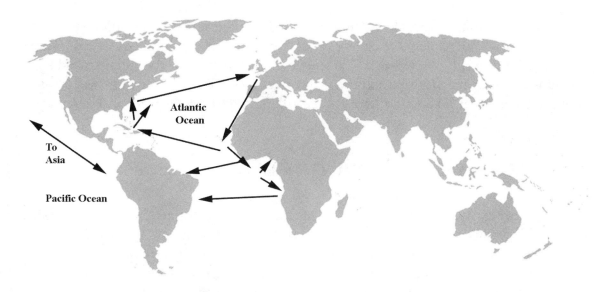

The Columbian Exchange. The European exploration and conquest of the Western Hemisphere in the late 15th and 16th centuries led to the exchange of products between Western and Eastern Hemispheres, with new trade routes across the Pacific and Atlantic Oceans connecting to established trade routes. For the first time in world history, trade routes encircled the globe.

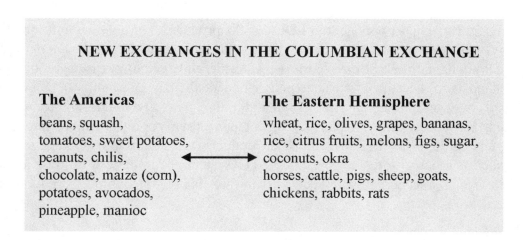

NEW EXCHANGES IN THE COLUMBIAN EXCHANGE

The Americas
beans, squash,
tomatoes, sweet potatoes,
peanuts, chilis,
chocolate, maize (corn),
potatoes, avocados,
pineapple, manioc

The Eastern Hemisphere
wheat, rice, olives, grapes, bananas,
rice, citrus fruits, melons, figs, sugar,
coconuts, okra
horses, cattle, pigs, sheep, goats,
chickens, rabbits, rats

SECOND AGRICULTURAL REVOLUTION

A **second agricultural revolution** began in Western Europe during the 1600s, which intensified agriculture by promoting higher yields per acre and per farmer. This agricultural revolution preceded the Industrial Revolution, making it possible to feed the rapidly growing cities. Some innovations included increased use of fertilizers and improved collars for draft animals to pull heavier plows.

Beginning in the early 1700s, wealthy landowners in England began to enlarge their farms through **enclosure**, or fencing or hedging large blocks of land (including "common" areas previously shared by all) for experiments with new techniques of farming. These scientific farmers improved **crop rotation** methods, which carefully controlled nutrients in the soil. They bred better livestock, and invented new machines, such as Jethro Tull's **seed drill** that more effectively planted seeds. The larger the farms and the better the production the fewer farmers were needed. Farmers pushed out of their jobs by enclosure either became tenant farmers or they moved to cities. Better nutrition boosted England's population, creating the first necessary component for the Industrial Revolution: labor.

Once the Industrial Revolution began, farming methods became much more efficient with the use of tractors for plowing soil, reapers for cutting crops, threshers for separating grain from stalks, and motors for pumping water to do the work of people and animals. Transportation for and storage of crops also improved dramatically, especially with the invention of refrigerated railroad cars and ships. Industrially-produced chemicals for fertilizers, weed killers, and pesticides were also introduced in the 20th century.

MAJOR AGRICULTURAL PRODUCTION REGIONS

Agricultural practices vary widely across the globe, but the most basic distinctions may be made between agriculture in less developed countries (LDCs) and more developed countries. Farmers in LDCs usually produce food through subsistence agriculture, and farmers in more developed countries usually practice commercial agriculture. Agricultural regions, then, may be divided broadly into these two types of agriculture, and then subdivided according to varying practices, types of crops, and climates.

SUBSISTENCE V. COMMERCIAL AGRICULTURE

Subsistence agriculture, most prevalent in LDCs, is the production of only enough food to feed the farmer's family, with no surpluses to sell. Some surplus may be sold to the government or to companies, but the surplus is not the farmer's primary purpose. **Commercial agriculture** is the production of food surpluses, with most crops destined for sale to people outside the farmer's family. Practiced mainly in more developed countries, farmers in commercial agriculture generally do not sell produce directly to consumers but to food-processing companies. Big companies sign contracts with commercial farmers to buy their grain, cattle, pigs, chickens, and other products that they in turn package to sell through food outlets (such as grocery stores) to consumers. The system of commercial farming found in more developed countries is called **agribusiness,** because farming is integrated into a large food-production industry.

Subsistence and commercial agriculture may be compared in several ways:

- **Percentage of farmers in the labor force** – Logically, in countries that practice subsistence farming a high percentage of people are engaged in farming. With no surplus to sell, all people must produce their own food in order to survive. In contrast, well-developed commercial agriculture allows people to pursue other activities, so a smaller percentage of people are farmers. For example, less than 2% of all workers in the United States and Canada (countries with a great deal of commercial agriculture) are farmers. In contrast, many countries in Africa have more than 60% of their citizens engaged in agriculture.

- **Use of machinery** – A key to successful development of commercial agriculture is the use of machinery to replace work done with hand tools and animal power. In more developed countries, tractors, combines, planters, and other farm machines have largely replaced manual labor. Transportation is also important to commercial farmers, who rely on railroads, highways, and rapid sea and air travel to facilitate their ability to get goods to consumers. Commercial farmers also have scientific advances – such as fertilizers, herbicides, and new breeds of plants and animals – that boost their crop yields and the health of their animals.

- **Farm size** – Because commercial farmers have machinery and scientific advances, they can efficiently farm far larger amounts of land than subsistence farmers can. Today commercial agriculture is increasingly dominated by a handful of large farms that can afford the expensive machinery needed to efficiently produce crops. Despite the fact that very few people are farmers, the amount of land devoted to agriculture is still quite significant in most developed countries.

SUBSISTENCE FARMING: SUBREGIONS

Subsistence farming varies according to adaptations to varying climates. Subregions for subsistence farming include:

1) **Intensive subsistence** – This type of agriculture yields a large amount of output per acre through concentrated farming, but still only provides a subsistence living for farmers. Sometimes they may sell a little to others, but usually they raise crops for their own consumption. Intensive subsistence farming is found in the large population concentrations of East and South Asia, with **wet, or lowland, rice** dominant in many areas. Wet rice is planted on dry land in a nursery and then moved as seedlings to a flooded field to promote growth. The crop requires a great deal of time and attention, but under ideal conditions it can provide large amounts of food per unit of land. Other products include wheat (grown in northern China), maize, millet, peas, and beans. A little less than half of the people of the world are engaged in this type of farming. This **labor intensive agriculture** employs large numbers of people and requires relatively little capital to produce food. Most work is done by hand, and although the crops the farmers raise form the basis of their diets, they often link to other regions for specialized products. Today production of food for sale in rapidly growing urban markets is increasingly important, a trend that is leading these areas away from strict "subsistence" farming.

2) **Shifting cultivation** – Often referred to as "slash and burn" or swidden agriculture, this farming method exists primarily in rain forest zones of Central and South America, West Africa, eastern and central Asia, and much of southern China and Southeast Asia. The obvious destruction to the environment is worsened by the frequency of the farmers' movements. As an extensive type of subsistence farming, by its very nature shifting cultivation agriculture still consumes a large percentage of arable land on the planet. At first, the soil in the burnt areas is very fertile, but when soil nutrients are depleted, farmers move on to slash and burn another piece of jungle. People who practice shifting cultivation generally live in small villages and grow food on the surrounding land, which the village controls. **Intertillage** – or the growing of various types of crops – is common. The village chief or council assigns a plot of land to each family and allows them to keep what they raise. Farming is done almost exclusively by hand, and plows and animals are not generally used. The main fertilizer is potash from burning the debris when the site is cleared. When the nutrients are depleted after a few years, the villagers identify another site and begin clearing it. They allow the old site to return to its natural vegetation, although they don't entirely abandon it because they will return after a few years to resume their farming.

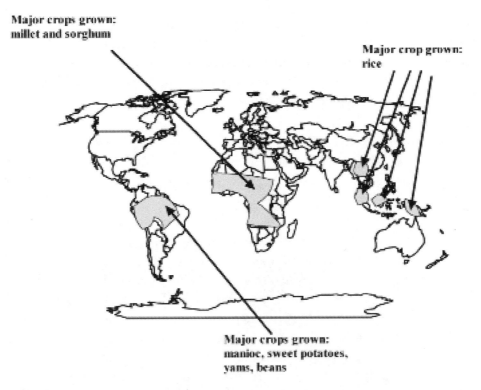

Major crops grown:
millet and sorghum

Major crop grown:
rice

Major crops grown:
manioc, sweet potatoes,
yams, beans

Major regions of shifting cultivation. Shifting cultivation is best suited to rain forest regions, where farmers fertilize the relatively infertile rain forest soils by burning the undergrowth and using the ash to allow cultivation of crops.

3) Pastoral nomadism – This alternative to sedentary agriculture is characterized by following the herds, just as the earlier hunters and gatherers did. A great deal of the earth's surface today is still devoted to pastoral nomadism. However, the herds are domesticated, and consists of sheep, goats, cows, reindeer, camels, and/or horses. **Nomadism**, or the practice of moving frequently from one place to the other, is dictated by the need for pasture for the animals. This life style first developed across the grassy plains of central Eurasia and nearby desert areas of the Arabian Peninsula and the Sudan, and formerly included reindeer herding in northernmost Scandinavia and along the Arctic fringe of Russia, where it is still sometimes practiced. The animals involved must be hardy and mobile, most commonly including sheep, goals, and camels, and sometimes cattle, horses, and yaks. For the herders, the animals provide their primary subsistence with milk, cheese, and meat for food, and hair, wool, and skins for clothing and shelter. Extended stays in one location are neither desirable nor possible because the herds follow seasonal availability of pasture.

Both shifting cultivation and pastoral nomadism are referred to as **extensive subsistence agriculture** because they involve large areas of land and minimal labor per land unit. Both product per land unit and population densities are low. In contrast, **intensive subsistence agriculture** involves the cultivation of small land plots through great amounts of labor, and yields per unit and area and populations densities are both high. A major issue for subsistence farmers today is the need to intensify farming because of rapidly growing populations. According to economist Ester Boserup, subsistence farmers intensify production by leaving land fallow for shorter periods and adopting new farming methods. In order to farm land more efficiently, plows must be used, more weeding must take place, and more ditches for irrigation must be dug. The increase in population provides more people for weeding and digging ditches, so yield per acre increases, and land may be left fallow for shorter periods of time.

COMMERCIAL AGRICULTURE: SUBREGIONS

In pure **commercial agriculture**, farmers and ranchers sell all of their output for money and buy their families' food at stores. Commercial farmers are part of a large, complex economy in which they are only one element of an integrated commodity chain that includes industrial and service sectors as well. Commercial agriculture generally is dominant in more developed countries, and may be divided into intensive types (dairy farming and truck farming) and extensive types (large grain farms and livestock farms). The seven types of commercial agriculture listed below may be categorized as intensive, extensive, or a combination of the two.

1. **Mixed crop and livestock farming** – This is the most common form of commercial agriculture in the United States west of the Appalachian Mountains and in much of Europe from France to Russia. As the name implies, farmers grow crops and raise livestock on the same land spread, with most of the crops fed to animals rather than to people. Most income comes from the sale of animal products, such as beef, milk, and eggs. Mixed crop and livestock farming permits farmers to distribute the workload more evenly through the year, with fields requiring attention in the spring when crops are planted, and in the fall, when they are harvested. Livestock require year-long attention, but unlike crop produce, livestock produce can be sold in the wintertime, too. Most farmers practice **crop rotation**, where each field is planted on a planned cycle. Different crops take different nutrients from the soil, but commercial farmers make more intensive use of their soil that shifting agriculturalists do, with the latter leaving fields fallow for long intervals. At any given time, commercial agriculturalists will have almost all of their fields planted, but with different crops from those of previous years. For example, one cycle might focus on **cereal grains**, such as oats, wheat, rye, or barley; a second cycle might feature a root crop, such as turnips; a third cycle would be a "rest" crop, such as clover, that helps to restore the field, but may be eaten by cattle. Then the farmer can start over with a cereal grain. In the United States today corn is most commonly raised, with soybeans (used as an ingredient in processed food) the second most important crop in mixed commercial farming regions.

2. **Dairy farming** – Dairy farms abound in the areas outlying large urban areas, where their products feed populations in cities across the United States (most frequently in the Northeast), Western Europe, and Southeast Canada. Dairy farms must be closer to their market than other products because milk spoils quickly, so a ring of milk production called a **milkshed** surrounds a major city. Today refrigerated rail cars and trucks have extended the reach of the milksheds, so that nearly every farm in the U.S. Northeast and Northwest Europe is within the milkshed of at least one urban area. Dairy farms also produce butter and cheese, with many specializing in one product or another. Since cheese and butter keep fresh longer than milk does, farms further away from urban centers tend to favor these products over milk. For example, New Zealand is the world's largest producer of dairy products, but they only devote a small share of their attention to liquid milk because it is too far away from North America and Western Europe to hold the milk market in those areas. Dairy farmers, like other commercial agriculturalists, usually do not sell their products directly to consumers, but to wholesalers or to butter and cheese manufacturers. A disadvantage of dairy farming is the expense of feeding cows in the winter. In contrast to mixed crop and livestock farmers, dairy farmers must purchase all feed, making it less likely that they will make a profit. Dairy farming is also labor intensive, since in addition to managing the care of their animals, cows must be milked regularly twice a day. The number of dairy farms has declined significantly since

Major grain-producing region of the United States. States like Wyoming and Nebraska that lie between regions often are able to produce both winter and spring wheat.

1980, with departing farmers citing long work hours and too little profit as reasons. However, despite the decreasing numbers of farms, overall dairy production rose, indicating that the farms that still exist are producing more.

3. **Grain farming** – The most important grain-producing areas in the world are in the United States in three regions: the **winter wheat area** in Kansas, Colorado, and Oklahoma, where the crop is planted in the autumn, survives the winter, and ripens the following summer; the **spring wheat area** of the Dakotas and Montana, where winters are too severe for winter wheat; and the Palouse region of Washington State. Other grain-producing countries are Canada, Australia, Argentina, France, and the United Kingdom. Large-scale grain production, like other forms of commercial agriculture, is heavily mechanized on large farms. The labor required for grain farming is concentrated during planting and harvesting seasons, although some farmers (depending on their locations) may combine winter and spring wheat to even out their work load over the year. Although much grain is sold to companies that eventually sell to consumers within the country, much wheat finds its way into the international market, where it serves as the world's leading export crop. As a result, the prairies of North America are often referred to as the **"world's breadbasket."**

4. **Livestock ranching** – Ranching is the commercial grazing of livestock over an extensive area, and is often practiced in arid or semi-arid regions where climate conditions make crop production impractical. Cattle ranching extends over much of the western United States, where the patterns of life associated with it have shaped the popular image of the West through stories of cowboys, round-ups, and trail-herding. In the early days, cattle roamed freely across vast extents of land, and were rounded up in the spring and then driven across land to railroad termini, such as Kansas City and St. Louis. However, by the late 19th century, cattle ranching became more sedentary as more and more railroads covered the landscape and farmers claimed more western lands. Today most cattle grazing is on land leased from the U.S. government. Although much land in the U.S. has been

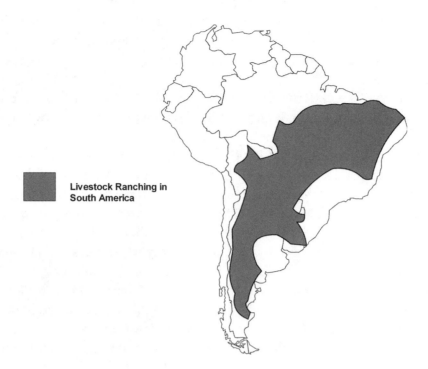

converted from ranching to crop production today, large ranches still exist, although some are now owned by meat-processing companies. In South America, large portion of the **pampas** (prairie) of Argentina, southern Brazil, and Uruguay are devoted to grazing cattle and sheep. Ranches in Australia, New Zealand, the Middle East, and South Africa are more likely to raise sheep than cattle. In all of these areas, as in the United States, irrigation has allowed conversion of ranch land to crops, with the remaining ranches experimenting with new methods of breeding, feeding, and watering in order to stay profitable. While livestock raised in the U.S. is sold primarily in the domestic market, livestock raised in other areas is more likely to be exported to high consumption developed countries.

5. **Mediterranean agriculture** – This type of agriculture exists not only in the lands that border the Mediterranean Sea, but also in California, central Chile, the southwestern part of South Africa, and southwestern Australia. These areas share a similar physical environment: they border seas, and are on the west coasts of continents, with moisture provided by prevailing sea winds and moderate winter temperatures. Summers are hot and dry, with hilly lands and mountains that plunge directly to the sea, leaving narrow strips of flat land along the coast. Some livestock is raised, but most effort is put into crop production for human consumption rather than for animal feed. **Horticulture** – the growing of fruits, vegetables, and flowers – and tree crops form the commercial base of Mediterranean farming. Major crop are olives, grapes, fruits, and vegetables. The hilly landscape encourages farmers to plant a variety of crops within one farming area. In the areas around the Mediterranean Sea, the most important cash crops are olives and grapes, with two-thirds of the world's wine produced there. Olives are an important source of cooking oil. California also produces grapes (and wine), and provides much of the citrus fruits and tree nuts for the United States market. California produces a wider variety of crops than other Mediterranean climate areas because of the extensive use of irrigation. During the winter months, many fruits and vegetables consumed in the United States are imported from Chile.

6. **Commercial gardening and fruit farming** – This type of agriculture predominates in the U.S. Southeast, a region with a long growing season and humid climate and accessibility to the large markets of the Northeast. It is often referred to as **truck farming**, because "truck" originally meant "bartering" in the English language. Products include apples, asparagus, cherries, lettuce, mushrooms, and tomatoes, with some sold fresh to consumers, but most sold to large processors for canning or freezing. Truck farms usually rely heavily on machinery and fertilizers, and labor costs are controlled by hiring migrant farm workers who work for very low wages.

7. **Plantation farming** – A **plantation** is a large farm that specializes in one or two crops, and is found today in Latin America, Africa, and Asia. Almost all crops are raised for export to high-consumption developed countries, and are called **cash crops** because they are raised to make money for their owners. Plantations are colonial legacies that persist in poorer, primarily tropical, countries along with subsistence farming. Cotton, sugarcane, coffee, rubber, and tobacco are usually grown on plantations in sparsely settled locations where owners import workers and provide them with food and housing. Until the 19th century, slave labor was employed, but today the workers are paid, although their room and board constitutes a large part of their salaries. Plantation agriculture predominated in the Southeastern United States until slavery was outlawed in the 1860s, when the land was subdivided and either sold to individual farmers or worked by tenant farmers. Today many plantations in former colonies are still owned by Western individuals or corporations.

RURAL LAND USE AND SETTLEMENT PATTERNS

As the variety of agricultural regions reflects, rural land may be put to many uses, including both subsistence and commercial farming. For subsistence farmers, the land and climate largely determine what crops may be grown as well as how they are cultivated. For commercial farmers rural land use is also influenced by access to markets, competition from other farmers, and government regulations and subsidies.

VON THÜNEN'S MODEL

A German farmer, Johann Heinrich von Thünen, developed a famous model for rural land use in the early 19th century. Von Thünen studied the spatial layout of farming around the town of Rostock in northeast Germany, where he noticed that within the landscape one crop gave way to another without any visible change in the soil, climate, or terrain. As he mapped this pattern, he discovered that each town was a market center surrounded by a set of roughly concentric rings that featured different crops.

Von Thünen identified these four rings that surrounded market centers:

- **Market gardening and dairy** – Nearest the town, farmers raised perishable products, such as garden vegetables and milk. These products are expensive to deliver and must reach the market quickly because they spoil rather quickly, so it makes sense that these farmers needed to choose locations close to town.
- **Forest** – In von Thünen's day, towns were still surrounded by belts of forest that provided wood for fuel and construction. Closeness to market is important because trees are bulky and heavy to transport.

- **Field crops** – The next ring was used for crops that were less perishable, such as wheat and other grains. Usually the crops were rotated from one year to the next.
- **Animal grazing** – The outermost ring was devoted to livestock grazing, which required lots of space. Beyond this ring, it generally became unprofitable to farm commercially because the transportation costs became too high.

The pattern of rings reflects the need to apply **intensive agriculture** methods for high-value and perishable crops in the first ring, where land is subdivided into relatively small units. Land far from markets, in rings three and four, may be farmed **extensively** and in larger units. Intensive vs. extensive agricultural techniques determine settlement patterns, with dairy and truck farmers seeking smaller plots of relatively expensive land relatively close to cities, and grain farmers and ranchers settling on larger, less expensive land farther away from urban areas.

Von Thünen's model assumed a flat terrain with uniform soils and no significant barriers to transportation to market. He did acknowledge that the spatial arrangement could vary according to topography. For example, towns located on rivers or on hilly terrain had to arrange their rings accordingly. Von Thünen published his model in 1826 in a book called *The Isolated State*, the first effort to analyze the spatial character of economic activity. Despite the fact that soil quality, terrain, and climate changes may alter the model significantly, von Thünen identified the interplay of transportation costs and value of the products on rural land use, a formula that is still at the heart of **location theory**, the general but logical attempt to explain how an economic activity is related to the land space where goods are produced.

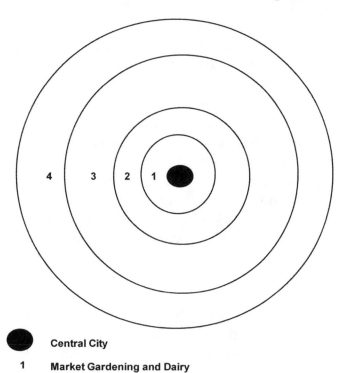

- ● Central City
- 1 Market Gardening and Dairy
- 2 Forest
- 3 Field Crops
- 4 Animal Grazing

Von Thünen's Model. According to this model, different types of farming are conducted at different distances from a city, or market center, depending on the cost of transportation and the value of the product.

GLOBAL PATTERNS OF RURAL LAND USE

Von Thünen applied his model to the relatively small land space around 19th century German towns, but his basic concern with the interplay of market location, transportation costs, and land use may be applied on different scales. Even with fast transportation available, many foods need to reach market within a short amount of time, especially with the growth in popularity of organic foods. Without added preservatives, organic products have a shorter freshness span, so von Thünen's model comes in to play in assessing rural land use for organic foods. For example, on a regional level, fresh organic chicken served in a New York City restaurant would most likely have a more limited area of profitability than chicken that is non-organic.

On a global scale, von Thünen's model is useful for understanding broad patterns of rural land use. Farmers in areas far away from the major markets of Western Europe and North America are less likely to grow highly perishable products or crops that are bulky and expensive to transport. However, other factors that affect rural land use include varying climate and soil conditions, farming methods, technology, and even historical influences. For example, many poor countries today still grow commercial crops, such as coffee and bananas, on soil that otherwise might be used for food for their own consumption. The historical roots of this practice are in colonialism, where entrepreneurs form powerful European countries and/or the United States established plantations for commercial agriculture.

PATTERNS OF SETTLEMENT

Clearly, the intensity of crop cultivation affects the density of housing in rural areas. Areas of extensive agricultural practices demonstrate a **dispersed settlement pattern**, with individual farmhouses lying quite far apart. Dispersed settlement patterns may also exist in areas where machinery makes intensive cultivation over large areas possible. For example, most farms across the Midwestern U.S. are large, houses are spaced far apart, and land is farmed fairly intensively by machines. In contrast, many rural areas in Indonesia are characterized by a **nucleated settlement pattern,** with villages located quite close together with relatively small surrounding fields. Land use is intense, but people and animals do the work. Nucleated settlement is the most common worldwide pattern of agricultural settlement. Houses are grouped together in **hamlets**, or small clusters of buildings, or in slightly larger settlements called **villages**. These arrangements reflect the historical need to band together for protection, but even though this need has changed in modern day, the patterns were established long ago and still persist.

Housing Styles and Geography

Geography has always influenced the types of houses that people build for shelter. For example, people in flood-prone areas learned how to build houses on stilts, and people in areas with lots of snow learned to build steep-sided roofs. Lifestyles also determine housing styles, such as the light-weight, transportable materials used by nomadic people for shelter. Until relatively recently, people were limited by their physical environments in their building materials for housing. For example, early settlers in the Midwestern United States built sod houses because trees were not readily available. Today migrations have carried housing styles far away from their origins, and building materials are shipped for long distances, so many areas have mixed housing styles.

Housing styles in rural areas tend to be more traditional than those in urban areas, especially if the areas are remote from or resistant to outside influences. Villages all over the world have mixtures of traditional and modified housing, with traditional styles ranging from sod-covered roofs in Scandinavia to hand-cut stone houses in the Andes Mountains to mud-walled houses in China.

Different building materials include:

- **Wood** – The use of wood in houses is still linked to the distribution of forests, but wood is now shipped to most corners of the globe. The log house probably originated in northern Europe where forests were plentiful, and its use spread to North America when Europeans first settled there. In those areas today wood is not usually the primary building material, but still is used for framing and trimming. Houses made primarily of wood are still found in a zone that extends eastward from Scandinavia through Russia to the Pacific coast.

- **Brick** – Although builders in the U.S. define bricks as oven-baked blocks of cement, bricks in other areas of the world are made from different materials. Wet mud mixed with straw is used in the Middle East, northern China, the southwestern United States, and Mexico. This mixture is sun-dried rather than oven-baked. Today brick is a major element of modern construction across the world.

- **Stone** – Natural stone has long been used in home construction. A distinctive feature of buildings in the Andes Mountains is that many have no mortar, but are stacked in puzzle-like pieces that have stood in some cases for centuries. More typically, houses of natural stone are built with cement mortar, usually in areas where building stone is plentiful.

- **Wattle** – The term **wattle** refers to poles and sticks woven tightly together and then covered with mud. Many African houses are constructed with wattle and a thick thatched roof. Other regions where wattle building is common also have plenty of bamboo, sticks, bark, and leaves for building, such as Southeast Asia and the Amazonian River Basin.

Villages

The definition of **village** varies across the world, but it usually describes a small number of people who live in a cluster of houses in a rural area. Other structures, such as places for religious gatherings, barns, markets, and government buildings, are commonly found in villages. How large may a village be? In Canada, the official definition limits a village to 1000 people; in the United States villages may have up to 2500 people. The numbers go way up in densely-populated areas, such as Japan and India. Another way to define a village is by the occupations of its inhabitants. In a village, most people work in the primary economic sector as farmers, herders, or fishers, and relatively few people have narrow, specialized jobs. Some villagers provide services to those who farm, herd, or fish, but the social organization is relatively simple.

Village forms include:

- **Round villages** – This most traditional style is found in East Africa and parts of Europe, and it features houses that circle around a central corral for animals, with fields extending outside the ring of houses. Clearly, the style was developed to protect domesticated animals, such as cattle.

Remains of a village wall. The photo above shows the remains of the wall and an old city gate that led to the city of Die in France. The wall provided protection from attack, and the gate was heavily fortified.

- **Walled villages** – This type of village developed in ancient days in order to protect villagers from attack. In Europe the villages were often surrounded by moats as well. Today remnants of these walls still exist, and in some cases walls are still intact.

- **Grid villages** – These more modern villages are laid out in straight street patterns that run in parallel and perpendicular lines. Grids are also used in cities, and work best in areas with flat land.

- **Linear villages** – These modern settlements follow major roads, often one single thoroughfare lined with houses, businesses, and public buildings.

- **Cluster villages** – These settlements may have more than one major road that they build along, and they also may have housing that clusters around large public buildings, such as churches, temples, mosques, livestock corrals, or grain bins.

The Influence of Land Ownership and Survey Techniques

One of the most important influences on land settlement patterns is land ownership. Parcels of land are divided by lines that clearly separate one person's land from another's. Rules about property inheritance often determine land distribution. For example, in areas where **primogeniture** is practiced, all land passes to the eldest son, resulting in large land parcels that are tended individually. This form of property distribution is found in northern Europe, the Americas, South Africa, Australia, and New Zealand. In other areas, such as much of Asia, Africa, and southern Europe, land is divided among heirs, resulting in smaller plots of land with scattered ownership.

Survey methods were first used in areas where settlement was regulated by law, such as European surveys of the Americas as settlers moved westward from the eastern coastline. For example, the U.S. government used the **rectangular survey system** to encourage settlers to disperse evenly across interior farmlands. The section lines were drawn in grids, often without reference to the terrain, that determined where people settled. The straight section lines often became the places where roads were built, shaping the landscape into familiar grid-like patterns still found across the U.S. today.

Other survey systems that have shaped the rural landscape are the **metes and bounds** approach where natural features are used to mark irregular parcels of land. This approach has been used along the eastern seaboard of the United States. The **long-lot survey system** divides land into narrow parcels that extend from rivers, roads, or canals. This approach gives more people access to transportation, and has been used in the Canadian Maritimes, Quebec, Louisiana, and Texas.

MODERN COMMERCIAL AGRICULTURE

Modern commercial agriculture has its roots in the commercial revolutions started in the 18th century by European powers. The economic system of **mercantilism** was developed most effectively by the British and the Dutch, with private companies under charter from the governments carrying out the trade. The main goal of mercantilism was to benefit the mother country by trading goods to accumulate precious metals to enrich the country. Major products included cotton grown in Egypt, Sudan, and India; tobacco and cotton in the American colonies; and sugar from plantations in the Caribbean and Brazil. These goods were marketed mainly in Europe, but sometimes they were manufactured in European factories and sold back to the colonists.

Although much has changed since colonial times, modern global agricultural patterns still follow colonial patterns. Poor countries still produce raw materials, including food, for consumption by people in the richer countries. For example, Colombians still produce a great deal of coffee, and Guatemala's economy is supported by banana sales. The production of cash crops in poor countries is perpetuated because many of them must repay loans from international organizations, such as the World Trade Organization, the International Monetary Fund, and the World Bank.

DIFFUSION OF INDUSTRIAL AGRICULTURE

Today **industrial agriculture** is the current stage of commercial agriculture resulting from the shift of the farm as the center of production to a position as just one step in a multiphase industrial process that begins on the farms and ends on the consumer's table. Commercial agriculture has spread to virtually all areas of the world through global trade and exchange markets, and almost all economies have adjusted to it in one way or another. Farmers produce not for their own subsistence but for a market that is part of a complex system that includes mining, manufacturing, processing, and service activities. They must act within the constraints of the market that set prices based on supplies and demands of the global economy, and not on their own immediate needs.

Agriculture now is characterized by **specialization**, or the growing of specialized crops because they seem to be the most profitable. Farmers must weigh in costs of production – such as machinery, fuel, fertilizer, and labor – and deal with unpredictable weather and/or disease. Also, market conditions may change by the time the crops are harvested, contributing to the risks. To minimize their risks, farmers in the 1950s in the United States began signing agreements with buyer-processors, who specified exact times and weights of products to be delivered, including chickens, cattle, wheat, potatoes, and other basic foods.

This **agribusiness** is now spreading to developing countries where small-size farmers are linking with foreign sources for advice, seeds, fertilizers, machinery, and profitable markets at stable prices. Contract farming in poorer countries has been criticized as exploitative of small farmers who receive too little money for their products. Farmers in wealthier countries are also concerned that competition from farmers in less developed countries will drive down market prices. As a result, some governments have placed controversial tariffs on foreign produce in order to protect their own farmers.

THE THIRD AGRICULTURAL REVOLUTION

The First Agricultural (Neolithic) Revolution began about 10,000 years ago when people changed from hunting and gathering to farming in several different areas of the world. The Second Agricultural Revolution occurred in the late 18th century as improved equipment and better farming methods greatly increased the productivity of European farms. The **Third Agricultural Revolution** began in the mid-20th century and is still going on today in the form of **industrial agriculture**, modern farming that refers to the industrialized production of livestock, poultry, fish, and crops. Methods of industrial agriculture include innovation in agricultural machinery and methods, genetic technology, techniques for achieving economies of scale in production, the creation of new markets for consumption, and global trade. These methods are widespread in developed nations and increasingly prevalent worldwide. Most of the meat, dairy, eggs, fruits, and vegetables available in supermarkets are produced using these methods of industrial agriculture. It is based on new, higher-yielding varieties of crops developed in laboratories and plant nurseries through **biotechnology,** the use of genetically altered crops in agriculture and DNA manipulation in livestock in order to increase production. The experiments began with hybrid rice initiatives in the U.S. Midwest in the 1930s, eventually leading to the development of "IR8," a cross developed in the Philippines between a dwarf Chinese variety of rice and an Indonesian variety. This led to other hybrids, so that by the 1980s "IR36" was developed, with the qualities of larger grains, a shorter growing cycle, and more resistance to pests. By the early 1990s IR36 was the most widely grown crop on earth. Meanwhile, a "miracle wheat seed" was developed that was shorter and stiffer, hardier, and faster-maturing than traditional varieties. More recently, scientists have developed new high-yield variations of corn.

By the 1970s the collection of new agricultural techniques was called the **Green Revolution**, which involved two important practices: the use of new higher-yield seeds and the expanded use of fertilizers. New miracle seeds diffused rapidly around the world, with many countries recording dramatic productivity increases. Biotechnologists don't just cross two varieties of plants or animals, hoping for the best. Instead, they identify the particular genes on the DNA molecules that produce the desirable characteristic and splice the gene directly into the chromosomes of the other plant or animal. During the 19th century scientists identified the critical elements in natural fertilizers (manure, bones, and ashes) as nitrogen, phosphorus, and potassium. Today these three elements form the basis for fertilizers that have boosted crop productivity even further. The Green Revolution has resulted in agricultural production outpacing population growth by the late 20th century.

THE IMPACT OF THE GREEN REVOLUTION

The Green Revolution has brought about dramatic changes in the world's food production, with consequences that have been both praised and criticized.

Whereas the Green Revolution appears to be contributing to the good health of many people around the world, it has failed to provide famine relief for people in Sub-Saharan Africa. Seriously affected countries include Somalia, Ethiopian, Sudan, Gambia, Senegal, Mali, Mauritania, Burkina Faso, Niger, and Chad. Part of the problem is lack of resources to buy seed, fertilizer, and machinery, but the situation is worsened by rapid population growth. Traditionally, this region supported limited agriculture, with pastoral nomadism prevailing. The land has now been overgrazed by animals, and soils have been exhausted from overplanting. These practices have led to an alarming rate of **desertification,** with the Sahara Desert continuing to claim more and more land space. Soil erosion has become a problem, with the limited number of trees cut for wood and charcoal for urban cooking and heating. Government policies have traditionally favored urban populations by keeping food prices low, giving farmers little incentive to increase their productivity. In recent years international aid for agriculture has dropped drastically, while aid for health and primary education has surged. However, in its 2007 annual report, the World Bank put agriculture and the productivity of small farmers – particularly in Africa – at the heart of its global agenda to reduce poverty. The African Union and the United Nations have also advocated major investments to increase the productivity of poor farmers in Africa, although a great deal of disagreement remains regarding the role that African government should play in spurring farm productivity.

ENVIRONMENTAL IMPACTS OF MODERN AGRICULTURE

From its very beginnings, agriculture has transformed the natural landscape. Forests have been cleared for agriculture, terraces built into hillsides, and natural vegetation removed in order to make room for desirable crops. However, the industrialization and commercialization of agriculture has strengthened agriculture's impact on the environment. More land has been cleared, and the land is farmed more intensely. As a result, the mix of plants and animals on any given plot of earth is often a far cry from what existed there naturally.

Other problems, beyond clearing the land, include:

- **Erosion** – Lands cleared for agriculture almost immediately begins to erode away, usually by wind or running water. The surface material removed is transported by rivers, and changes valley contours, extending areas subject to flooding, and clogging irrigation and drainage channels.

- **Changes in the organic content of soil** – Crops take nutrients from the soil, so they change its organic content, especially if fields are not allowed to remain fallow long enough to restore the nutrients removed, or if crops are not rotated on a regular basis. The more pressure there is on land to be farmed intensely, the more likely it becomes for soil to lose its fertility.

PRAISE AND CRITICISM OF THE GREEN REVOLUTION

PRAISE	CRITICISMS
Agricultural production now outpaces population growth, almost certainly avoiding disastrous famines that have plagued the past.	Poor countries cannot always afford the machinery, seeds, and fertilizers necessary to raise the new crops, leading to problems in getting the new foods to their citizens.
Nitrogen-based fertilizers, now widely used, have greatly increased farm productivity in many countries of the world.	Farmers in poor countries cannot afford the fertilizers, increasing inequalities between rich and poor countries. Fertilizers also lead to groundwater pollution and the reduction of organic matter in the soil.
Scientists continue to invent new food sources, including cultivating the oceans, developing higher-protein cereals, and improving palatability of rarely consumed foods.	Many fishing areas are already over-fished, and populations of many breeds of fish are dwindling. Cultural preferences shape food consumption, and production of rarely eaten foods will not change eating habits.
Higher productivity is primarily responsible for reducing dependency on imports in Asia, including China and India. In both areas populations are balanced fairly well with food resources.	Many people in Sub-Saharan Africa are not getting enough to eat, with millions of people facing famine. Green Revolution techniques have made too few inroads, and population is increasing faster than food production.
New irrigation processes have greatly increased crop yields.	Irrigation has led to serious groundwater depletion, negatively impacting water supplies for urban populations.
Agribusiness has increased the productivity of cash crops, yielding profits for farmers and raising large amounts of basic crops to feed the world.	Agribusiness often means that land is devoted to raising one type of crop, rather than the variety needed for a balanced diet, especially in poorer countries.

Food Supply Crisis in Africa. Production of most food crops is lower today in Africa than it was forty years ago, whereas populations are increasing. Particularly hard hit are the countries that formerly were inhabited by nomadic herders shown in gray shading on the map above. The problem has been worsened not only by increasing population, but also by desertification, as the Sahara Desert continues to grow.

- **Depletion of natural vegetation** – This problem is especially acute when commercial agriculture expands into marginal environments. For example, when livestock herding moves into arid or semi-arid areas, the natural vegetation in these areas cannot always sustain the herds. This can lead to ecological damage and, in some areas, to desertification.

- **Presence of chemicals in soils and ground water** – Concern about the presence of chemicals from fertilizers and pesticides has sparked a recent trend toward **organic agriculture**. Crops are grown without fertilizers and pesticides, ensuring that the consumer will not suffer adverse health effects from them. Sales of organic food in the United States, Western Europe, and Japan have soared in recent years, benefiting farmers in those areas, but not those in other parts of the world.

Some have called the depletion of farmlands a "quiet crisis" that threatens to undermine the foundations of civilization today.

SUSTAINABLE AGRICULTURE

In recent years, a movement to practice farming using principles of ecology has gained strength. **Sustainable agriculture** attempts to integrate plant and animal production practices that will protect the ecosystem over the long term. It promotes the idea that human needs can be met without sacrificing environmental quality and depleting natural resources.

Sustainable agriculture emphasizes human intervention in terms of soil quality and water. Suggested techniques for soil conservation include recycling crop waste and livestock manure, growing peanuts or alfalfa to enrich soil with nitrogen, and producing nitrogen artificially. Another option is long-term crop rotations that return to natural cycles that annually flood cultivated lands.   In some areas, sufficient rainfall is available for crop growth, but many other areas require irrigation. For irrigation systems to be sustainable they must not use more water from their source than is naturally replenished. Improvements in water well drilling technology and submersible pumps combined with the development of drip irrigation and low pressure pivots have made it possible to regularly achieve high crop yields. However, in that in many areas where these practices have been applied, the water is being used at a greater rate than its rate of recharge.

Several steps that support drought-resistant farming systems include improving water conservation and storage measures, providing incentives for selection of drought-tolerant crop species, using reduced-volume irrigation systems, and managing crops to reduce water loss.

FUTURE FOOD SUPPLIES

Food supplies are a crucial component of every economy, and throughout history almost all other accomplishments have rested on the availability of food surpluses. Today several strategies are used to ensure and improve the production and distribution of adequate food products around the world:

- **Expansion of agricultural land** – This is the historical method of increasing food production – clear and plow more land for planting. When the world's population began to increase rapidly in the late 18th and early 19th centuries, people migrated to sparsely-inhabited land in western North America, the pampas of Argentina, and central Russia to farm new land. However, this method is not as likely to increase food supplies as it once was. Only about 11 percent of the world's land area is currently cultivated, but most of the remaining land – especially in Europe, Asia, and Africa – is not arable. In fact, some land has been lost to **desertification**, a deterioration of land to a desert-like condition by over-grazing and over-planting. Irrigation can also ruin land in dry areas because it cannot drain properly from the hard soils. Urbanization also cuts down on available land space, as farms are replaced by homes, roads, and shops.

- **Increase in land productivity** – The Green Revolution has made this alternative for increasing food supply a viable one. Land produces more crops and supports more animals as new hybrids are introduced and nutrients are added to soil through fertilizer. Farming methods also have made land more productive, and many anticipate that higher-yielding fields will be developed in the future.

- **Identification of new food sources** – Many things in the world that are edible are not chosen as food for a number of reasons. Oceans and seas have provided only a small percentage of world food supply historically, and many plants and creatures live in these waters. In recent years, fish catches have increased significantly, causing over-fishing in some areas. With improved access to ocean food away from shore, more food sources almost certainly may be found there. Many people avoid food for social reasons. Americans prefer hamburgers and hotdogs to tofu, sprouts, and other soybean products, but that preference doesn't make the soybean products any less nutritious. New food sources are also discouraged by the fact that they are not connected to the established commodity chains that instead favor more established sources.

- **Improved distribution of food** – Today the top three export grains are wheat, corn, and rice, and most of those grains come from the United States. About half of global corn exports and a quarter of all wheat exports come from the United States. Other major exporters of wheat are Argentina, Australia, France, and Canada. Thailand has replaced the United States as the leading exporter of rice, and now other Asian countries, such as Vietnam, India, and China, also export rice. In countries that export, food sometimes goes to waste, either because markets are not coordinated properly or because the government subsidizes crops. Meanwhile, countries that need food cannot buy it, either from lack of resources or poor coordination of markets.

Despite increasing urbanization and globalization in today's world, farming is still the major occupation of people in less developed countries. In more developed countries, fewer people are farmers, but many are employed in the food business, including processing plants, supermarkets, restaurants, and food wholesalers. Farming continues to alter the earth's landscape, leaving the human imprint deeply ingrained on the land.

TERMS AND CONCEPTS

agribusiness
agricultural hearths
agriculture
biotechnology
cereal grains
Columbian Exchange
commercial agriculture
desertification
dispersed settlement pattern
enclosure
erosion
extensive agriculture
extensive subsistence agriculture
Green Revolution
hamlets, villages
horticulture
hunters and gathers
industrial agriculture
intensive agriculture
intensive subsistence agriculture
irrigation
job specialization
labor intensive agriculture
location theory
long-lot survey system
Mediterranean agriculture
mercantilism
metes and bounds
milkshed
mixed crop and livestock farming
Neolithic Revolution

nomadism
nucleated settlement pattern
organic agriculture
pampas
pastoral nomadism
patriarchal system
plantation farming
post-industrial societies
primary sector
primogeniture
quaternary sector
rectangular survey system
Second Agricultural Revolution
secondary sector
seed agriculture
seed drill
shifting cultivation (swidden agriculture)
specialization
subsistence agriculture
sustainable agriculture
tertiary sector
Third Agricultural Revolution
truck farming
vegetative planting
von Thünen's model
wattle
wet (lowland) rice
winter wheat area, spring wheat area

UNIT FIVE MULTIPLE-CHOICE QUESTIONS

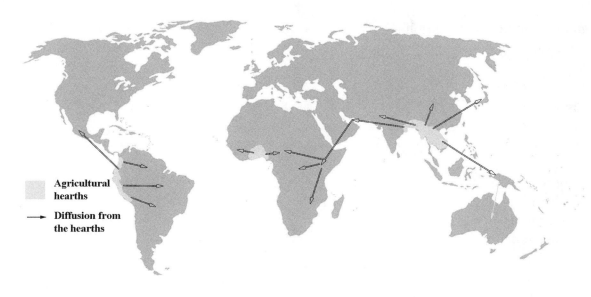

Agricultural hearths

Diffusion from the hearths

1. The map above shows the origin and diffusion of

   (A) commercial agriculture
   (B) vegetative planting
   (C) swidden agriculture
   (D) plantation farming
   (E) pastoral nomadism

2. In which of the following areas is livestock most likely to be sold in the domestic market?

   (A) Argentina
   (B) the Middle East
   (C) the United States
   (D) New Zealand
   (E) Uruguay

3. Two independent seed agriculture hearths that originated in the Western Hemisphere were

   (A) western India and northern China
   (B) North America and the Caribbean
   (C) southern Mexico and North America
   (D) southern Mexico and Peru
   (E) Peru and western Africa

4. Which of the following may NOT be categorized as a primary activity?

(A) refining petroleum into gasoline
(B) agriculture
(C) fishing
(D) raising animals
(E) forestry

5. Labor-intensive intertillage is most likely to take place in areas were farmers practice

(A) pastoral nomadism
(B) dairy farming
(C) grain farming
(D) livestock ranching
(E) shifting cultivation

6. In the Mediterranean area, the most important cash crops are

(A) olives and grapes
(B) citrus fruits and tree nuts
(C) tomatoes and lettuce
(D) cotton and sugarcane
(E) rubber and tobacco

7. A farmer who produces only enough food for the immediate family is practicing

(A) shifting cultivation
(B) intensive agriculture
(C) vegetative planting
(D) subsistence farming
(E) seed agriculture

8. According to von Thünen, which of the following activities would take place in the outermost ring around a market center?

(A) market gardening
(B) dairy farming
(C) forestry
(D) raising field crops
(E) animal grazing

9. The land survey system that makes use of natural features to mark irregular parcels of land is called

   (A) the rectangular survey system
   (B) the metes and bounds approach
   (C) the long-lot survey system
   (D) primogeniture
   (E) the township and range survey system

10. Both shifting agriculturalists and commercial farmers practice crop rotation, but commercial farmers

   (A) make less use of fertilizers
   (B) do not raise livestock
   (C) are less likely to allow fields to remain fallow
   (D) do not feed their crops to animals
   (E) do not distribute their workload evenly over the year

11. Which of the following are both forms of extensive subsistence farming?

   (A) hunting and gathering and pastoral nomadism
   (B) shifting cultivation and pastoral nomadism
   (C) dairy farming and plantation farming
   (D) truck farming and shifting cultivation
   (E) grain farming and livestock ranching

12. Early hunter and gatherer societies differed from early agricultural societies in that hunter and gatherer societies were

   (A) less likely to be characterized by gender inequality
   (B) more likely to require more hours of work per person
   (C) more likely to practice polytheism
   (D) less likely to base division of labor on gender
   (E) more likely to have job specialization

13. The Green Revolution has had the least impact on people who live in

   (A) Southeast Asia
   (B) China
   (C) Sub-Saharan Africa
   (D) India
   (E) the Philippines

14. On the map above, the shaded area is associated with which of the following types of agriculture?

(A) dairy farming
(B) plantation farming
(C) grain farming
(D) fruit farming
(E) livestock ranching

15. Which of the following does NOT characterize modern industrial agriculture?

(A) specialized crops
(B) signing agreements with buyer-processors
(C) global exchange
(D) prices met by individual needs of farmers
(E) participation by farmers in less developed countries

16. Increasing global food production by expanding the amount of land under cultivation is limited by the fact that

(A) technology is lacking in many less developed countries
(B) most of the world's arable land is already under cultivation
(C) few young people want to be farmers
(D) governments are unwilling to give up public lands
(E) global warming has put many previously cultivated areas under water

17. In which of the following areas was rice probably domesticated earliest?

(A) Southeast Asia
(B) northern China
(C) Japan
(D) Central America
(E) Mongolia

18. Refrigerated ships and railroad cars most directly benefitted the long-distance transportation to global markets of

(A) wheat
(B) fruit
(C) rice
(D) cotton
(E) beef

19. In which of the following areas has desertification had the strongest negative impact on food production?

(A) Mexico
(B) eastern China
(C) the African Sahel
(D) India
(E) Peru

20. Which of the following accurately describes the evolution of food production from the earliest development to the latest?

(A) seed agriculture, vegetative planting, the Columbian Exchange
(B) vegetative planting, the Columbian Exchange, seed agriculture
(C) the Columbian Exchange, vegetative planting, seed agriculture
(D) seed agriculture, the Columbian Exchange, vegetative agriculture
(E) vegetative agriculture, seed agriculture, the Columbian Exchange

21. In what area of the United States are land parcels most likely to be rectilinear?

(A) along the Pacific Coast
(B) the Southeast
(C) the Northeast
(D) the Midwest
(E) the Southwest

22. In which of the following countries is the largest percentage of workers employed in the primary sector?

   (A) the United States
   (B) China
   (C) Nigeria
   (D) Mexico
   (E) the United Kingdom

23. Which of the following was NOT a commodity first raised in the Americas and traded to the Eastern Hemisphere during the Columbian Exchange?

   (A) beans
   (B) wheat
   (C) squash
   (D) maize (corn)
   (E) potatoes

24. One difference between subsistence and commercial agriculture is that with commercial agriculture

   (A) more people work in the primary sector of the economy
   (B) farm sizes grow smaller
   (C) less machinery is used
   (D) crop yields are smaller
   (E) more extensive use is made of fertilizers

25. The "world's breadbasket" is located in

   (A) the coastal areas of India
   (B) northern China
   (C) the pampas of South America
   (D) the prairies of North America
   (E) Australia

UNIT FIVE FREE-RESPONSE QUESTION

From its beginning agriculture has transformed the landscape. However, the industrialization and commercialization of agriculture has strengthened its impact on the environment.

a. Identify and explain two problems that modern agriculture has caused for the environment.

b. Define organic agriculture, and explain one way that it lessens agriculture's impact on the environment.

c. Define sustainable agriculture, and explain one way that it lessens agriculture's impact on the environment.

UNIT SIX: INDUSTRIALIZATION AND ECONOMIC DEVELOPMENT

Since humans first began to farm about 10,000 years ago, the earth's landscape has constantly changed as economic activities have evolved. For thousands of years, agricultural practices were most responsible for the transformation of land areas. Then in the late 18th century, less than 300 years ago, another economic development – industrialization – began to reconfigure the landscape in dramatic ways, creating a vast panorama of farmlands punctuated by growing cities. The growth of cities is one consequence of industrialization, an economic change so recent in earth's history that we cannot possibly understand how far-reaching its influence will be in the future.

Industrialization is a topic of great interest to **economic geography**, a discipline that studies the impact of economic activities on the landscape and investigates reasons behind the locations of economic activities. Geographers are also interested in the changes that industrialization has brought to the cultural and social landscapes as well, especially in the different patterns of wealth that it has created. Largely as the consequence of industrialization, not only has the gap between rich and poor people of many nations grown, the divide between rich and poor nations has become much more pronounced.

KEY CONCEPTS IN INDUSTRIALIZATION AND DEVELOPMENT

Industrialization is the process by which economic activities on the earth's surface evolved from producing basic, primary goods (such as food products) to using factories for mass-producing goods for consumption. Whereas agriculture is a **primary economic activity** that directly extracts products from the earth, industry is composed of **secondary economic activities** that transform raw materials into usable products. Industrialization involves the production of goods using advanced sources of energy to drive large machinery and specialized labor to produce standardized goods. Secondary activities also pose different locational problems than those for primary activities. They often involve the assembly and the processing of inputs (raw materials) and the distribution of outputs (finished products) to other points, so location of industry usually requires more spatial levels of consideration than primary activities require.

The **Industrial Revolution** began this process in England during the late 18th century. **Economic development,** the process of improving the material conditions of people through diffusion of knowledge and technology, has occurred as a result of industrialization. Economic development may be traced by examining three types of economic activities as they have developed through time:

- **The primary sector (agriculture)** is the part of the economy that draws raw materials from the natural environment. The primary sector – agriculture, raising animals, fishing, forestry, and mining – is largest in low-income, pre-industrial nations. This type of economic activity first appeared about 10,000 years ago, and continued to be the main type of human economic activity on earth until the 20th century. Even today farming is the major occupation in many countries of the world.

- **The secondary sector (industry)** is the part of the economy that transforms raw materials into manufactured goods. This sector grows quickly as societies industrialize, and includes such operations as refining petroleum into gasoline and turning metals into tools and automobiles. Historically this sector was first created in the late 18th century by the Industrial Revolution, which replaced human and animal muscle with energy generated by machines. As industrialization spread to other areas of the world, it has transformed societies beyond economic activities, dramatically changing lifestyles, values, beliefs, and customs.

- **The tertiary sector (services)** is the part of the economy that involves services rather than goods. The tertiary sector grows with industrialization and comes to dominate **post-industrial societies,** or countries where most people are no longer employed in industry. Whereas production in industrial societies centers on factories and machinery generating material goods, post-industrial production is based on computers and other electronic devices that create, process, store, and apply information. With post-industrialism, a society's occupational structure changes significantly. Examples of tertiary jobs include construction, trade, finance, real estate, private services, government, and transportation. **The quaternary sector** is often seen as a subset of the tertiary sector. It includes service jobs concerned with research and development, management and administration, and processing and disseminating information.

Countries of the world may be categorized by the evolution of economic activities. Those that have experienced industrialization may be called **more developed countries (MDCs)**, and those that have not may be categorized as **less developed countries (LDCs).** More countries in today's world belong to the latter category, but some may be subcategorized as **newly-industrializing countries.** During the last few decades, some countries, mostly in Asia and parts of Latin America, have experienced economic growth, so that they appear to be somewhere in between MDC and LDC status. An example is South Korea, a country that only fifty years ago was a relatively poor agricultural country. During the late 20th and early 21st century, South Korea has developed into one of the world's largest economies and also has experimented with democratic institutions. The process that it has experienced is sometimes called **compressed modernity** – rapid economic and political change that transformed the country into a stable nation with democratizing political institutions, a growing economy, and an expanding web of nongovernmental institutions. Mexico is often cited as newly-industrializing, with its dramatic economic growth that began in the 1980s based on its abundance of oil.

ECONOMIC INDICATORS OF DEVELOPMENT

Economic development may be measured in several ways, including the following:

- **Gross Domestic Product Per Capita – The Gross Domestic Product (GDP)** is the value of the total output of goods and services produced in a country during a year. Dividing the GDP by total population creates the **Gross Domestic Product Per Capita**, a measure of the average

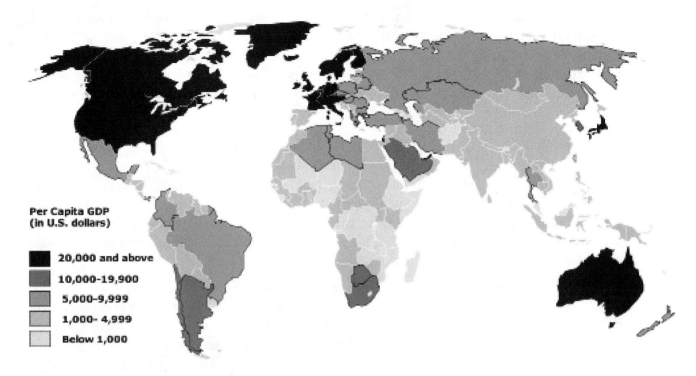

Per Capita GDP (in U.S. dollars)

- 20,000 and above
- 10,000-19,900
- 5,000-9,999
- 1,000- 4,999
- Below 1,000

Annual gross domestic product (GDP) per capita. This measure exceeds $20,000 in most MDCs, compared to less than $5,000 in most LDCs. In between are newly industrializing or middle-income nations.

person's contribution to generating a country's wealth in a year. Annual per capita GDP exceeds $20,000 in MDCs, compared to about $1,000 in LDCs, with newly-industrializing countries somewhere in between. GDP Per Capita is strongly related to many social characteristics, including literacy rates and education levels, since economic development is dependent on a skilled work force.

- **Types of jobs** – More developed countries usually have the fewest workers in the primary sector, and the most in the tertiary sector. Less developed countries have a larger percentage of their workers in the primary sector, generally occupied as farmers. Middle-income nations have an in-between spread of workers in the three economic sectors.

- **Worker productivity** – Workers in more developed countries are more productive than in less developed countries, largely because they have access to more machines, tools, and equipment to perform their work. Workers in LDCs must rely more on human and animal power. Productivity can be measured by the **value added** by each worker. The value added in manufacturing may be figured by subtracting the costs of raw materials and energy from the gross value of the product. The value added in MDCs is much higher than in LDCs.

- **Access to raw materials** – Development requires access to raw materials, such as minerals and trees, which can be transformed into useful products. Energy to operate the factories is also necessary, and it takes the forms of oil, coal, water, or natural gas. One reason that the Industrial Revolution began in England was the country's abundance of coal. A motivation for European empires was control of natural resources in other areas, so even though the countries had limited resources within their boundaries, they came to control raw materials in other areas of the globe. Today countries have access to raw materials through world trade.

- **Availability of consumer goods** – MDCs not only have enough wealth for essential goods and services, they also have money for nonessentials. Whereas food, shelter, and clothing are essential for human life, other products are not. Three indicators commonly used to measure consumption of nonessential goods are cars, telephones, and televisions. These products are accessible to most people that live in MDCs, and their production and sale are vital to the functioning of the economy. Few people in LDCs have the means to buy nonessential goods, and so the growth potential of their economies is limited.

Economic development is often accompanied by **social development**, such as high rates of literacy, access to formal education, and good health care. Economic development also changes demographic characteristics, such as life expectancy, birth rates, and death rates.

THEORIES OF ECONOMIC DEVELOPMENT

What factors explain differences in levels of economic development? Two conflicting theories guided social scientists in the 20th century in answering these questions:

- **Modernization model** – According to this theory (also called the westernization model), Britain was the first country to begin to develop its industry. The Industrial Revolution was spurred by a combination of prosperity, trade connections, inventions, and natural resources. Max Weber explained that the cultural environment of Western Europe favored change. Wealth was regarded as a sign of personal virtue, and the growing importance of individualism steadily replaced the traditional emphasis on kinship and community. Once started, the British model spread to other European nations and the United States, which prospered because they built on British ingenuity and economic practices. By extension, any country that wants its economy to grow should study the paths taken by industrialized nations, and logically they too can reap the benefits of modernization, or "westernization." Modernization theory identifies tradition as the greatest barrier to economic development. In societies with strong family systems and a reverence for the past, the culture discourages people from adopting new technologies that would raise their standards of living.

- **Dependency theory** – This analysis puts primary responsibility for global poverty on rich nations. In contrast to the modernization model, dependency theory holds that economic development of many countries in the world is blocked by the fact that industrialized nations exploit them. How can a country develop when its resources (natural and human) are controlled by a handful of prosperous industrialized countries? Inequality has its roots in the colonial era when European nations colonized and exploited the resources of other areas around the world. Although virtually all colonies gained independence by the late 20th century, political liberation has not translated into economic health. Dependency theory is an outgrowth of Marxism, which emphasizes exploitation of one social class by the other. The same dynamic is at work in assessing relationships among countries. Problems, then, cannot be solved by westernization, but must be addressed by establishing independence. In reaction to this theory, many LDCs have experimented with forms of socialism, with the intent of nationalizing industry and narrowing the gap between the rich and the poor.

Modernization Theory: Rostow's Stages

Modernization theory holds that economic prosperity is open to all countries. According to W.W. Rostow, modernization occurs in four stages:

1) **Traditional stage** – People in traditional societies build their lives around families, local communities, and religious beliefs. Their lives are often very similar to those of their ancestors, and they generally have very limited wealth. Most people are subsistence farmers. A century ago, most countries of the world were in this initial stage of economic development, and some still are.

2) **Take-off stage** – Often with the encouragement of political leaders, people start to experiment with producing goods not just for their own consumption but also for trade with others for profit. The country experiences something like an industrial revolution, and sustained growth takes hold. Urbanization increases, and technological and production breakthroughs occur. Greater individualism, a willingness to take risks, and a desire for material goods also take hold, often at the expense of family ties and traditional customs.

3) **Drive to technological maturity** – During this stage, economic growth is widely accepted, and people focus on attaining higher living standards. The economy diversifies as people become more prosperous and can afford some luxuries. Many miss the security of family and local community life, but poverty has been reduced greatly and material goods are much more common. Cities grow, as more people leave the farms, and modernization is evident in the core areas of the country. The rate of population growth is reduced as children require more years of schooling in order to survive in the increasingly complex society, and become more expensive to raise. International trade expands.

4) **High mass consumption** – Economic development steadily raises living standards as mass production encourages consumption of industrial products. Items that may have been luxuries in previous stages now become necessities as the society is structured on the expanding array of goods produced. This stage is marked by high incomes, with a majority of workers involved in the service sector of the economy.

Modernization theory claims that high-income countries can help poorer countries by encouraging them to control population growth, increase food production, and take advantage of industrial technology. They also may provide poorer countries with foreign aid. Socialist countries have criticized modernization theory as a justification for capitalist systems to continue to exploit non-capitalist countries. Critics point out that modernization simply has not occurred in many poor countries. Another criticism is that modernization theory fails to recognize that rich nations, which benefit from the status quo, often block paths to development for poor countries. Poor countries today have to develop from a position of global weakness, so they have a much more difficult task than the industrialized countries did during the 19th century. Another criticism of modernization theory is that it suggests that the causes of poverty lie almost entirely in the poor societies themselves, which is like blaming victims for their own plight.

Dependency Theory: Wallerstein's Capitalist World Economy

Immanuel Wallerstein first explained economic development in 1974 using a model of the **capitalist world economy**, a global economic system that is based in high-income nations with market economies. As a dependency theorist, Wallerstein traced economic inequality among nations to the colonial era when Europeans first took advantage of the wealth of the rest of the world. He divided today's countries into three types, according to how they fit into the global economy:

1) **Core countries** – These are the rich nations that fuel the world's economy by taking raw materials from around the world and channeling wealth to North America, Europe, Australia, and Japan through multinational corporations that operate worldwide.

2) **Countries of the periphery** – Low-income countries were drawn into the world economy by colonial exploitation, and they continue to support rich ones today by providing inexpensive labor and a large market for industrial products.

3) **Countries of the semiperiphery** – The remaining countries of the world are somewhere in between. They exert more power than peripheral countries, but are dominated to some degree by the core countries.

According to Wallerstein, the world economy benefits rich societies and harms other countries by making them dependent on the core countries. Their dependency is perpetuated by narrow, export-oriented products, such as oil, coffee, and fruit. They lack industrial capacity, so they are caught in a cycle of selling inexpensive raw materials and buying expensive manufactured goods, forever spending more than they take in. As a result, they often have high foreign debt that cripples their economies even further.

In contrast to modernization theory that puts most responsibility for development on individual countries, dependency theory emphasizes the idea that no country develops in isolation because the global economy shapes the destiny of all nations. Critics say that dependency theory wrongly treats wealth as a zero-sum commodity, as if no one gets richer without someone else getting poorer. They say that in reality new wealth is created through ambition, hard work, and new uses of technology, so no developed country "blocks" others from success. Another criticism of dependency theory is that it places too much blame on rich countries that have a long history of supporting economies of nations such as India, South Korea, and Japan, through foreign investments that foster economic growth. Dependency theorists are also criticized for ignoring cultural factors in poor countries that discourage economic growth, such as values that emphasize family and tradition rather than innovation. Corrupt national leaders may also contribute to the poor economic health of countries that lack a strong rule of law, since the country's wealth is squandered or monopolized by the elite.

The Self-Sufficiency Model

Whereas the Rostow development model encourages LDCs to identify and develop products that they can successfully trade in international markets, the **self-sufficiency model** encourages them to isolate fledgling businesses from competition of large international corporations. According to self-sufficiency advocates, LDCs can only escape global inequalities by shielding local businesses from trade in the international market and encouraging internal growth. Countries promote self-sufficiency by setting barriers that limit the import of goods from other places. Some governments have set high taxes on imported goods to make them more expensive than domestic products, and others have fixed quotas on imported goods. Another approach is for a country to require international companies to purchase expensive licenses in hopes of discouraging them from selling within its borders. For example, India used all of these methods for years to encourage internal economic development. Although many Indian companies grew under the self-sufficiency model, one problem that emerged was inefficiency. With government subsidies and import protections in place, businesses had little incentive to improve quality, lower production costs, or reduce prices, and so their products were sometimes inferior to – but more expensive than – those on the international market. Another problem was the development of a highly complex bureaucracy that set and enforced government regulations that restricted the growth of businesses.

In contrast to India, the four "Asian Tigers" adopted the international trade alternative. Hong Kong, South Korea, Taiwan, and Singapore – whose economies boomed starting in the 1960s – used **export-oriented industrialization**, a strategy that seeks to directly integrate the country's economy into the global economy by concentrating on economic production that can find a place in international markets. The countries have watched the "product life cycle" that follows stages: first an innovator country produces something new; next that country moves on to other innovations. Meanwhile, other countries think of ways to make the first product better and cheaper, and export it back to the innovator country. For example, Asian countries have prospered from this strategy with automobiles and electronics in their trade with the United States.

GROWTH AND DIFFUSION OF INDUSTRIALIZATION

Industry existed in many areas of the world before the late 18th century, but the Industrial Revolution intensified it greatly. Examples of industrial centers before the Industrial Revolution were silk factories in China and metal workshops in India. Goods in many other parts of the world were superior to those produced in Europe, although most of the work was done by hand and power was provided by water and/or wind. The early factories in 18th century Britain were run by water running downslope. The big breakthrough came with the steam engine, invented by **James Watt**, which allowed much more flexible use of energy to drive new machines. Watt's engine could pump water much more efficiently than the watermills then in use. At the same time new methods for smelting iron were discovered that transformed coal into high-carbon coke.

THE INDUSTRIAL REVOLUTION

The textile industry was one of the first to benefit from the new steam-powered machines and smelting processes. A series of inventions meant that thread and cloth could be woven together much more quickly than before, and British factories began to demand more raw materials – such as wool, linen, and cotton – for their ever-increasing capacity to manufacture. The textile industry was transformed from a large collection of scattered home-based industries to a small number of large factories centered in a few locations. Britain's stable government and wealth gathered from overseas ventures, as well as an abundant supply of coal, helped spread the new technologies to other industries, including transportation and communications. The first railroad in England was opened in 1825, and soon its major cities were connected by rail. Ships also benefited from steam engines, and England expanded its growing industrial power as steam-powered vessels began crossing the Atlantic.

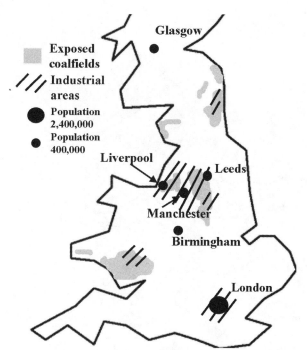

Industrial Britain by 1850. The first industries arose in northern and western England around abundant coal and iron-ore deposits. Railroads connected the major cities to one another and to the coast for shipping.

Industrialization Through the Early 20th Century

As industrialization diffused during the 19th century, Britain had an enormous comparative advantage over other areas, allowing it to expand its colonial empire to further prosperity and power spawned by its creator role in the Industrial Revolution. The new industries transformed England's landscape. Cities grew dramatically, especially in the Midlands of north-central England, where a belt of major coalfields extended from west to east. In mainland Europe, another industrial belt developed around coalfields that stretched from northern France, southern Belgium, and the Netherlands , through Germany, to Poland. Iron ore was also found in this area, and economic activity developed accordingly.

Western Europe's industrial success was not based exclusively on its abundant raw materials, but also on the ability of France, Britain, and the Low Countries to access resources around the world through their colonial empires. Europe also had comparatively skilled laborers as well as established trade routes to facilitate exchange of new products. By the turn of the 20th century, industry had diffused as far as northern Spain, southern Scandinavia, and the Ukraine.

Industrialization also diffused westward across the Atlantic to North America, where natural resources and available land space encouraged economic development. The first U.S. textile mill was built in Rhode Island in 1791 by Samuel Slater, a former worker in an English factory. Industry grew in response to the U.S. government's protection of industry through embargoes on European trade, and the industry grew accordingly. Before 1860 industry concentrated on processing North America's abundant food and lumber resources, and iron and steel industries rapidly developed during the late 19th century. Most early industry flourished in the northeastern United States, where despite a lack of abundant natural resources, the large populations from Boston in the north to Washington D.C. in the south provided a large market for consumption of industrial products. New York City became one of the world's great ports, with a huge skilled and semiskilled labor force, and a fine natural harbor for **break-of-bulk** (transfer of cargo from one type of carrier to another) from ships to trains and trucks and vice versa.

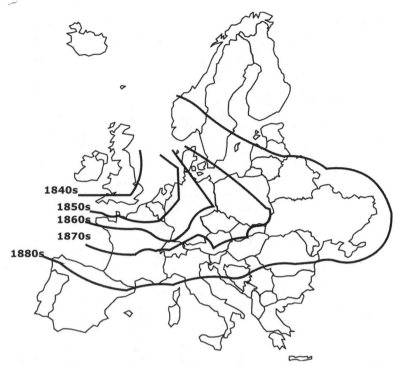

The diffusion of the Industrial Revolution. The Industrial Revolution began in England in the late 18th century, and diffused across Europe, following belts of coalfields and iron ore.

By the time that World War I began in 1914, Europe had developed a huge industrial base, and the United States was rapidly catching up. However, industrialization had not diffused to the rest of the world, except for areas settled by Europeans, such as Australia.

20th Century Industrialization After World War I

The earlier industrialization of Europe and the eastern United States gave those regions a huge economic advantage by the early 20th century, but the picture changed dramatically as key resources of the world became oil and natural gas. During the mid-20th century, the use of coal as an energy source in industry diminished, and the use of oil and natural gas greatly increased. Industrialized nations needed these products to run their power plants, machinery, cars, airplanes, and ships. Oil and natural gas also became common forms of energy for heating homes and providing household conveniences, such as hot water and cooking stoves.

This reliance on oil and natural gas meant that the United States and industrialized Europe increasingly turned to foreign countries to provide for their needs, vesting new economic power to those that had these natural resources. Today these countries include Saudi Arabia, Kuwait, Iran, Russia, China, Mexico, Venezuela, and Nigeria. While oil has enriched them, they have also played host to American and European multi-national companies that have established production centers within their border. Most oil-rich nations signed agreements with these companies that have allowed a great deal of the wealth to return to the U.S. and Europe, producing international tensions between developing countries and the established industrialized powers.

THE EVOLUTION OF ECONOMIC CORES AND PERIPHERIES

The Industrial Revolution greatly impacted the regions that it reached, but it totally bypassed other areas. Areas of industrial activity marked the earth's surface, while others remained much the same as before. **Location theory** explains the locational pattern of economic activities by identifying factors that influence this pattern. First, **primary industry** develops around the location of natural resources, such as the industrial belt in the British Midlands. Next, as transportation improves, **secondary industry** develops, which is less dependent on resource location. Raw materials may be transported to the factories for manufacture. The location of secondary industries depends on several factors:

- **Variable costs** – Energy, labor, and transportation is less expensive in some areas than others, encouraging industries to develop.

- **Friction of distance** – Although secondary industry may transport raw materials to factories, the cost usually goes up the farther the distance of transport from source to factory. At some point, the distance is too great for practical transportation.

- **Distance decay** – Largely because of the friction of distance, industries are more likely to serve markets of nearby places than those far away. As distance increases, business activity decreases until it becomes impractical to do business.

The patterns formed by primary and secondary industries divide the world into regions based on their economic activity: core, semi-periphery, and periphery. Immanuel Wallerstein first used these terms in 1974 to promote dependency theory among nations, and many economic geographers now use the core-periphery model to describe economic spatial patterns in general. Core regions have concentrations of primary and secondary industries, peripheral regions do not, and semi-peripheral regions have some industries but not as many as core regions do. Even within "core countries" wealthy urban cores lie in contrast to depressed rural peripheries. For example, in the modern-day United States, "high-tech" concentrations, such as those that exist along the Pacific coastline, in the Northeast, and in some interior cities (such as Austin, Texas), create wealth that contrasts to rural areas or "rust belt" industrial areas that provide few job opportunities for young people. With more jobs in the service sector, people move to areas where those jobs are provided, leaving the peripheral areas with even fewer resources than they had before. Another country with distinct core/peripheral distinctions is India, where high-tech jobs (often outsourced by Western companies) are growing rapidly in urban centers, as contrasted to peripheral areas that still adhere to traditional customs and occupations.

WEBER'S MODEL FOR THE LOCATION OF INDUSTRIES

In his *Theory of the Location of Industries* published in 1909, German economic geographer **Alfred Weber** developed a model for the location of secondary industries. Weber's industrial model is often compared to von Thünen's agricultural model because they both are examples of location theory that explain why economic activity is patterned as it is. Weber identified points for particular inter-related activities, such as manufacturing plants, mines, and markets. Weber's **least cost theory** explained location of industries in terms of three factors:

- **Transportation** – The site of industry is chosen based partly on the cost of moving raw materials to the factory and finished products to the market. Business owners look for the least expensive transportation costs. Today, for most goods, truck transport is cheapest over short distances; railroads are most cost efficient over medium distances; and ships are cheapest over long distances. However, transportation involves terminal costs, which vary considerably, and are least expensive for trucks and most expensive for ships.

- **Labor** – The cost of labor is also taken into consideration, and cheap labor may allow an industry to make up for higher transportation costs. For example, a factory may relocate from the United States to Mexico, where transportation costs to market increase, but are more than made up by cheaper labor costs.

- **Agglomeration** – If several industries cluster (or agglomerate) in one city, they can provide support by sharing talents, services, and facilities. A restaurant needs furniture and equipment, and the companies that provide those products have workers that bring business to the restaurant. All the workers need clothes that may be provided by a clothing store that also needs furniture and equipment and employs people that eat at the restaurant. The point of agglomeration explains location of industry, but excessive agglomeration may lead to an increase in labor and transportation costs, leading to a process called **deglomeration**, or the exodus of businesses from a crowded area.

Some economic geographers have criticized Weber's model as too inflexible, particularly in considering costs over time. The **substitution principle** suggests that business owners can juggle expenses, as long as labor, land rents, transportation, and other costs don't all go up at one time. If labor costs go up, they may be offset by a decline in transportation and rent costs, encouraging the owner to stay put. This balancing of expenses allows a business to be profitable within a larger area than Weber's model suggests.

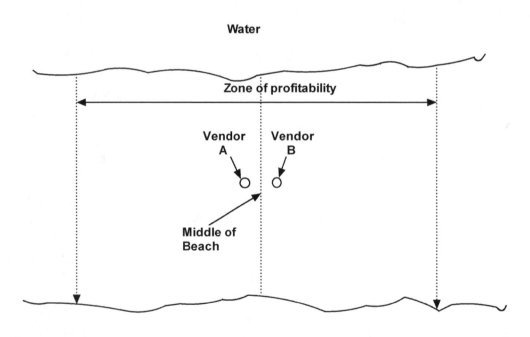

LOCATIONAL INTERDEPENDENCE THEORY

Another approach to location theory is **locational interdependence**, or the influence on a firm's locational decision by locations chosen by its competitors. In contrast to Weber's reliance on variable costs, this model is concerned with **variable revenue analysis**, or the firm's ability to capture a market that will earn it more customers and money than its competitors. One example provided by economist Harold Hotelling is a stretch of beach with two ice cream vendors selling identical products, with a fixed demand for ice cream among its customers (those on the beach). Where should each vendor locate? Logically you might say that each should locate in the middle of her half of the beach, but in reality what generally happens is that both will cluster in the middle. That way each can have her half, but can also compete for those in the middle, maximizing the customer base. The problem is that some customers will have to walk further to get their ice cream, so they may change their minds about wanting ice cream. If that happens, the vendors might have to relocate.

CONTEMPORARY PATTERNS AND IMPACTS OF INDUSTRIALIZATION AND DEVELOPMENT

Today traditional location theories, such as Alfred Weber's model, are limited by their focus on particular points of local economic interactions. Globalization means that every country's industrial development is related to conditions in the global economy. **Space-time compression** describes the reduction in the time it takes to diffuse something to a distant place as a result of improved communications and transportation systems. Although situation and site factors are still important for understanding economic activities, globalization has altered their meaning so that position of places in the global web is also crucial. For example, the role of agglomeration in location decisions has reached new dimensions as urban areas have grown much larger and international contacts have increased. If you wish to locate a sock factory in China to benefit from low-cost labor, you would have many needs, ranging from transportation facilities to markets (both in China and overseas) to telephones, electricity, and water services. Both surface and ocean transportation has to be taken into consideration, for getting raw materials (such as cotton) to the factory and shipping the finished socks out to market. These all are examples of **infrastructure,** or services that support economic activities. Without all of these things in place, a sock factory would be difficult to operate. The growth of economic activities conducted via the internet makes express package delivery systems more important, so that consumers in one part of the world may buy goods sold by companies in far-distant areas.

MAJOR INDUSTRIAL REGIONS

Due to many factors – such as historical patterns of development and colonization, current power relations among nations, and geographical context – the distribution of industry around the world is quite uneven. For example, industrialization patterns in Europe are still based on the diffusion of industry from its origins in Britain across to France and Germany. Only a few countries have become major industrial economies through a confluence of factors, including abundant natural resources, favorable relative location, stable political circumstances, economic leadership, and high levels of educated and trained executives and workers.

SITUATION AND SITE FACTORS

Geography provides companies with two types of production costs:

Situation factors have to do mainly with transportation – bringing raw materials or parts into a factory and shipping the finished goods to consumers or retailers. The farther something has to be carried, the higher the cost, so a manufacturer tries to locate a factory as close as possible to both buyers and sellers. If the cost of transporting the finished product is higher than the cost of shipping raw materials, then the factory shoud be located closer to the buyer than to the seller, and vice versa. For example, **bulk-reducing industries,** such as the North American copper industry, usually locate factories close to raw materials because the raw materials are heavier and bulkier than the finished products. The U.S. steel industry has located factories around iron and coal deposits and has repositioned its locations as sources have changed. More recently, with more iron ore coming from Canada and Venezuela, steel factories have moved to the East and West coasts, away from previous plants in the Midwest. For **bulk-gaining industries,** such as most canned food and beverage products, factory locations are usually determined by accessibility to the market. Cans, bottles, and ingredients are brought to the factory, and emerge packaged for consumers. Weight is gained, especially with products (such as soda) that have a significant amount of water added. Also, cars are much more difficult to ship out of factories than the parts coming into the factory are, so automobile assembly plants are generally located near large metropolitan areas. **Single-market manufacturers,** such as clothing manufacturers shipping to New York City, also cluster near their markets. As von Thünen noted for farmers, perishable products need to be close to large urban markets.

Site factors are particular to a geographic location and focus on varying costs of land, labor, and capital. Modern factories are located in suburban or rural areas, and not in center cities, where land costs are prohibitive for the space necessary for production. Factories are usually more efficient if they operate on one or two levels, and land costs in center cities encourage businesses that can locate in skyscrapers. Climate may also impact location decisions, with some industries drawn to relatively mild climates and opportunities for year-round outdoor recreation activities. Some executives may prefer sites with good access to cultural or sports events. The cost of labor is another consideration, especially for **labor-intensive industries,** such as fiber-spinning, weaving, or cutting and sewing of fabric into clothing. Textile industries require skilled workers, and so they often choose locations where labor costs are low. In recent years, this factor has encouraged clothing manufacturers to move to China and other Asian countries where labor is cheaper. Businesses typically borrow money to expand, so sometimes location is influenced by the willingness of banks in a geographical location to provide loans to entrepreneurs. For example, in the late 20th century, high tech companies clustered in California's Silicon Valley partly because banks sometimes offered large incentive packages to persuade businesses to locate within their city limits.

For some businesses, transportation of both resources and finished products are a negligible part of their total costs. Such firms are said to be **footloose,** or neither resource or market-oriented. For example, both parts and finished products in the manufacture of computers are expensive, so that transportation costs are only a small part of total production costs.

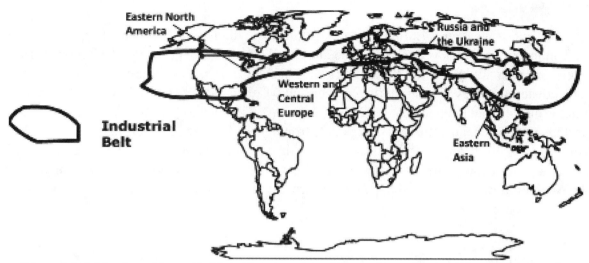

Primary industrial regions of the world. Most of the primary industrial areas of the world exist within a "belt" that stretches from North America, through Europe, southern Russia, China, South Korea and Japan. Even within this belt, many other uses of land exist, including primary economic activities such as farming. Secondary industrial regions lie outside the belt in concentrated areas of South America, Africa, Southeast Asia, and Australia.

When industrial centers are mapped, four areas emerge as **primary industrial regions,** or areas of the largest agglomeration of industry:

- Western and Central Europe
- Eastern North America
- Russia and the Ukraine
- Eastern Asia

Each of these regions includes a core of industrial activities with other clusters some distance away. Industries are also located in **secondary industrial regions**, where agglomeration is somewhat less, but still significant. These secondary regions include Venezuela, Argentina, and Brazil in South America, South Africa and Nigeria in Africa, coastal areas and the Ganges River area of India, Malaysia, and southern Australia.

Western and Central Europe

Despite the devastation of World War I, European industry recovered and expanded rapidly in the post-war years. In the industrial core itself, the Ruhr River area of Germany became Europe's greatest industrial complex, combining proximity to large markets, accessible transportation, and abundant natural resources to spark its growth. Products of heavy industry, including tanks and weapons for Hitler's armies, poured from the region by the 1930s. German industry became specialized, as Saxony produced optical equipment, cameras, textiles, and ceramics – products of light manufacture. World War II virtually destroyed the German industrial base and damaged industrial infrastructure all over the continent, leaving Europe's industrial future in question. However, with American aid to new factories, much has been rebuilt, incorporating new technologies that have revived European economies overall. Even with colonial empires dwindling during the 1950s and 1960s, Europe's economic and political influence have allowed it to withstand the damage, although other parts of the world would come to challenge its industrial preeminence.

North America

World Wars I and II weakened Europe's economy, allowing the United States to emerge as the world's strongest industrial power by the mid-20th century.   Despite damage to Pearl Harbor in 1941, the wars were fought mainly outside the borders of the U.S., and at the same time, production of war materials bolstered its developing industrial economy. Canada also benefited, with a major American Manufacturing Belt that included southeastern Canadian cities such as Windsor, Toronto, and Montreal. The North American Manufacturing Belt extends from its northeastern edge around the cities of Boston and New York south through Philadelphia and Baltimore, westward through Upstate New York and Pennsylvania, and through the states that bound the Great Lakes. Canadian and U.S. manufacturing complexes meet in two horseshoe-shaped zones around the western ends of Lakes Ontario and Erie.

North American Manufacturing. North American manufacturing has dispersed to other regions, but the core area pictured above remains dominant.

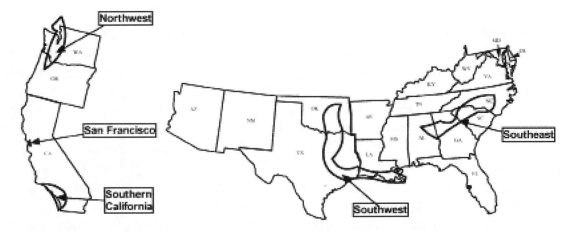

Other North American Manufacturing Regions. During the 20th century manufacturing spread to other areas of North America from the Manufacturing Belt in the Northeastern United States. These newer areas include the Southeast, Southwest, Northwest, the San Francisco area, and Southern California.

Other important industrial areas developed in North America during the 20th century. The Southeastern district extends from Birmingham, Alabama, to Richmond, Virginia, with Birmingham producing iron and steel, and the area eastward from Atlanta, Georgia, to Richmond manufacturing cotton, tobacco, and furniture. Another area stretches from Oklahoma southward to the Dallas-Fort Worth area, Houston, and New Orleans. Originally rooted in meat packing and flour milling, this area has become more and more important for the oil industry. Other industrial districts are in northern California (around San Francisco), southern California (from Los Angeles to San Diego), and the Pacific northwest from Portland Oregon, north through Seattle, Washington, and Vancouver, British Columbia in Canada.

Russia and the Other Former Soviet Republics

By the end of the 19th century Ukraine in the western Russian Empire had been affected by the diffusion of the Industrial Revolution as it spread eastward across Europe. When Russia became the Soviet Union in the 20th century, Ukraine produced much of the country's coal, and it grew into one of the world's largest manufacturing complexes by the mid-20th century. Other manufacturing areas grew around Moscow and Leningrad (now St. Petersburg) which provided large markets for industrial products. Although the communist government controlled industrial development, industrial patterns still followed logical patterns based on geographic location, markets, transportation, and natural resources. Much manufacturing during the 1930s followed the Volga River, an area that combined accessibility to raw materials and ease of transportation by the river. After World War II a series of dams were constructed along the Volga, making electrical power plentiful. Canals linked the Volga to both Moscow and the Don River, making it easy to transport raw materials, including plentiful oil and natural gas from nearby reserves. Other regions in Russia follow the Trans-Siberian Railroad that connects the western cities across southern Siberia all the way to the Pacific coastline.

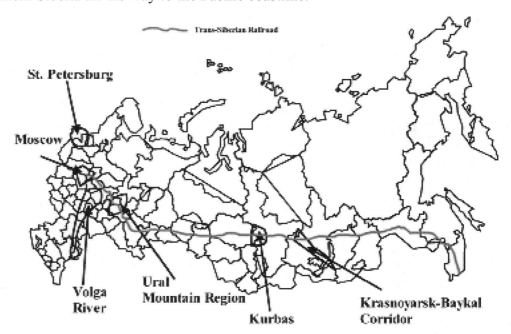

Russian Industrial Areas. Although many of the industrial regions of the former Soviet Union are outside the boundaries of the modern Russian Federation, several industrial areas remain, including the region around the capital city of Moscow, St. Petersburg, the Volga River, the Ural Region, the Kurbas Region, and the Krasnoyarsk-Baykal Corridor. The eastern regions follow the Trans-Siberian Railroad.

Eastern Asia

- **Japan** – The first country in Eastern Asia to industrialize was Japan, partly because its geographical location in the northern Pacific Ocean placed it out of the path of most 19th century imperialist powers. As a result, it was never colonized. Its economic development began during the second half of the 19th century with the **Meiji Restoration**, a remarkable government-sponsored campaign for modernization and colonization. Under the leadership of a few **oligarchs**, or industrial and military leaders that came to political power, Japan modernized industries, organized armed forces, and transformed education and transportation systems to follow the western model. The Japanese also established colonies to provide raw materials that were not available in their homeland. After the setbacks caused by the massive destruction of World War II, Japan managed to rebuild its economy so that by the 1980s it was a major post-industrial society. Japan's dominant region of industrialization is the **Kanto Plain**, which includes Tokyo and other nearby cities and suburbs that form a huge metropolitan area. Many industries and businesses chose Tokyo as their headquarters in order to be near government decisions makers. Japan has three other key industrial districts, each surrounding major metropolitan areas.

- **The "Four Tigers"** — Japan's economic dominance of East Asia was first challenged in the late 20th century by the "Four Tigers" of East and Southeast Asia: South Korea, Taiwan, Hong Kong, and Singapore. Britain transferred control of Hong Kong to China in 1997, fueling the already developing economy of China. All Four Tigers used the strategy of **export-oriented industrialization** to directly integrate their economies into the global economy by concentrating on economic production to find a place in international markets. The countries have watched the "product life cycle" that follows stages: first an innovator country produces something new; next that country moves on to other innovations. Meanwhile, other countries think of ways to make the first product better and cheaper, and export it back to the innovator country. For example, Asian countries have prospered from this strategy with automobiles and electronics in their trade with the United States.

- **China** – China has long been a political power, but its major industrial expansion did not begin until the mid-20th century under communist leaders. Industrial development occurred first under the supervision of Soviet planners, and again under the Chinese Communist Party, especially since 1979. Its earliest industrial heartland was the **Northeast District** in Manchuria, centered on the region's coal and iron deposits near the city of Shenyang. Other major industrial areas developed around the cities of Beijing, Shanghai, and Hong Kong. In recent years industry has increased at a very rapid pace in many other Chinese cities, so that China had successfully challenged Japan for economic and political leadership in East Asia by the early 21st century.

Tokyo Fish Market. These giant tuna were brought to the central fish market in Tokyo to be sold to wholesalers who service the vast population centered on the Kanto Plain.

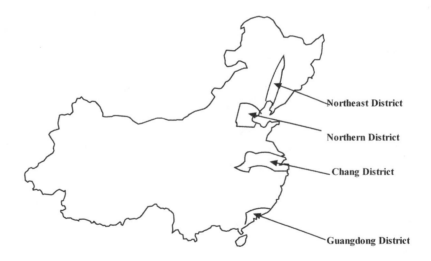

Chinese Industrial Areas. China's first large industrial area was the Northeast District, centered on coal and iron deposits located in the basin of the Liao River. Today three other regions are growing rapidly: the Northern District around the capital city, Beijing; the Chang District around the cities of Shanghai and Nanjing; and the Guangdong District around Hong Kong and Guangzhou.

In recent years other parts of the **Pacific Rim** (countries that border the Pacific Ocean on their eastern shores) have also experienced industrialization. More and more cities of China are industrializing, partly through government-designated areas called **Special Economic Zones** where foreign investment is allowed and capitalistic ventures are encouraged.

SECONDARY INDUSTRIAL REGIONS

Several **secondary industrial regions** lie south of the world's primary industrial region. These regions developed later, and their industrial centers are not as large, but their economies are growing. One region is Southeast Asia – including Thailand, Malaysia, Indonesia, and Vietnam – that shares the growing prosperity of the Pacific Rim. In northern Africa an industrial region exists around Cairo, and in South Africa around Johannesburg. In the Western Hemisphere, Mexico and Brazil have substantial manufacturing industries that have grown up around major cities. In Brazil a manufacturing triangle has formed between São Paulo, Rio de Janeiro, and Belo Horizonte, and in Mexico industry has developed along a corridor from Mexico City to Guadalajara.

Maquiladora

A manufacturing zone was created in the 1960s in northern Mexico just south of the border with the United States. Workers in this *maquiladora* district have produced goods primarily for consumers in the U.S., and a number of U.S. companies have established plants in the zone to transform imported, duty-free components or raw materials into finished industrial products. Industrialization of the zone was promoted by the **North American Free Trade Agreement (NAFTA)**, a treaty signed in 1995 by Mexico, the United States, and Canada, which eliminated barriers (including most tariffs) to free trade among the three countries. Today hundreds of thousands of workers are employed in the *maquiladora* district, and their interactions with the U.S. market provide a good example of the new **international division of labor** in which some components of products are made in one country and others in another. U.S. companies have been criticized for avoiding employment and environmental regulations imposed within the borders of the U.S., hiring young women for low pay, no benefits, and work in buildings that are environmentally questionable.

Since globalization and physical restructuring have encouraged the building of low-cost offshore assembly factories in places like China, and countries in Central America, maquiladoras in Mexico have been on the decline for the past few years. According to U.S. federal sources, approximately 529 maquiladoras shut down and investment in assembly plants decreased by 8.2 percent during 2002. Despite the decline, over 3,000 maquiladoras still operate along the 2,000 mile-long United States–Mexico border, providing employment for approximately one million workers, and importing more than $51 billion in supplies into Mexico. Maquiladoras, in general, are best represented among operations that are particularly assembly intensive.

Industrialization and Tertiary Development in India

Very important changes are occurring in India, where industrialization is expanding as a result of recent government policies. The development is occurring in several urban areas around the country. Although India has no major oil reserves, it does have much hydroelectric potential and large coal and iron ore deposits. It also has a large labor force and a geographical location midway between Europe and the Pacific Rim.

NAFTA: A BOON OR HINDRANCE TO NORTH AMERICAN ECONOMIES?

The North American Free Trade Agreement (NAFTA) between Mexico, the United States, and Canada in 1995, was hailed as a free trade area that would rival the European Union as the world's wealthiest and most populous market. However, integrating the markets of such three different countries has been problematic, considering Mexico's lower standard of living and wage structure. U.S. and Canadian labor unions are concerned that with the removal of tariffs, more manufacturers will relocate to Mexico to take advantage of lower wages for workers, leaving many U.S. and Canadian workers without jobs. Environmentalists fear that firms will move to Mexico in order to avoid costly government regulations for pollution in the United States and Canada. Even though Mexico has passed environmental protection laws, enforcement is lax, and companies are infrequently fined for violations. Many fear that this loss of industry will hurt the U.S. and Canadian economies in the long run. Meanwhile, Mexico faces a new problem: maquiladora jobs are now being lost to countries where wages are even lower. For example, Mexican wages are about twice those in China, where wages are only about $1 an hour. Since wage rates constitute an important site factor in deciding the location of industries, many firms are moving from Mexico to China.

In recent years India has benefited from increased global access to and cost reductions of information technology and electronic data transmission. Computer software development is rapidly growing around Bangalore and Hyderabad, and many back-office jobs have been outsourced from western companies to India. Customer interaction services ("call centers") formerly based in the United States have relocated to India, processing claims for life and health insurance, and taking care of banking transactions, airline tickets, and medical appointments. There the companies hire Indians with good English-speaking skills to talk with customers halfway across the globe in the United States and Europe. As a result, the Indian economy has developed a strong tertiary sector, increasingly integrating it into the world market.

GLOBAL INEQUALITIES

The Industrial Revolution set in motion the dramatic global inequalities that exist among people and nations today. Areas that industrialized early are generally still the most prosperous, with many other areas still largely untouched by industry, often resulting in poverty for the people that inhabit them. Today an increasingly integrated global economy provides challenges for all countries, despite their levels of development, although the problems for more developed countries generally differ from those of less developed countries.

CHALLENGES FOR MORE DEVELOPED COUNTRIES

An important challenge for more developed regions is the protection of their markets from new competitors, with competition now occurring more and more frequently within regional **trading blocs**, or conglomerations of trade among countries within a region.

Impact of Trading Blocs

The three most important trading blocs are:

1) **North America** – Most trade barriers between the United States and Canada have been eliminated over the past few decades, and Mexico was brought into the bloc by the North American Free Trade Agreement (NAFTA) in 1995. Since then, the three NAFTA countries have been negotiating with other Latin American countries to extend the trading bloc to new areas of the Western Hemisphere.

2) **The European Union** – Most barriers to trade have been eliminated among the members of the EU, with membership extended to Bulgaria and Romania in January of 2007. Even European nations that are not members of the EU (such as Switzerland and Sweden) depend heavily on trade with members.

3) **East Asia** – No formal organization of states exists in East Asia, but Japanese companies play leading roles in the economies of other countries in the region. Although many political tensions exist among the nations, the rapid economic development of many Pacific Rim countries has created a strengthening trade bloc in East Asia.

The free movement of most products across the borders has led to closer integration of industries within North America and within Europe. For example, parts of complex products (like cars) are made in different countries within each bloc, and are transported freely across borders to assembly plants. However, at the same time, competition among blocs has increased in many ways. Trade barriers, such as taxes, lengthy permit procedures, and quotas on exports, have been placed between blocs. For example, the Japanese government maintains quotas on the number of cars that Japanese companies can export to the United States. Most cooperation and competition within and among trading blocs takes place through **transnational corporations,** or companies that operate factories in countries other than the ones in which they are headquartered. Most transnational corporations are also **conglomerate corporations** comprised of many smaller firms that support the overall industry. For example, a car company like General Motors actually consists of many smaller firms that produce car parts and other products that automobiles need. Most transnational corporations are headquartered in the U.S., but others are located in Japan or Europe.

Disparities within trading blocs are problematic in all three areas. Within the European Union industrialization is concentrated in Germany, France, and the United Kingdom. Within those individual countries, some areas are more industrialized (and thus richer) than others. For example, in France most industry and wealth are concentrated around Paris, creating economic disparities between Paris and the rest of France. In Germany, the eastern part (formerly the communist-run German Democratic Republic) drags far behind the western region. Within the NAFTA countries, Mexico's economy lags behind those of the United States and Canada.

Deindustrialization

During the past few decades, employment in manufacturing as a share of total employment has fallen dramatically in the more developed countries, a phenomenon widely referred to as "**deindustrialization**." Generally, the number of jobs has increased in the service or tertiary sector as the percentage of jobs in industry has decreased. The trend, particularly evident in the United States and Europe, is also apparent in Japan and more recently in the Four Tiger economies of East Asia (Hong Kong, South Korea, Singapore, and Taiwan). Deindustrialization has caused considerable concern about the affected economies and has given rise to a debate about its causes and likely implications. Many regard deindustrialization with alarm and suspect it has contributed to widening income inequality in the United States and high unemployment in Europe. Some suggest that deindustrialization is a result of the globalization of markets and has been fostered by the rapid growth of trade between the advanced economies and the developing world. These critics argue that the fast growth of labor-intensive manufacturing industries in the developing world is displacing the jobs of workers in the advanced economies. Others are more optimistic, believing that the adjustments between industrial and service sectors will work themselves through, and that advances in the service sector, rather than in the manufacturing sector, are likely to encourage the growth of living standards in advanced economies in the future.

CHALLENGES FOR LESS DEVELOPED COUNTRIES

Less developed countries face the challenge of reducing the disparity in wealth between them and the more developed countries. Industrial development not only lifts the value of exports, it often generates money to buy other products. Problems that LDCs encounter include:

- **Distance from markets** – Wealthy consumers in more developed countries are generally far away, so industrializing countries have had to invest scarce resources in constructing and subsidizing transportation facilities, such as airports, docks, and ships.

- **Inadequate infrastructure** – Support services for industrial development are often lacking in less developed countries. These include not only direct support, such as transportation, communications, and equipment production, but also fewer schools and universities to educate industrial workers, technicians, managers, and executives.

- **Competition with existing manufacturers in other countries** – Particularly problematic for LDCs is the control exerted by transnational corporations headquartered in MDCs but doing business globally. These companies have sought out low-cost labor in LDCs, but have kept highly skilled jobs in the MDCs. This selective transfer of some jobs to LDCs is called the **new international division of labor**, a process that keeps global inequalities in place, discourages new industries from developing in LDCs, and prevents wealth from flowing from MDCs to LDCs.

INDUSTRIALIZATION AND THE ENVIRONMENT

As a result of the Industrial Revolution, coal replaced wood as the leading energy source in North America and Western Europe. Whereas this change relieved the environmental pressure of deforestation apparent in both areas before the Industrial Revolution, it increased the likelihood that coal, and eventually petroleum and natural gas, would be depleted as natural resources. Population growth has exacerbated the problem but energy use in more developed countries is far greater than it is in less developed countries. **Fossil fuels**, including coal, petroleum, and natural gas, are residues of plants and animals that were buried millions of years ago. When these substances are burned, they generally cannot be replaced because the process of creating the fuels takes millions of years. The world faces an energy sustainability problem partly because the three fossil fuels, especially petroleum, are rapidly being depleted.

FOSSIL FUEL RESERVES

Just how much petroleum, coal, and natural gas remains on earth is uncertain. Energy deposits that have been discovered are called **proven reserves.** These may be measured with reasonable accuracy. However, we don't know how many **potential** (undiscovered) **reserves** there are. New deposits are being discovered each year, but petroleum is being consumed at a more rapid rate than it is being found, and world demand is increasing rapidly, especially with the acceleration of industry and wealth in China and India. Extraction of fossil fuels is also an issue, since most of the more accessible resources have already been used. Today more off-shore drilling is going on, as companies try to extract petroleum under ocean and sea floors. Likewise, oil companies are considering the challenge of removing oil from under the frozen tundra of Siberia. In both cases, extraction is more time-consuming and expensive. The hazards of off-shore drilling are illustrated by the Deepwater Horizon oil spill in the Gulf of Mexico which flowed unabated for three months in 2010, and continues to seep. It is the largest accidental marine oil spill in the history of the petroleum industry, and all of the environmental consequences of the disaster will not be clear for years.

CONSUMPTION OF FOSSIL FUELS

Not surprisingly, more developed countries, with about ¼ of the world's population, consume about ¾ of the world's fossil fuels. People in these countries have more cars and larger homes to heat, and businesses and industries need energy to run their machinery and their plants. However, this traditional pattern is changing. As countries with large populations, such as China and India, develop industries, their share of the world's consumption of energy is increasing. Some estimates show that LDCs may soon consume half or more of the world's energy, putting more pressure on the finite fossil fuel reserves.

TOP CONSUMERS OF OIL

1.	United States	20,700,000 bbl/day
2.	China	6,534,000 bbl/day
3.	Japan	5,578,000 bbl/day
4.	Germany	2,650,000 bbl/day
5.	Russia	2,500,000 bbl/day
6.	India	2,450,000 bbl/day
7.	Canada	2,294,000 bbl/day
8.	South Korea	2,149,000 bbl/day
9.	Brazil	2,100,000 bbl/day
10.	France	1,970,000 bbl/day

Source: NationMaster.com

SUSTAINABLE DEVELOPMENT

A major issue for industrial development is the ability of the environment to sustain it. **Sustainable development** may be defined in many ways, but its basic premise is that people living today should not impair the ability of future generations to meet their needs. Irreparable harm to the environment would of course compromise the earth's future. Many critics today believe that the pace of economic development today is no longer sustainable, despite the fact that natural resources still abound.

POSSIBLE SOLUTIONS TO ENVIRONMENTAL PROBLEMS

Both individually and collectively humans may respond to environmental problems in many ways, including the following:

1) **Prevention** – Some government policies have encouraged destruction of the environment, including low livestock grazing fees, cheap gasoline, or company access to government lands and forests. These policies may be reversed, but of course not without protests from people and companies affected. The Chinese One-Child Policy is an example of prevention of over-use of natural resources through limiting population growth.

2) **Technological change** – Technological possibilities include installing pollution-capturing filters for industrial runoff and recycling of industrial wastes.

3) **Mitigation** – Damage may be undone or reduced once it has occurred. For example, chemical spills may be cleaned up, lakes may be deacidified, and fish ladders may be added to dams.

4) **Compensation** – Political bodies may negotiate compensation for those negatively impacted by industrial wastes. If workers successfully sue companies in government-sponsored courts for damages done due to careless treatment of the environment, companies will be encouraged to avoid those damages. For example, a company whose chemical wastes have resulted in illness and/or death among its workers may be held legally responsible for their damage.

INDUSTRIAL POLLUTION

Industrial development has greatly increased air, water, and land pollution, adding waste that cannot be accommodated. Some pollution is natural, such as ash and gases from volcano eruptions and erosion from natural flooding. Pollution is also a consequence of agricultural practices. However, industrial products have greatly added to the overall pollution of air, water, and land resources on earth.

One concern is **global warming**, or the increase in earth's temperature caused primarily by the burning of fossil fuels. Earth is warmed by sunlight that passes through the atmosphere, strikes the surface, and is converted to heat. When fossil fuels are burned, carbon dioxide is discharged into the atmosphere, where it traps some of the heat leaving the surface heading back to space. This process is called the greenhouse effect, an anticipated warming of earth's surface that could melt the polar icecaps and raise the level of the oceans enough to destroy coastal cities. Consequences could include massive migrations inland and countless economic and political disasters.

Another by-product of air pollution is **acid rain**, which forms when sulfur dioxide and nitrogen oxides are released into the atmosphere by burning fossil fuels. These pollutants combine with water vapor and eventually work their way into lakes and streams. Results include corrosion of buildings and monuments, fish kills, stunted growth of forests, and loss of crops. Countries of the former Soviet Union, including Russia and Ukraine, are especially impacted by acid rain. Aging factories from the Soviet era still emit chemicals that make their way across the region and beyond. In the United States and Western Europe, government regulations on emissions are having positive results, with water and air pollution levels in many areas testing considerably lower than they did before the regulations were put in place. This evidence is now supporting stricter controls over factory emissions in the developing world.

TERMS AND CONCEPTS

acid rain
agglomeration
break-of-bulk
bulk-reducing industries, bulk-gaining industries
capitalist world economy
compressed modernity
conglomerate corporations
deglomeration
deindustrialization
dependency theory
distance decay
economic development
economic geography
export-oriented industrialization
footloose industry
friction of distance
fossil fuels
global warming
GDP, GDP per capita
greenhouse effect
industrialization
Industrial Revolution
Infrastructure
international division of labor
Kanto Plain
labor intensive industries
location theory
locational interdependence theory
maquiladora district
Meiji Restoration
modernization model
more developed country, less developed country
NAFTA
new international division of labor
newly industrializing country
Northeast District (China)
Oligarchs (Japan)
Pacific Rim
post-industrial societies
primary economic activities, primary sector
primary industry, secondary industry
proven reserve, potential reserve
quaternary sector
Rostow, W.W., Rostow's stages
secondary economic activities, secondary sector

secondary industrial region
single market manufacturers
site factors
space-time compression
Special Economic Zones
substitution principle
sustainable development
tertiary sector
trading blocs
transnational corporations
value added productivity
variable revenue analysis
Wallerstein, Emanuel
Watt, James
Weber, Alfred

UNIT SIX MULTIPLE-CHOICE QUESTIONS

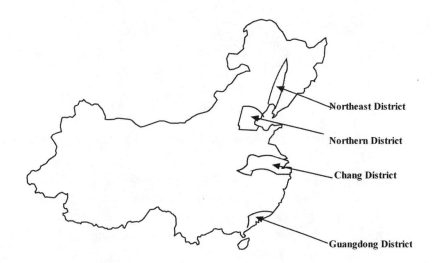

(Questions 1 and 2 are based on the above map):

1. Which of the Chinese industrial areas pictured above was the earliest to develop?

   (A) Northeast District
   (B) Northern District
   (C) Chang District around Nanjing
   (D) Chang District around Shanghai
   (E) Guangdon District

2. The earliest industrial area identified in #1 centered on the region's

   (A) plentiful labor supply
   (B) oil deposits
   (C) coal and iron deposits
   (D) ready access to water transportation
   (E) access to consumer markets

3. The establishment of maquiladoras is an example of the new international division of labor
   between

   (A) laborers and supervisors
   (B) North and South American countries
   (C) NAFTA member-states and EU member-states
   (D) the United States and Mexico
   (E) China and Mexico

4. Which of the following pairs of countries are rapidly increasing their share of the world's consumption of energy today?

  (A) the United States and Russia
  (B) China and India
  (C) Japan and the United States
  (D) Germany and Britain
  (E) Canada and Australia

5. Alfred Weber's least cost theory explained location of industries of terms of the three factors of

  (A) deglomeration, labor, and locational interdependence
  (B) locational interdependence, variable revenue analysis, and transportation
  (C) raw materials, transportation, and agglomeration
  (D) situation factors, site factors, and locational interdependence
  (E) transportation, labor, and agglomeration

6. A country that experiences a process called compressed modernity is most likely to be a

  (A) more developed country
  (B) democratic country
  (C) newly industrializing country
  (D) dictatorship
  (E) less developed country

7. The main goal of NAFTA has been to

  (A) more closely integrate the economies of Mexico, Canada, and the United States
  (B) increase tariffs and trade restrictions between Mexico, Canada, and the United States
  (C) make safety regulations for trade more uniform across North America
  (D) strengthen the competitiveness of the Mexican economy
  (E) restrict immigration across international borders in North America

8. Which of the following types of government would be most likely to be guided by dependency theory in setting public policy?

  (A) a conservative government of a newly industrializing country
  (B) a left-leaning government of a less developed country
  (C) an authoritarian government that wishes to emulate the development of the United States
  (D) a right-leaning government of an advanced democracy
  (E) a government that wishes to strengthen its country through membership in a supranational organization

9. According to modernization theory, less developed countries can improve their economies by

   (A) experimenting with socialism in order to narrow the gap between the rich and the poor
   (B) strengthening traditions, especially those that are family-based
   (C) forbidding more developed countries from exploiting their resources
   (D) nationalizing their major industries
   (E) following the paths taken by industrialized nations

10. Which of the following sectors of the economy grows the fastest as a country industrializes?

   (A) primary sector
   (B) tertiary sector
   (C) quaternary sector
   (D) secondary sector
   (E) retail sector

11. The primary cause of global warming in recent years has been the

   (A) burning of fossil fuels
   (B) formation of acid rain
   (C) increase in slash and burn agriculture
   (D) changes in heat emissions from the sun
   (E) melting of polar icecaps

12. Which of the following countries has NOT been significantly impacted by the modern trend toward deindustrialization?

   (A) United States
   (B) Britain
   (C) Japan
   (D) Egypt
   (E) South Korea

13. The location decision of a bulk-reducing industry is most likely to be affected by the

   (A) cost of labor
   (B) close proximity to raw materials
   (C) close proximity to customers
   (D) good access to railroad lines
   (E) good access to warm water ports

14. Which of the following is negatively correlated with Gross Domestic Product (GDP) Per Capita?

(A) education levels
(B) literacy rates
(C) infant mortality rates
(D) worker productivity
(E) number of workers in the tertiary sector of the economy

15. Which of the following countries is NOT located in one of the world's primary industrial regions?

(A) Russia
(B) Japan
(C) China
(D) South Korea
(E) Australia

16. A clustering of hotels and restaurants near airports is BEST explained by the benefits of

(A) agglomeration
(B) deindustrialization
(C) economic development
(D) space-time compression
(E) value added productivity

17. Which of the following strategies have the "Four Tigers" used most successfully in their economic development?

(A) import-oriented industrialization
(B) deglomeration
(C) the substitution principle
(D) export-oriented industrialization
(E) sustainable development

18. According to Rostow's modernization theory, one consequence of the drive to technological maturity is a(n)

(A) re-emphasis of traditional values
(B) unwillingness to experiment with producing goods for profit
(C) shift in emphasis to primary sector activities
(D) narrowing of the gap between the rich and the poor
(E) slowing in the rate of population growth

19. In contrast to less developed countries, more developed countries have

   (A) a larger proportion of workers employed in the primary sector
   (B) higher worker productivity
   (C) less access to raw materials
   (D) less access to nonessential goods
   (E) less reliance on industrial agriculture

20. Dependency theory puts primary responsibility for global poverty on

   (A) political leadership in less developed countries
   (B) lack of productivity of workers in less developed countries
   (C) rich nations
   (D) powerless international organizations
   (E) weak modernization models for less developed countries

21. One impact of the Industrial Revolution on Britain during the 19th century was to

   (A) stimulate the growth of seaports in the north
   (B) promote a general migration of people from the cities to the suburbs
   (C) stimulate the growth of cities at railroad hubs
   (D) shift economic power from cities in the north to cities in the south
   (E) push farmers out of business by the end of the century

22. The most important single invention that stimulated the growth of the Industrial Revolution in Britain during the early 19th century was

   (A) the steam engine
   (B) the spinning jenny
   (C) the combustion engine
   (D) electricity
   (E) the cotton gin

23. In contrast to primary industry, secondary industry is less dependent on

   (A) labor supplies
   (B) friction of distance
   (C) reliability of transportation
   (D) agglomeration
   (E) location of natural resources

24. Both Weber's least cost theory and von Thünen's agriculture model are examples of

   (A) variable revenue analysis
   (B) the substitution principle
   (C) modernization theory
   (D) location theory
   (E) dependency theory

25. All of the following are examples of infrastructure that support economic activity EXCEPT:

   (A) water transportation
   (B) inventory of goods
   (C) telephone systems
   (D) electricity
   (E) surface transportation

UNIT SIX FREE-RESPONSE QUESTION

Sustainable development is a growing concern in the modern world.

a. Define sustainable development.

b. Identify and describe one specific challenge that modern industry has created for sustainable development.

c. For the challenge identified in b, explain one solution that has been proposed to meet the challenge.

d. Identify and describe one specific challenge that modern agriculture has created for sustainable development.

e.   For the challenge identified in d, explain one solution that has been proposed to meet the challenge.

**UNIT SEVEN:
CITIES AND URBAN
LAND USE**

The natural landscape of the earth's surface has been transformed by human activities of all kinds, but perhaps none more profoundly than the building of great cities. The first cities were built in cradles of civilization thousands of years ago, and their numbers and locations have steadily grown, so that by the early 21st century they exist in almost all areas of the world. As the number of cities has grown, so has the number of people who live in them, so that today about half of the world's population lives in cities or towns. The field of **urban geography** focuses on how cities function, their internal systems and structures, and the external influences on them. Two sub-fields of urban geography are:

- **The study of systems of cities** – This sub-field focuses on where cities are located and why they are there, including such topics as current and historical distribution of cities, the functions of cities, and reasons for differential growth among cities. This study takes an external view of how cities influence the landscape around them, how they connect to one another, and how they are distributed nationally and globally.

- **The study of internal cities** – This sub-field focuses on the internal workings and structures of cities, as well as the analysis of patterns of land use, racial and ethnic segregation, architectural styles, types of intracity transportation, and cycles of construction and development. This sub-field makes use of both quantitative data, such as that gathered by the U.S. Census Bureau, and qualitative data, such as narrative accounts and field studies.

DEFINING URBANISM

What is an **urban area**? Many definitions exist, and they come in many different types, structures, and sizes. Their common characteristics are that they are **nucleated**, with one or more clear core areas, and that people who live in them work in nonagricultural jobs. The words "**city**" and "**town**" describe nucleated settlements that perform multiple residential and nonresidential functions, and include a central business district and surrounding residences. Towns are smaller and less complex than cities, but they still have nuclear business concentrations. Cities are usually surrounded by **suburbs**, areas that are also nucleated, but use much land space for residences of people that work in or near cities. Suburbs are not self-sufficient; most would not exist except for their locations near cities. Even though they are economically dependent on cities, suburbs usually have their own governments and are separated from the **central city** by political boundaries.

In many parts of the globe today cities and towns are located so close together that they form an **urbanized area** of continuously built-up landscapes of buildings and populations so that political boundaries are simply imaginary lines that separate them. The **physical city**, then, is a continuous development that contains a central city and many nearby cities, towns, and suburbs. Physical cities may be separated by less developed landscapes, but they may still be part of a larger **metropolitan area**, a large-scale functional entity that operates as an integrated economic whole. The U.S. Bureau of Statistics currently defines a **metropolitan statistical area** as a central county or counties with at least one urbanized area of at least 50,000 people, plus adjacent outlying counties with a large number of residents that commute in.   A **micropolitan statistical area** is a similar but smaller version of a metropolis, with at least one urban cluster between 10,000 and 50,000 people plus outlying counties with considerable social and economic integration.

URBAN HIERARCHY

Clustered settlements range in size from hamlets to megalopolises, and they may be arranged in a hierarchy according to the complexity of their centralizing functions.

From smallest to largest the hierarchy includes:

- **Hamlet** – A hamlet is a small cluster of farmers' houses with perhaps a few basic services, such as a gas station, a general store, or a coffee shop.
- **Village** – This next smallest urban settlement is likely to offer several dozen services that are more specialized than those of a hamlet. Stores sell only certain goods (as opposed to "general stores") and gas stations may sell competing brands of gasoline.
- **Town** – A town is not only larger than a village, its structures have more specialized functions. It may have a bank, a post office, a hospital, schools, and a library. A town also has a **hinterland**, or a surrounding area of smaller villages and hamlets that are economically dependent on it. People that live in the hinterland depend on the town for these services, and may also work in town.
- **City** – A city has a larger population, more functional specialization, larger hinterlands, and greater centrality than a town. Whereas towns often have clustering of businesses as well as outskirts, cities have well-defined **central business districts (CBD)**, as well as suburbs that may also have their own commercial centers or shopping malls.
- **Megalopolis** – Multiple cities that have grown together form the highest level of the urban hierarchy – the megalopolis. For example, a megalopolis spreads on the east coast of the United States from Boston to beyond Washington, D.C., the so-called **Bosnywash** megalopolis.

SOCIAL CHARACTERISTICS OF URBAN AREAS

In the 1930s social scientist **Louis Wirth** defined a city as a permanent settlement that has three characteristics that create living experiences for urban residents that are different from residents in rural areas:

- **Large size** – Because cities are large, a resident can know only a small percentage of the other residents. Acquaintances are those that urban dwellers come into contact with through work, living arrangements, and daily routines. In contrast, people in rural areas know almost everyone that lives nearby, and they usually know a great deal about their neighbors. This basis difference means that social contacts are very different in urban areas, where one comes in contact with many people, but does not get to know most of them very well.`

Bosnywash. One big megalopolis spreads along the east coast of the United States. Although it includes many large, distinct cities, the area is economically integrated, and the hinterlands around each city overlap to create a single urban expanse that stretches from Boston to Washington D.C. and beyond.

- **High density** – Wirth also notes that people in cities have highly specialized jobs, a characteristic that allows a large number of people to live in one place. Each person in a city plays a special role or performs a specific task that allows the urban system to function smoothly. At the same time, high density encourages people to compete for space, causing some social groups to dominate others. It also leads to higher prices for property and rents, further distinguishing between rich and poor.

- **Social heterogeneity** – By their very nature, large settlements include people with diverse backgrounds. Cities allow more anonymity, so people that are uncomfortable with their all-knowing neighbors in rural areas will flock to cities to live freer lives. Cities attract people with unusual occupations only available in urban areas, sexual orientations unacceptable in rural areas, or cultural interests that are fed by the city's museums, theaters, and libraries. Wirth notes that despite the freedom and independence that cities offer, a downside of urban living is that people may feel lonely and isolated, thinking that others around them are indifferent to their neighbors.

SYSTEMS OF CITIES

Cities appear on earth's surface in response to human needs and activities, and their locations are important in determining their growth. Political, economic, and cultural factors all play roles in determining which hamlets will grow into villages, villages into towns, and towns into cities. For example, a decision as to where to locate the political capital may cause one town to grow into a city with specialized businesses and employment opportunities, and another town to lose population, businesses, and employment. A settlement located on a good harbor may grow economically through trade, causing it to climb the urban hierarchy to a more complex, larger community. A town may also establish itself as a cultural center by fostering museums, theatres, libraries, and/or universities that encourage artists, scholars, actors, and literary figures to settle in the area. Many large cities combine these factors, so that political, economic, and cultural growth is complemented. Geography plays a key role in determining urban growth because location and topography influence where people settle, causing some cities to grow and others to stagnate.

ORIGIN AND EVOLUTION OF CITIES

Our modern world is so centered on urban life that it is hard to imagine the world without cities; however, cities first appeared on earth in relatively recent times. Assuming that human beings first appeared about 100,000 years ago, they formed no permanent settlements for about 90,000 years. Once the Neolithic (Agricultural) Revolution occurred about 10,000 years ago, people established permanent settlements, but the communities remained small and relatively simple. In Southwest Asia things began to change about 3000 B.C.E. as irrigation and larger-scale farming caused agricultural societies to become more complex. These practices allowed them to raise a surplus, or more crops than farmers needed to feed their own families. As a result, job specialization was possible because everyone did not have to be a farmer, and food supplies became more reliable. Their populations grew larger, and evidence of inequality appeared, with some houses and landholdings growing larger than others. Job specialization also began, with most people continuing as farmers, but others becoming craftsmen, priests, or government officials. Government buildings appeared, and the villages became more diversified.

The Role of Government

Partly as a result of geographic features, by 3000 B.C.E. some villages were larger and more specialized than others. The period between about 4000 and 2000 B.C.E. is called the **formative era** for both the development of states and urbanization. The more complex the settlements grew, the need for central authority increased, and so **states** (organized territories under governments) appeared along the Nile River in northern Africa (Egypt), the Tigris and Euphrates Rivers in Southwest Asia (Mesopotamia), and the Indus River in South Asia. Other early civilizations appeared along rivers in East Asia (early

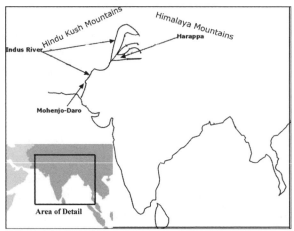

Cities of the Indus River Valley Civilization. Archaeological excavations make it clear that an advanced urban civilization flourished in the major cities of Harappa and Mohenjo-Daro for hundreds of years, beginning about 3000 B.C.E. Both cities were carefully planned, with broad streets, large walled neighborhoods, and narrow lanes separating the rows of houses. Houses differed in size, with some reaching as high as three stories. Only a well-organized government could have maintained such carefully structured cities.

China), and eventually around the Aegean Sea (the forerunners of the Greeks). The rise of the earliest states is closely linked to the evolution of the first cities. All of these civilizations had major cities that increased in size and complexity as farming techniques improved and trade up and down the rivers (or across the sea) developed.

Function and Location of Ancient Cities

The ancient city was the organizational focus of the state. Agriculture had to be planned and controlled so as to guarantee a flow of food into the city, especially once irrigation systems developed. Governments collected taxes and tribute as civilizations expanded, and they also built fortified walls around cities to protect them from outside invaders. Cities were located near productive farmlands along rivers for availability of water for agriculture and transportation. Sites were also chosen for their defensibility, as well as their location along travel and trade routes. Less accessible, more isolated places were at a disadvantage.

Job specialization and social inequality grew along with the need to acquire, store, and distribute food. A group of **urban elite** (decision makers and organizers) controlled the resources, and sometimes the lives, of others. These leaders saw that the gods looked favorably upon the people and their food production, and they also developed a system of writing and record-keeping to help organize resources. Eventually some early civilizations codified laws to ensure that society functioned smoothly, and the urban elite organized the construction of public buildings, such as temples, government centers, and granaries for storing food. Functions of ancient cities included:

- **Centers of power** – Cities were often the headquarters for early heads of state.
- **Religious centers** – Priests, temples, and shrines were generally located in cities.
- **Economic centers** – Most cities had markets for trade, with wealthy merchants, land and livestock owners, and traders operating and living in urban areas.
- **Educational centers** – City residents included teachers and philosophers to educate new generations of the urban elite.

How large were the ancient cities? Many of the sites are still being excavated, but estimates indicate that the cities of Mesopotamia and the Nile Valley had between 10,000 and 15,000 inhabitants after nearly 2000 years of growth and development. Cities could not have grown much larger than this because the existing systems of food gathering, storing, and distribution would not have supported a larger population.

Early Urbanization Around The Mediterranean

Settlements were first established in the area around the eastern Mediterranean Sea about 2500 years ago by forerunners of the ancient Greek civilization. They were organized into **city-states**, self-governing communities that included the nearby countryside. The settlement provided the government, military protection, and other public services for the surrounding hinterland. The number of urban settlements grew rapidly during the 8th and 9th centuries B.C.E., and by the middle part of the first millennium Greek settlements were as far west as present-day Spain. Meanwhile, the Phoenicians established communities on the southwest coastline in modern-day Africa. Athens was probably the first city to

Ruins of a Roman City. Roman ruins in Vaison-la-Romaines in southern France reflect the widespread network of Roman cities connected by land and sea routes. Ruins such as these may be found in many parts of Europe and other areas that were controlled by Ancient Rome.

reach a population of 100,000, during the 5th and 4th centuries B.C.E. When the Romans succeeded the Greeks as rulers of the region, their **urban empire** incorporated not only the Mediterranean shores but also a large part of interior Europe, North Africa, and the former Mesopotamian lands. Although much of the empire was still rural farmlands, numerous cities dominated the hinterlands, with Rome reaching at least 250,000 inhabitants at its height in the second century C.E. The cities of the empire were connected by a network of land and sea routes, with Roman roads built so expertly that many still remain intact today.

Urban Growth In China

The earliest civilizations in East Asia grew from a central region around the Huang River and its tributaries. By the time of the Han Dynasty (202 B.C.E. to 221 C.E.), the city of Chang'an on the Wei River had become one of the great cities of the world, rivaling Rome in its size and complex organization. Chang'an and its successor capital Luoyang lay at the eastern end of the great Silk Road that stretched to the Mediterranean Sea, and the trade route brought much wealth and diversity to the Chinese cities. These cities became economic, governmental, cultural, and educational centers that were connected by an intricate system of roads, rivers, and canals. During the Tang era (618-907 C.E.), Chang'an was the hub of a vast trade network enhanced by the building of the 1100-mile Grand Canal that linked the Yellow and Yangzi Rivers as a key component to internal trade routes within the empire. Other urban areas grew along the trade routes, and urban life was quite diverse, with perhaps as many as 100,000 west Asians living in Chang'an by the early 10th century. By the 11th century, the greatest of the trading cities of the south was Hangzhou, which was home to merchants, craftsmen, and government officials. Its primary exports included silks, copper coins, and ceramics.

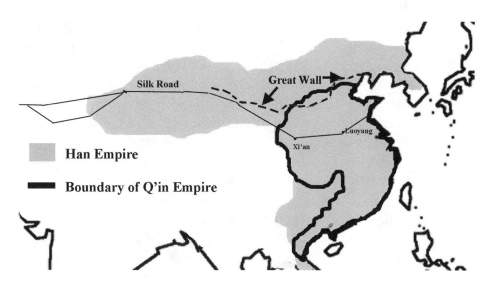

Early Urban China. China's government strengthened greatly under the Q'in Empire, and by the time of the Han Dynasty (202 B.C.E. – 221 C.E.) an urban empire had developed in China, with Xi'an serving as the political capital during the early years and Luoyang during the later dynastic rule. An urban elite controlled the political, economic, and cultural systems, and roads and canals connected the natural river waterways.

Medieval, Preindustrial, And Industrial World Cities

After the fall of the Western Roman Empire in 476 C.E., urban settlements declined across Europe and other areas around the western Mediterranean Sea. Once the city of Rome was sacked, the empire fragmented under hundreds of rulers, trade diminished, and large urban settlements shrank or were abandoned. Urban life began to revive during the 11th century, and was stimulated by the trade that developed between the Italian cities of Venice and Genoa and the Middle East as a result of the Crusades. The largest medieval European urban settlements served as centers for government, church, and markets, and roads connected them to smaller towns in the hinterlands. The tallest and most elaborate structures were usually churches that often took decades to build. Most medieval European cities were surrounded by walls, although by the 15th century, cannonballs could destroy them. Medieval cities were very different from today's cities. The streets were narrow and winding, and occupational groups such as bakers, carpenters, and metalworkers clustered together in distinct sections. Ethnicity also defined communities as residents sought to keep out people who differed from themselves. The term "ghetto" first described the segregation of Jews in Venice.

 Many other parts of the world remained far more urbanized as Europe recovered from Rome's fall. Just before the first millennium ended (1000 C.E.), the largest cities were in Asia, not Europe, including Baghdad (in present-day Iraq), Constantinople (later named Istanbul, in modern-day Turkey), Kyoto (in Japan), and Chang'an and Hangchow (in China). Not until the early 1800s did a European city (London) become the most populous city in the world.

Cities in the preindustrial world often became urban centers for a whole cultural region. Geographer Mark Jefferson named these **primate cities**, larger than other cities in the area and representing a national culture. For example, Kyoto became the primate city for old Japan; Paris reflected French culture; and London came to represent all that is English. Some scholars believe that world cities varied so significantly that it is a mistake to categorize them all together as "preindustrial." For example, religious buildings dominated the landscapes in Muslim lands, Europe, and the Americas, but not in Africa or East Asia.

During the preindustrial era, long distance trade networks developed across the Sahara Desert, Sub-Saharan Africa, the Indian Ocean, the Silk Road, and the South China Sea. By the 16th century, significant trade routes connected the western and eastern hemisphere via the Atlantic and Pacific Oceans. These networks stimulated the growth of the **mercantile city** where trade became central to city design. No matter where the city was located, its central square was fronted by government and religious buildings, as well as housing for the rich. Streets leading to the central square were arteries of commerce, lined with shops that specialized in products brought in by the trade routes.

The Industrial Revolution created the **manufacturing city**, where factories attracted laborers from rural areas and other countries to tenements constructed to provide housing for factory workers. Older winding streets gave way to broad, straight boulevards to accommodate the flow of commercial traffic, and eventually, automobiles. Steam and electric trolleys crisscrossed the streets. Because land came to be seen as a commodity to be bought and sold, developers divided cities into regular-sized lots. Although some cities retained their historic town squares, others lost that organization, and most all of them suffered from problems of sanitation, overcrowding, pollution, and disarray. Unlike pre-industrial cities that were usually located near navigable waterways, manufacturing cities grew along railroad lines that connected them to their markets. Cities grew rapidly during the 19th and early 20th centuries, and the problems multiplied, although conditions improved as a result of government intervention, legislation, and the introduction of city planning and zoning.

RURAL-URBAN MIGRATION AND URBAN GROWTH

Urbanization accelerated in the 1800s in the countries of Europe and North America largely because of industrial development. For example, the percentage of people living in urban areas in the United States increased from 5% in 1800 to 50% in 1920. Today about three-fourths of people in developed countries live in urban areas.

In more recent years migration from rural to urban areas has rapidly increased in less developed countries in Africa, Asia, and Latin America. This migration has meant that the percentage of people in poor countries that live in cities has risen from 25% in 1950 to an estimated 50% by 2010. By 2000, 48 cities in the world had passed the 5 million population mark, and 32 of them were in less developed nations. Part of the reason for the growth of cities in poor countries is that longevity has increased, but much of it results from a migration from rural to urban areas by people looking for jobs, education, and conveniences, such as electricity and running water. As the countries begin to industrialize, opportunities shift from rural to urban areas, and the pull to the city stimulates migration.

The amount of urban growth differs from continent to continent and from region to region, but nearly all countries have two things in common: the proportion of their people living in cities is rising, and the cities themselves are large and growing. Whether or not the United Nations projection that world urban populations have now become the majority has actually come to be, the trend toward urbanization is still holding strong today.

WORLD CITIES AND MEGACITIES

During the second half of the 20th century, manufacturing cities stopped growing, with many factories relocating outside cities or closing their doors as economies adjusted to the post-industrial world. New transportation systems, such as railroads, automobiles, and subways allowed workers to

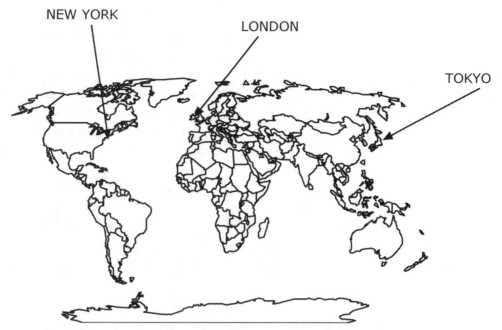

live farther away from factories, so all could relocate to areas less expensive and more spacious than accommodations in the center city. In the place of the great manufacturing cities are modern world cities that have become centers of business, consumer, and public services.

World Cities

World cities exist all over the globe, but the three that serve as the largest regional centers are London, New York, and Tokyo. All three house important stock exchanges and contain major concentrations of business services, and all are characterized by a polarized social structure with larger than usual numbers of the wealthy on one end and the very poor on the other end. A second tier of world cities includes Chicago, Los Angeles, and Washington in the United States; Brussels, Frankfurt, Paris, and Zurich in Western Europe; São Paolo in Brazil; and Singapore in Southeast Asia. Only São Paolo and Singapore are in the less developed world, although a third tier of world cities includes Bangkok, Bombay, Hong Kong, Manila, Osaka, Seoul, and Taipei in Asia; Buenos Aires, Caracas, Mexico City, and Rio de Janeiro in Latin America; and Johannesburg in Africa. These "tiers" of world cities are based on the centrality of these services in each city:

- **Business services** – As factories relocated outside city centers, many business services that took up less space remained there. Corporate directors and support staff do much of their work in offices in world cities, as do people that provide the financial services of banks and insurance companies. Stock exchanges for corporations are also located in world cities, as are legal and accounting firms. Transportation services converge on world cities that lie at the junction of rail and highway networks, and also center on airports and busy harbors.

- **Consumer services** – Partly because business services are located in cities, a disproportionately large number of wealthy people live in cities. As a result, many retail businesses concentrate their organizations and efforts in world cities. Entertainment and cultural offerings are also more varied and numerous in cities, where audiences are larger, more varied, and wealthier. As a result, cities have concentrations of plays, concerts, operas, restaurants, museums, and libraries that are often lacking in smaller cities or towns.

- **Public services** – Most world cities are national or international seats of political power. Since governments are headquartered in these cities, ambassadors from other countries, as well as lobbyists from interest groups, also locate here, increasing the centralization of political power. New York is an exception among world cities because it is not the U.S. capital, but it does house the United Nations, and so it serves as an international center of political power. Brussels is the national capital of the small country of Belgium, but its rank as a world city is based on the fact that the European Union is headquartered there.

Megacities

By 2017 nineteen metropolises in the world had populations of more than 10 million, earning them the title, **"megacities,"** a term created by the United Nations in the 1970s. In 1900, no cities were that large. Just how large they will grow in the future is debatable, but rapid expansion of many megacities seems to be slowing today. The United Nations predicts that by 2015, the number of megacities will rise to 24, and by 2025 to 27.

Many megacities, especially those in less developed countries, house new arrivals in overpopulated apartment buildings, tenements, and slums. Shantytowns have grown up around many of them, where despite miserable living conditions, many new migrants continue to arrive. During the 1990s, Africa had the world's fastest growing cities, followed by those in South Asia, mainland East Asia, and South and Central America. In contrast, cities in North America, southern South America, and Australia were growing more slowly, and those of Western Europe were not growing at all. Megacities offer some stark contrasts in inequality. There the richest people in the world reside virtually next door to the poorest. Cities in poorer parts of the world generally lack enforceable zoning laws to ensure the space is used in ways beneficial to the community. Without zoning laws, many growing megacities are

Ten Largest Megacities in the World

Tokyo, Japan	35,700,000
New York-Newark	19,000,000
Mexico City	19,000,000
Mumbai (Bombay)	19,000,000
São Paulo	18,800,000
Delhi	15,900,000
Shanghai	15,000,000
Kolkata (Calcutta)	14,800,000
Dhaka	13,500,000
Buenos Aires	12.800,000

The other megacities are Los Angeles, Karachi, Cairo, Rio de Janeiro, Osaka-Kobe, Beijing, Manila, Moscow, and Istanbul

Source: AN OVERVIEW OF URBANIZATION, INTERNAL MIGRATION, POPULATION DISTRIBUTION AND DEVELOPMENT IN THE WORLD*, United Nations Population Division, 2008

unable to control expansion and haphazard development that seriously affect the quality of life within the urban area.

FUNCTIONS OF CITIES

Urban centers are functionally connected to other cities and to rural areas. Cities usually provide services for themselves, and for others outside their city limits. Some are **transportation centers** where major routes converge – roads, railroads, sea traffic, and air transportation. Others are **special-function cities** engaged in mining, manufacturing, or recreation. Most large cities are multi-functional, even if they began their growth because of one function that they originally served. A common property of all settlements is centrality, so that cities become **central places** that provide goods and services for the surrounding area. Cities also carry on activities that are necessary simply to support the city itself. These two levels of activities – those that connect to the outside and those that support the internal structure – make up the economic base of an urban sector.

THE ECONOMIC BASE OF A CITY

Some city workers produce goods or services for areas outside the city. These **"export activities"** result in money flowing into the city, and are collectively called the **basic sector** of the city's economy. Others produce goods or services for residents of the city itself, and their work collectively forms the **nonbasic,** or **service sector,** of the economy. Despite the name of the latter sector, these workers are crucial to the operation of the city's businesses, professional offices, city government, schools, and intracity transit systems. Many workers produce goods or services in both sectors, making it difficult to separate the two sectors. Some cities specialize in one sector or the other, but the larger the city, the more likely it is to be multi-functional, with workers from both sectors.

Economists and geographers often compare cities by function by creating a **base ratio,** or a ratio between workers employed in the basic sector and those employed in the nonbasic sector. Usually the larger a city grows, the larger its ratio of nonbasic workers, mainly because the city takes more workers to support its growth. Eventually a **multiplier effect** takes hold in which new basic sector employment is accompanied by a larger share of nonbasic workers, decreasing the ratio of basic sector workers to nonbasic. For example, if a new industry locates to a city that produced goods for people outside the city (like automobiles), the new workers need services from nonbasic workers, such as grocery clerks, gasoline station attendants, and medical doctors and nurses. As a result, more of the total number of new jobs created are in the nonbasic sector.

In 1943 Chauncy Harris published an article in which he classified cities in the United States into three types according to their functions:

- manufacturing-dominated cities in the Northeast
- retail centers scattered across the country
- diversified cities with multiple functions

Today these categories are very much blurred because growing size has brought greater diversification. Specialization is still apparent. For example, Boston has a disproportionate number of universities, and Las Vegas is still a center for gambling. However, both cities have diversified considerably as they have grown.

URBAN INFLUENCE ZONES

Urban influence zones are the areas outside the city that are affected by it. As the distance away from the city increases, its influence on the surrounding countryside decreases. The larger the city is, the larger the sphere of influence outside its borders grows. A large city will usually encompass smaller cities with their own influence zones, so there is an overlapping hierarchical arrangement, so that individuals will often feel the pull of multiple zones. For example, a world city like New York influences people in suburban New Jersey by providing work places and cultural attractions for many people in outlying areas. However, residents of New Jersey are also in the influence zone of smaller cities like Newark or Trenton, where local newspapers cover "New Jersey" events and the state government makes decisions that affect their children's educations. The urban hierarchy is almost always at work, as individuals may also be in the influence zone of a town or village.

THE CHANGING CITY

As cities grow older, they inevitably change, creating different mixes of employment opportunities and demographic characteristics. In 1967 John Borchert recognized four stages in the evolution of the American metropolis:

1) The Sail-Wagon Epoch, 1790-1830, when trade took place by ships across the sea or along coastlines, or by wagons overland. The technologies determined job opportunities of people that came to work in cities.
2) The Iron-Horse Epoch, 1830-1870, when railroad technology changed the nature of trade and employment.
3) The Steel-Rail Epoch, 1870-1920, when the steel industry transformed urban America and job opportunities of workers.
4) The Auto-Air-Amenity Epoch, 1920s-1960s, when the internal combustion engine came to dominate life styles, employment opportunities, and the economic base of cities.

Today many would add an epoch initiated by computer technology, another revolutionary innovation that changed people's lives and employment opportunities. With these changes come demographic shifts, such as those that took place when the new industries of the late 19th century Industrial Revolution attracted immigrant groups from Europe and Asia. Enclaves based on nationality formed in coastal cities, so that Italian, Chinese, Polish, Greek, and Russian neighborhoods emerged. As technologies changed, or moved to new areas, and as new immigrants assimilated into the culture, so the neighborhoods changed as well.

MODELS OF URBAN SYSTEMS

Two theories of **settlement geography**, or the patterns of settlement on the earth's surface, are the **rank-size rule** and **Christaller's central place theory.**

Rank-Size Rule

The urban hierarchy identifies settlements of differing sizes and complexities from the hamlet to the megalopolis. For many large countries, the city-size hierarchy is summarized by the **rank-size rule.** It tells us that the *n*th largest city will be $1/n$ the size of the largest city. For example, the 2nd largest city will be ½ the size of the first-ranked city, and the 5th largest city will be 1/5 as large as the first-ranked city. The rank-size ordering often describes the pattern of urban area sizes in complex economies where urbanization is well-established, such as the United States. It does not usually describe areas where urbanization is more recent, as in many less developed countries. In some countries the **primate city** is so dominant that no other cities fit the rank-size rule; they are far smaller than the primate city. An example is South Korea, where Seoul is the primate city with all other cities being far smaller. Even in more developed countries in Europe, the rank-size rule does not apply – London dominates Britain, and Paris dominates France. In countries where a primate city dominates, the rest of the country depends on it for cultural, economic, political, and major transportation needs. On the other hand the primate city depends on the rest of the country as paying consumers of the cultural, economic, and political services produced in the city.

Rank-size often reflects the distribution of wealth in a country. If an urban hierarchy exists according to the rank-size rule, it often means that economic goods and services are spread throughout the countryside, and inequalities between rural and urban living standards are lessened. In contrast, countries with primate cities often have a large gap between standards of living in the city and the countryside. It may mean that there is not enough wealth in the society to pay for a full variety of services.

Central Place Theory

Central place theory views urban settlements as centers for the distribution of economic goods and services to surrounding nonurban populations. The theory is based on the work of Walter Christaller in a 1933 book entitled *The Central Places in Southern Germany*. Christaller provided a model for settlement patterns that rested on several assumptions:

- No topographic barriers
- No difference in farm productivity
- An evenly dispersed farm population
- People with similar life styles and incomes
- Differing thresholds, or minimum number of consumers necessary to support different products (lower threshold for inexpensive items, higher threshold for expensive items)
- Purchase of goods and services at the nearest center

Christaller made these assumptions for the sake of developing a consistent model to explain settlement patterns, even though he knew that in reality these factors vary. His results have formed the basis of central place theory ever since:

1) The landscape is divided into noncompeting market areas – **complementary regions** – where each individual urban center and its merchants have a sales monopoly.
2) The market areas form a series of hexagons that cover the area, with no area unserved and no area with equal service from two centers.
3) The central place is at the center of each hexagon, and it will supply all the goods and services to consumers in that area.
4) The size of the market area of a central place is based on the number of goods and services offered; the larger the number of goods and services, the larger the market area.

5) Within each hexagon, or around its edges, lie smaller hexagons with central places that serve smaller areas. This nesting of small hexagons within larger ones creates a **hierarchy of central places**, with small centers providing lower-order services than the large centers do. The small centers may provide goods with low thresholds (like bread, milk, and other basic foodstuffs), and the larger centers provide more expensive items, like automobile or farm machinery.

Christaller came to two important conclusions regarding settlement patterns:

1) Towns of the same size are evenly spaced because they are in the center of like-sized market areas. Larger towns will be farther apart than smaller towns because their market areas are larger.
2) Towns are part of an interdependent system. If a central place is eliminated, the entire system readjusts, altering the spatial pattern to meet the needs and demands of the inhabitants. A smaller town might grow to be larger, or a new town might appear, but changing one hexagon will automatically alter the arrangement of all the others because customers will be willing to travel further distances for luxury items than for everyday necessities.

Christaller's conclusions apply to widely differing areas of the world. They describe agricultural areas particularly well. In areas where cities are multi-functional, the model is less applicable, but it does fairly accurately describe special-function cities as well as transportation-based cities.

INTERNAL CITIES

A second sub-field of urban geography is the study of internal cities. Whereas the rank-size rule and central place theory focus on systems of cities and how they are located, other geographers analyze the internal land space of cities and the varying uses that it serves. Cities are often arranged in similar ways, allowing geographers to develop models for urban land use. These models are influenced by several factors:

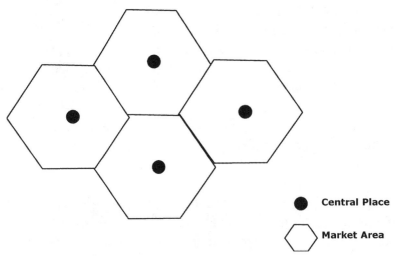

● Central Place

⬡ Market Area

Complementary Regions. According to Christaller's central place theory, market areas form hexagons in order to cover all markets without overlap. Circles would create overlap and areas not served by the central place, so markets tend to form hexagons instead. Smaller hexagons form within the larger ones with smaller central places, forming a hierarchy of central places.

1) **Accessibility** – In order to operate effectively, the city requires that its functions be fulfilled in spaces accessible to its inhabitants. For example, in early industrial cities, factories had to be within walking distance of where workers lived. As a result, high-density housing built up around the factories in as compact a space as possible.

2) **High cost of accessible space** – Because city functions must be located in close proximity, the cost of land goes up because space is at a premium. With the advent of mass transportation (subways, automobiles), the amount of usable space grew, allowing workers to move farther away from the places where they worked. However, competition among inhabitants generally has remained keen for the best, most accessible places to live, so population density has pushed prices of land and other commodities higher.

3) **Transportation** – Since uses of land are determined by accessibility, lines of transportation often determine the growth of the city. When subway lines are built, houses and stores tend to be built within walking distance of those lines. Houses and stores also follow roads (and eventually highways) that lead to the center city, with accessibility again the key to the city's development. Land with the highest accessibility is the most desirable, and as a result, generally more expensive.

4) **Societal and cultural needs** – Economic competition is an important determinant of land use, but some highly desirable land is usually set aside to meet societal and cultural needs. Examples include schools, libraries, and parks.

MODELS OF URBAN LAND USE

Three models help explain different land uses within cities: the concentric zone, sector, and multiple nuclei models. The three models were all developed in Chicago, a city on flat land, with only Lake Michigan to the east to disrupt the physical landscape. All the models include a **central business district (CBD)** and residential areas by various income levels of inhabitants. The concentric zone model was developed first, and the sector and multiple nuclei models built on and altered the ideas first presented by the concentric zone model.

Concentric Zone Model

The **concentric zone model** was created in 1923 by sociologist **E.W. Burgess**, and it views cities as growing outward from a central area in a series of concentric rings, much like the growth rings of trees. The size and width of the rings vary from city to city, but Burgess believed that the model fit most cities of the time. The zones he identified are:

- **Zone One** – The innermost zone is the central business district, where nonresidential activities are concentrated. Very few residences exist in this ring, and property costs are quite high.

- **Zone Two** – The **zone in transition** contains light industry and housing for the poor, and serves as a transition zone between the businesses in the CBD and the more purely residential areas in the outer zones. Industries located in Zone Two may be too large to fit into the relatively small Zone One, or their owners may be seeking cheaper land. Houses may have been formerly occupied by the wealthy, who have moved farther out, leaving the homes to deteriorate.

- **Zone Three** – This zone contains working-class homes, modest older houses on small lots occupied by stable, working-class families. Housing here is less expensive than in the outer rings.

- **Zone Four** – As rings get further from the CBD, the homes get larger and more expensive. Zone Four consists of middle-class residences, either single-family homes or high-rent apartments occupied by those wealthy enough to choose location and afford the higher cost of transportation into the CBD.

- **Zone Five** – A commuter's zone is the final ring, the farthest away from the CBD. It is beyond the continuous built-up area of the city, and people live in small villages where they spend their leisure and sleep hours and commute into the CBD for work.

Burgess's model is dynamic and ever-changing, as inner rings grow larger, invading spaces of rings further out. He explains that neighborhoods change through a process of *invasion* and *succession*, with succeeding poorer inhabitants driving wealthier residents further away from the center city.

The Sector Model

Land economist **Homer Hoyt** developed the **sector model** in 1939 as a variant of the concentric zone theory. According to Hoyt, the city develops in a series of sectors, not rings, as Burgess described. The sectors may be determined by environmental factors (like hills or bodies of water), or they may simply develop by chance. As a city grows, particular activities expand outward in a wedge-like sector from the center. Once a district is established for industry, other industry will cluster around it, creating the wedge. Likewise, a district where wealthy people live will attract other wealthy people, so the sector becomes a concentration of their residences. Middle class residences are adjacent to the high-income areas, and low-income residents occupy the left over areas. Hoyt's sectors are similar to Burgess's circles, but the overall pattern of land use does not reflect unbroken circles around the central business district. Hoyt, like Burgess, notes that as the city grows, residential areas once occupied by the wealthy "filter down" to the middle class, and eventually to the lower class, as property is sold (or rented) from one owner to another.

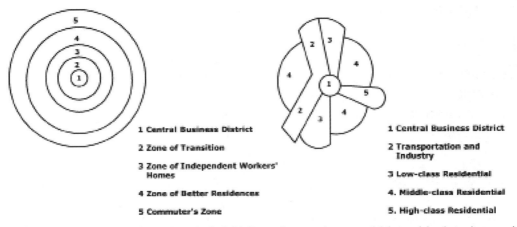

1 Central Business District

2 Zone of Transition

3 Zone of Independent Workers' Homes

4 Zone of Better Residences

5 Commuter's Zone

1 Central Business District

2 Transportation and Industry

3 Low-class Residential

4. Middle-class Residential

5. High-class Residential

Concentric Zone and Sector Models of Land Use. On the left is Burgess' concentric zone model that explains that a city grows in a series of rings that surround the central business district. On the right is Hoyt's sector model that demonstrates that a city grows in a series of sectors, or wedges, out from the central business district.

The Multiple-Nuclei Model

The concentric circle and sector models assume urban growth and development outward from a single central business district, which originally had been the site of first settlement. The **multiple-nuclei model,** developed in 1945 by geographers **C.D. Harris** and **E.L. Ullman**, counters that large cities develop by spreading from several nodes of growth, not just one. Individual nodes usually have special functions, like ports, neighborhood businesses, universities, airports, and different levels of residences. This model explains that incompatible land use activities do not cluster in the same locations, so the nodes influence the type of development that occurs around them. The clusters expand as the city grows, and when the clusters come into contact, incompatible land uses develop along the lines of juncture.

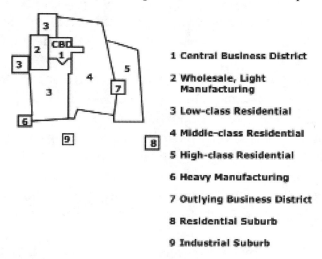

1 Central Business District

2 Wholesale, Light Manufacturing

3 Low-class Residential

4 Middle-class Residential

5 High-class Residential

6 Heavy Manufacturing

7 Outlying Business District

8 Residential Suburb

9 Industrial Suburb

Multiple-nuclei Model of Land Use. According to this model, a city grows from multiple nodes, not just from one central business district. Different types of people and activities cluster around each node.

The three models help to explain not only land use in cities, but also the different social characteristics of people that live in particular areas of a city. The models may be used along with census information to describe individual neighborhoods. Urban areas in the United States are divided into **census tracts**, areas of approximately 5,000 people that correspond whenever possible to neighborhood boundaries. Every ten years the U.S. Bureau of the Census publishes reports on the demographic characteristics of each tract, including ethnicity, race, median income, and education levels of residents.

PATTERNS OF CLASS, AGE, GENDER, RACE, AND ETHNICITY

The distribution of social characteristics in a census tract may be plotted on a map by a computer that stores vast amounts of data about the inhabitants. This type of study is called a **social area analysis** that puts together information from census tracts to create an overall picture of how various types of people are distributed within a broader area, like a city. Although the models for urban land use do not explain why particular people live in specific areas of a city, they all support the concept that most people prefer to live near others with similar characteristics. The larger and more economically and socially complex cities are, the stronger the tendency for residents to segregate themselves into groups based on social class, race, and ethnicity. Perhaps this pattern is a response to the anonymity of cities and the desire to be with people with familiar lifestyles, or it may be attributed to income restraints.

Many of these social-area groups are influenced by the size and the value of available housing. Land developers, especially in high-density areas, mass produce homes of similar price and quality in specific areas. Once social divisions are in place, they tend to carry over from one generation to the next. Even when change does occur, it tends to take place all over the area, so that "mixed" neighborhoods are often just in temporary transition to domination by another group.

- **Social class** – Social class is multi-dimensional, and is often measured by a combination of income, education, and occupation. People in higher social classes generally buy homes that are larger, in neighborhoods with people of similar status. One indicator of social class is the number of people that live per room in a house. A low number of people per room tends to indicate high status. Of the three models of urban land use, Hoyt's sector model is most reflective of clustering patterns by social status.   If people from a lower social status move into an area, the higher status residents tend to move away from the central city along a corridor connecting them with their old neighborhoods, creating the sectors that Hoyt describes.

- **Age and marital status** – Younger families tend to live farther from the city center because they are seeking space for child rearing. They tend to cluster according to social status as well, and so child-friendly businesses tend to locate near or in these neighborhoods. Houses are larger with green space around for children's play. In contrast, groups that need less living space often live closer to city center. Older families who may have lived on the city's outskirts when they were younger now may relocate to retirement communities or suburbs, or move toward city center to access the cultural and business life of the city. Young professionals, unmarried or without children, are also more likely to live close to the city center.

- **Gender** – A growing phenomenon in American society is the increase in the number of one-parent families. According to the 2000 census, 28% of U.S. families with children under eighteen have only one parent in the household, and 78% of all one-parent families are headed by women. Because of a combination of lower-paying jobs for women and the limitation of only one income in the family, these families are generally poorer than two-parent families. As a result, they are less likely to be able to afford large houses in the outer areas of the city, and so a disproportionate number of one-parent families live in low-income neighborhoods. This trend is called the **feminization of poverty**, or the increasing proportion of the poor who are women. Because their incomes are lower, women rely more heavily upon public transportation than do men, so they tend to be concentrated in or near central cities.

- **Race and ethnicity** – The multiple-nuclei model of urban land use best explains the tendency for ethnic and racial groups to cluster together in particular areas. Once a group moves into an area, that "node" tends to attract others, so that growth takes place around multiple nodes, each with a different ethnic or racial base. Examples are "Little Italies" or "Chinatowns" that attracted the groups as they immigrated into cities on the East and West Coasts of the United States. In many American cities, black Americans and Latinos are segregated into nuclear communities that are frequently among the most undesirable neighborhoods (called **ghettos**), with dilapidated housing, high crime rates, and inadequate schools. Social and economic barriers to movement outside the area have always been high. Because schools and social services are often neighborhood-based, this racial and ethnic segregation tends to create a vicious cycle of poverty that is hard to break. Segregation patterns in cities show a great resistance to change, so that today, the average black city dweller lives in a census tract that is more than 75% minority. Contrary to popular stereotypes, black-white separation is highest in metropolitan areas in the Northeast and Midwest, and lowest in metropolitan areas of the South and West.

GHETTOIZATION

The changing pattern of ethnic clustering within metropolitan areas is determined partly by residential choice and partly by discrimination. Growing ethnic groups that voluntarily live in the same area frequently expand the area where they live by growing outward from the core of the city in a radial pattern. Where forced segregation limits residential choices, ethnic or racial minorities may be confined to the older, low-cost housing areas typically close to the city center, a process called **ghettoization.** Patterns of ghettoization of African Americans historically have differed by region:

- **Early southern ghetto** – In pre-Civil War cities such as Charleston and New Orleans, African Americans were confined to small houses in alleys and back streets, which were nearby the white communities where they worked as house and garden slaves.
- **Classic southern ghetto** – After slavery was banished, newly-free blacks lived in small houses of poor quality on undesirable land, such as swampland or areas adjacent to industry or railroad tracks. The ghettos were far enough from white neighborhoods to maintain full spatial and social segregation.
- **Early northern ghetto** – As African Americans migrated to northern cities in the early 20th century, they competed with other groups for living space. They often ended up in high-density, deteriorating housing on the margins of the central business district.
- **Classic northern ghetto** – From their early centers, the black ghettos grew, often surrounding the CBD and penetrating nearby areas with low-rent housing. Their growth was shaped by white neighborhoods or suburbs that strongly resisted blacks moving into their areas. The resistance tended to make the ghettos overcrowded, further contributing to the deterioration of the housing.

Until the 1960s there were few legal regulations to curb racial discrimination that reinforced racial ghettos. Banks that loaned house buyers money clearly identified "risky" neighborhoods by **redlining** them and refusing to give out loans for houses there. This technique kept property values down in these ghettos and restricted the necessary flow of money for repairs and upkeep in the redlined neighborhoods. Another practice that insured racial segregation was **blockbusting,** when real estate agents would seek to sell a house in a white neighborhood to an African American for a very low price, and then use scare tactics to try to get white neighbors to sell. Real estate agents earned commissions, and neighborhoods rapidly transitioned to ghettos. Blockbusting became illegal in the 1960s, but was replaced by **racial steering,** an attempt to change ghetto boundaries by showing houses to blacks in white neighborhoods and to whites in black neighborhoods. All of these practices have eased with greater political oversight, but city neighborhoods still remain highly segregated.

TRANSPORTATION AND INFRASTRUCTURE

Infrastructure refers to all the facilities that support basic economic activities to such a degree that a city cannot function without them. Structures that specialize in support activities include banks, post offices, hotels, cable networks, television and radio stations, and other communications companies. A city's infrastructure includes its transportation systems, such as airports, roads, docks, railways, taxis, and intracity transit systems. In modern urban areas people are dependent on transportation systems for access to work, shopping, and leisure activities. More than half of the trips that people make are work related – commuting between work and home, business travel, or delivery services. Historically cities were forced into compact shapes until new forms of transportation were invented and built. The shapes of cities changed dramatically once streetcars, railroads, automobiles, subways, and airplanes made it possible for people to live further distances away from their places of work.

Some modern forms of transportation that impact the demographic layout and functions of cities include:

- **Motor vehicles** – People in the suburbs usually rely more on motor vehicles than railroads, especially in the United States. In the 19th century rail and trolley lines restricted housing development to areas within walking distance of the stations, but cars have permitted people to live in less restricted spaces. For people living outside cities in the United States, cars are a near necessity because public transportation facilities are often very limited. The U.S. government – national, state, and local levels – has encouraged car ownership by funding road building so that driving a car is usually the most efficient way to get from one place to another. Cities must allow for the large number of cars that go in and out, and the average city allocates about ¼ of its land to roads and parking lots. Multi-lane freeways cut huge swaths through the heart of cities, and elaborate interchanges consume even more space.
- **Public transportation** – In the United States public transportation systems other than roads for automobiles are much more common in cities than in suburban and rural areas. A large percentage of population movement in and out of and within cities takes place during **rush hours**, or the two-hour period in the morning when people are going to work and the two-hour period in the afternoon when they are coming home. In large cities, public transportation is more efficient than personal automobiles for moving people around because each traveler takes up far less space. Public transportation includes buses, trains, and subways. Despite the fact that most Americans still prefer to commute by car, public transportation is cheaper, less polluting, and more energy-efficient than the automobile. Buses have a declining number of passengers, but in recent years more U.S. cities have been adding heavy rail (subways) or fixed light rail (streetcars) to their infrastructure. Established systems, such as those in Boston, New York, and Chicago, have been expanding subway lines and improving service. New systems have been built in recent years in Atlanta, Washington, D.C., Baltimore, and Denver. In contrast to the United States, public transit is much more developed and funded by government in most European countries and Japan.

POLITICAL ORGANIZATION AND URBAN PLANNING

Over the past century, and particularly since World War II, governments have become more active in controlling land-use arrangements and growth patterns of most U.S. cities. National, state, and local governments have passed laws to restrict ways that property and city areas can be developed and used. In U.S. cities, emphasis has been on land-use planning, zoning ordinances, and building, health, and safety codes.

Zoning

Zoning ordinances, first developed in Europe and North America in the early 20th century, encourage spatial separation by preventing mixing of land uses within the same district. Usually they separate single-family houses, apartments, industry, and commerce into different areas because locating one activity near another is considered unhealthy and inefficient. One effect has been to make it difficult for poor residents to escape their neighborhoods, and some critics believe that zoning has reinforced class, racial, and ethnic lines in these countries. Bitter court battles have been waged, with mixed results, over zoning practices that restrict access to exclusive neighborhoods or business areas. Government actions are also criticized by business interests because they interfere with the market allocation of urban land.

In most of Asia there is no zoning, and it is quite common to have mixed neighborhoods, both by economic level and business vs. residential use. Often homes serve as businesses as well, with no interference by the government. In Europe and Japan, neighborhoods often contain a wide variety of building types from many different eras, all in close proximity. In the United States and Canada, such mixing is not nearly as common.

Local Government Fragmentation

Urban problems usually don't end with political borders, but tend to characterize the entire urban sprawl. Yet local governments are fragmented, with a city's local government operating separately from those of each of its suburbs. Even city governments are broken up, as is reflected in the fact that New York City has five mayors, one for each of its five boroughs. Chicago has 1,100 different local governments within its urban area. This fragmentation makes it very difficult to solve regional problems, such as traffic, solid waste disposal, and provisions of social services.

In recent years more metropolitan areas are calling for cooperation among local governments, with many forming **councils of government**, cooperative agencies consisting of representatives from local governments in the region. One example is the federation system formed in Toronto, Ontario, where local government has two layers. On the first layer, each of the six local governments is responsible for police and fire services and for tax collection. On the second layer is the Metropolitan Council, a regional government that sets the tax rate for the region as a whole, assesses property values, and manages money for new projects. Other services, such as transportation, parks, water, and sewage, are shared responsibilities. Another example is a consolidated metropolitan government, so that city and county boundaries match. Indianapolis has such consolidated governments, so that no differences exist between city and county governments.

Planning For Growth

On the state level in the United States, steps to curb sprawl, limit traffic congestion, and reverse inner-city decline have led to a movement called **smart growth.** The goal is to produce a pattern of controlled development, while protecting rural lands for agriculture, wildlife, and recreation. Smart growth legislation and regulations have been enacted in Maryland, Oregon, Tennessee, New Jersey, Rhode Island, and Washington. Some provisions have limited highway funding, and others have defined growth boundaries for new development and designated "urban growth areas."

Urban Renewal And Gentrification

Many cities have targeted blighted inner-city neighborhoods through **urban renewal** plans that allow the government to buy properties from the owners, relocate residents and businesses, clear the sites, and build new roads and utilities. The land is then turned over to private developers or to public agencies to construct new buildings and services. The national government has helped cities pay for urban renewal through federal grants. Often **public housing** – reserved for low-income households – has been built and funded by the federal government, but managed by a local government authority. In the United States the percentage of people that live in public housing is far less than in Britain, where more than one-third of all housing is publicly owned. In other countries in Western Europe, governments do not own the housing, but instead subsidize construction cost and rent for many privately built housing units.

Today many public-housing projects built in the United States and Europe during the 1950s and early 1960s are rapidly deteriorating. Because of poor living conditions, public-housing authorities have demolished high-rise public-housing projects, and have begun experimenting with construction of smaller buildings and/or dispersal of low-rent housing throughout the city. By 1980 the U.S. government had stopped funding construction of new public housing, although some federal money remained in place for renovation of public buildings and rent subsidy. The demolition of housing projects has sometimes been criticized because African Americans were most often the people displaced.

An alternative to demolishing deteriorated inner-city houses is to renovate them. Once housing in an area has been renovated, the neighborhood often begins to attract middle-class residents, a process called **gentrification.** Middle-class people are often drawn to these areas because they are conveniently located close to downtown where job opportunities, restaurants, and cultural opportunities abound. Others are attracted by older, substantially-built homes with architectural features and individual detail not available in newer houses in the suburbs. Cities often encourage gentrification by providing low-cost loans and tax breaks. These public expenditures are sometimes criticized as subsidies for the middle class at the expense of poor people, who are forced to move out because rents increase once gentrification begins. By law, cities must reimburse families forced to move both for moving expenses and for rent increases over a four-year period.

Suburbanization And Edge Cities

For many years cities expanded their borders as they grew by annexing nearby land. Suburbs in the United States began expanding before World War II as more people bought cars made more affordable by mass assembly-line production. Suburbs expanded rapidly in the post-World War II era, as demand for new homes grew, the interstate highway system improved, and the GI Bill of Rights provided government-sponsored loans for veterans to buy houses. The suburbs were linked to center cities by highway transportation, and few cities provided public transportation to their rapidly growing suburbs. As more people moved to the suburbs, businesses followed, with retailing increasingly concentrated in planned suburban shopping malls with plenty of space around them to build parking lots for cars. Chain stores, which had developed as early as the 1920s, filled these malls with shopping experiences and store architecture that were similar no matter where the malls were located. The availability and low cost of land in the suburbs eventually led to the construction of **megastores,** huge stores with a wide variety of products designed for one-stop shopping. Megastores organized as giant chains that first spread across the United States and eventually throughout the world.

Today U.S. cities have stopped their spatial growth because residents in outlying areas organize their own services rather than pay city taxes for them. These legally independent suburban areas may grow to become **edge cities**, defined by their own CBDs and other concentrations of office and commercial buildings that provide jobs for residents within their boundaries. Edge cities now exist in all regions of urbanized Anglo America. Chauncy Harris – creator of the multiple nuclei model – describes the formation of edge cities through his **peripheral model,** an urban area consisting of an inner city surrounded by large suburban residential and business areas. The parts of the city are often connected by a beltway or ring road. As the distance increases from the center of the city, the density of residents and houses decreases, a change called the **density gradient.**

The progressive development of landscape in the suburban areas (called **sprawl)** allows people to have larger houses and more land, but it also brings problems. The cost of new roads and utilities often leads to higher taxes and home prices. Sprawl is criticized for wasting agricultural land as well as energy, since automobiles must burn fuel for transporting residents to their jobs long distances away from their homes. In Europe, the supply of land for construction of new housing is more restricted than in the U.S., so many cities surround themselves with **greenbelts,** or rings of open space where houses may not be built. Despite the fact that greenbelts preserve land, they tend to drive house prices up in the cities that they protect.

COMPARATIVE URBANIZATION

As megacities have multiplied all around the world, hundreds of cities now number their inhabitants in the millions. As a result, the North American and European models for urban patterns are today often difficult to apply to cities in Africa, Asia, and Latin America. In many areas that were once colonized, Western styles and layouts are still apparent, but in today's postcolonial megacities, the patterns have been altered by modernization and immigration, so that they have been transformed. In response to these changes, geographers have developed regional models that more accurately reflect the spatial arrangements of urban areas.

European Cities

As in the United States, the upper-class residential areas cluster around a sector that extends out from the CBD. In many cases these clusters date back many centuries, as in Paris, where the rich moved to the southwestern hills to be near the king's palace. European cities are different from most U.S. cities because wealthy Europeans are more likely to live close to center city, not just in the suburbs. Here they live in elegant, older residences that are carefully and expensively restored to their former splendor. Because they don't have large private yards, Europeans frequent public parks that also have deep historical roots. Many wealthy Europeans have weekend homes in rural areas out from the cities, causing an exodus from the cities on Fridays, with all returning on Sunday nights.

In the past, poor people also lived in the central European city. As cities expanded with the Industrial Revolution, housing for workers was constructed in areas near the factories and away from the rich. Now most poor people live on the outskirts of the cities. Many live in high-rise apartment buildings and have long commutes by public transportation to reach jobs and other attractions in the center city. Many European suburbs are centers for crime, violence, and drug dealing, and the residents are often recent immigrants from Africa or Asia who face discrimination and prejudice in the larger society.

Latin American Cities

Latin American cities are growing faster than those in most other areas of the world. Ernst Griffin and Larry Ford have devised a model that blends traditional elements of Latin American culture with forces of modernization that are changing them rapidly. The central business district is the main focus of business, employment, and entertainment, just as it is in the North American models, but it is divided into a market sector, where old-fashioned markets are set up; and a high rise sector, where more modern businesses are headquartered. From this area, a commercial spine radiates away from the city, and is surrounded by the elite residential sector. This corridor includes upper-end restaurants, theaters, parks, and golf course, and it leads to a mall, or an edge city.

The remaining concentric zones are residential areas for the poor and the middle class. Socioeconomic levels and housing quality decrease as distance from the center city increases. Closer in are the middle classes, who form a "zone of maturity" where they generally maintain their homes well enough to keep them from deteriorating. They are ringed by a zone *"in situ accretion"* that contains much more modest housing and transitions to the outer-ring poverty. The **disamenity sector** is a relatively stable slum area that radiates from the central market to the outermost zone of peripheral squatter settlements consists of high-density shantytowns.

The African City

Cities in Africa are shaped by the fact that many are located in the periphery of the world system, as described by Wallerstein (p. 167). Many of the cities are huge, and they are characterized by squatter settlements on their outskirts. However, Africa is a diverse continent with many different geographical and historical influences, so it is difficult to formulate a model of African cities. Cities in the north are influenced heavily by Islamic traditions, with a mosque at the center, with a nearby marketplace or bazaar, which serves as the commercial core. Government buildings and the homes of wealthy families surround the commercial core. Narrow streets lead from the core to neighborhoods of the less wealthy located farther from the core. Cities in South Africa are essentially Western, since they were colonized and built by Europeans. The largest city in Africa is Lagos, Nigeria, which is rapidly growing into a world-class megacity. Lagos presently is a confused landscape of shanty developments

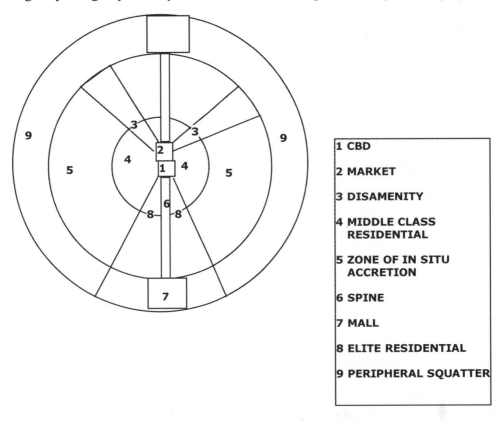

1 CBD
2 MARKET
3 DISAMENITY
4 MIDDLE CLASS RESIDENTIAL
5 ZONE OF IN SITU ACCRETION
6 SPINE
7 MALL
8 ELITE RESIDENTIAL
9 PERIPHERAL SQUATTER

A Model of Latin American City Structure. This model combines the concentric zone and sector models, but it differs from the North American models partly because the outermost ring consists of a ring of low-income people living in shantytowns. Middle class residents are close to the center city, whereas in North American cities, they often live in the suburbs.

with no running water or sewers that coexist with areas of modern high-rise buildings, paved streets, and modern facilities. Near its harbor are older, lower buildings, mixed with government facilities and residences.

One model of Sub-Saharan cities indicates that the central city often consists of three CBDs: the remains of the colonial CBD, an informal open-air market zone, and a transitional business center where business is conducted in less transitory, but somewhat makeshift, buildings, stalls, or storefronts. Residential zones based on ethnicity ring the CBDs, and, like Latin American cities, the outermost ring tends to be squatter settlements.

Asian Cities

Many large cities of Asia were founded and developed by Europeans, so they often follow the European model, but the spatial arrangements vary by region. The large Southeast Asian city is centered on a port, usually developed by European colonialists. Around the port is a Western-style central business district with European shops, hotels, and restaurants, and one or more "alien commercial zones" where merchants from other areas (such as China or India) have established themselves. Out from this center is a widespread zone of mixed residences, businesses, and light industries, with central slums and peripheral squatter zones housing the majority of the city's population. Market gardening and recent industrial development mark the outer metropolitan limits. The South Asian city may take two forms: colonial based with clearly segregated neighborhoods and businesses for natives and for Europeans, or the traditional city centered on a bazaar or marketplace from pre-colonial times.

Many parts of Asia are still on the periphery of the world system, but others – such as Hong Kong, Singapore, and Shanghai – are quite central to world trade. Asia's urban growth is explosive, with millions of people migrating from rural areas to the cities every year. China has nearly tripled its urban population since the late 1970s, and the government has adopted policies encouraging the growth of intermediate-sized cities to disperse urbanization. Today many of those secondary cities have populations in the millions.

Urbanization is a global phenomenon that presents challenges to modern citizens and governments. Although cities have been part of human geography for thousands of years, only in the past century have they become the home of the majority of people in the industrialized world. Today the developing world is also rapidly urbanizing, with cities generally struggling to keep up with demands for jobs, housing, safe water, sanitation, and other services and facilities.

TERMS AND CONCEPTS

base ratio
basic, nonbasic sectors
Burgess, E.W.
Bosnywash
census tract
central business district (CBD)
center city
central place theory
Christaller, Walter
city
city-state

complementary regions
concentric zone model
councils of government
disamenity sector
edge cities
export activities
feminization of poverty
formative era
gentrification
ghettos, ghettoization
greenbelts
hamlet
Harris and Ullman
hierarchy of central places
Hoyt, Homer
infrastructure
in situ accretion
manufacturing city
megacity
megalopolis
megastores
mercantile city
metropolitan area
metropolitan statistical area
micropolitan statistical area
multiple-nuclei model
multiplier effect
nucleated
peripheral model
physical city
primate cities
public housing
rank-size rule
rush hours
sector model
settlement geography
smart growth
social area analysis
special-function cities
sprawl
states
suburbs
town
transportation centers
urban area
urban elite
urban empire

urban geography
urban hierarchy
urban influence zone
urban renewal
Wirth, Louis
world city
zone in transition
zone of maturity
zoning ordinances

UNIT SEVEN MULTIPLE-CHOICE QUESTIONS

(Questions 1 and 2 are based on the following model):

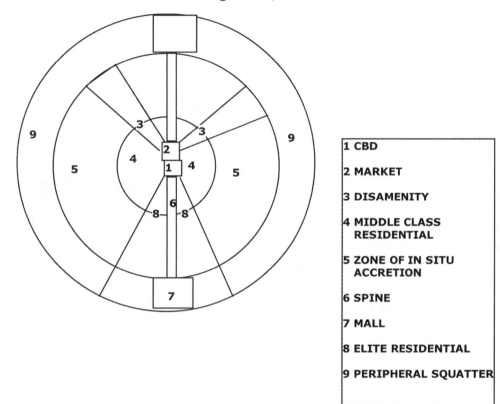

| 1 CBD |
| 2 MARKET |
| 3 DISAMENITY |
| 4 MIDDLE CLASS RESIDENTIAL |
| 5 ZONE OF IN SITU ACCRETION |
| 6 SPINE |
| 7 MALL |
| 8 ELITE RESIDENTIAL |
| 9 PERIPHERAL SQUATTER |

1. The model above reflects the structure of cities in

   (A) North America
   (B) Latin America
   (C) Africa
   (D) Asia
   (E) Europe

2. The model is influenced by

   (A) the concentric zone model only
   (B) the sector model only
   (C) a combination of the sector and multiple nuclei models
   (D) a combination of the multiple nuclei and peripheral models
   (E) a combination of concentric zone and sector models

3. Chauncy Harris's peripheral model is focused on describing a central city in relation to

   (A) surrounding edge cities
   (B) residential neighborhoods
   (C) surrounding rural areas
   (D) manufacturing areas
   (E) zones of transition

4. In contrast to a country with a primate city, a country whose cities follow the rank-size rule is more likely to have

   (A) wealth concentrated in urban areas
   (B) fewer cultural centers
   (C) more equality between urban and rural living standards
   (D) unequal living standards between larger and smaller cities
   (E) a smaller overall population

5. The growth of the earliest cities in world history was made possible primarily by the development of

   (A) job specialization
   (B) large concentrated populations
   (C) governments capable of control
   (D) the ability of farmers to raise a surplus
   (E) diversification of villages

6. Today many U.S. cities have stopped their spatial growth primarily because

   (A) many people are moving from urban to rural areas
   (B) residents in outlying areas organize their own services rather than pay city taxes for them
   (C) geographic barriers do not permit further development
   (D) infrastructure expenses have overwhelmed many city governments
   (E) they are responding to demands for more greenbelts

7. The primary reason that more women than men live in or near central cities is the

   (A) feminization of poverty
   (B) growing number of employment opportunities for women
   (C) superior level of city services that meet family needs
   (D) gentrification of many urban neighborhoods
   (E) lack of available housing in the suburbs

8. Christaller's central place model is least likely to be applicable to

(A) rural areas
(B) special-function cities
(C) regions with multiple towns
(D) multi-function cities
(E) regions where people have similar life styles and incomes

9. Which of the following is a correct statement about the megacities of the world?

(A) The largest by far is New York-Newark.
(B) Most are either in North America or Europe.
(C) None are in Latin America.
(D) Megacities are located in many parts of the world.
(E) The largest megacities are located in China.

10. The spatial design of cities in northern Africa is influenced heavily by

(A) European traditions, with a cathedral at the center
(B) a historical aversion to trade
(C) Islamic traditions, with a mosque at the center
(D) trading patterns with Sub-Saharan Africa
(E) traditional governments, with palaces for monarchs at the center

11. Which of the following was the first model of urban land use to be developed?

(A) Burgess's concentric zone model
(B) Hoyt's sector model
(C) Harris and Ullman's multiple-nuclei model
(D) Harris's peripheral model
(E) Griffin and Ford's Latin American model

12. Which of the following was one of the original urban hearth regions?

(A) the Mississippi River Valley
(B) Indus River Valley
(C) Rome
(D) France
(E) South Africa

13. The smallest, least complex type of settlement in the urban hierarchy is the

(A) farm
(B) village
(C) town
(D) hamlet
(E) suburb

14. All of the following were factors that encouraged suburban growth in the United States after World War II EXCEPT:

(A) more affordable automobiles
(B) the GI Bill of Rights
(C) public transportation systems that were built in most cities
(D) better roads and highways
(E) construction of megastores and malls

15. Which of the following is the best example of a central place with a large hinterland?

(A) Minneapolis
(B) Buffalo
(C) Fort Worth
(D) Tampa
(E) Denver

16. In the United States, neighborhoods are divided into areas of approximately 5,000 people that are called

(A) census tracts
(B) basic sectors
(C) complementary regions
(D) edge cities
(E) greenbelts

17. Which of the following is NOT a defining characteristic of a world city?

(A) important stock exchanges
(B) a non-polarized social structure
(C) concentrations of business services
(D) concentrations of cultural offerings
(E) national and international seats of political power

18. During the course of the 19th century, the growth of cities in the United States became increasingly dependent on access to

(A) navigable waterways
(B) water power
(C) shorelines
(D) railroad transportation
(E) highway transportation

19. Which of the following describes the growth of a city in a series of wedges out from the central business center?

(A) Burgess's concentric zone theory
(B) Christaller's central place theory
(C) Harris and Ullman's multiple nuclei theory
(D) core periphery model
(E) Hoyt's sector model

20. As a city grows, it usually experiences an increase in the size of its

(A) basic sector
(B) manufacturing areas
(C) nonbasic sector
(D) export activities
(E) deglomeration

21. The rank-size rule and Christaller's central place theory both are important theories that help explain

(A) settlement geography
(B) rural land use
(C) patterns of urban planning
(D) comparative urbanization
(E) the urban hierarchy

22. Which of the following is least likely to live close to a city center?

(A) unmarried young professional
(B) young married couple without children
(C) one-parent family headed by a female
(D) older married couple
(E) young family with children

23. Which of the following settlement types is likely to use the largest percentage of land space for residences?

(A) town
(B) suburb
(C) physical city
(D) hamlet
(E) village

24. Which of the following types of cities was created by the Industrial Revolution?

(A) city-state
(B) mercantile city
(C) manufacturing city
(D) primate city
(E) megacity

25. All the facilities that support basic economic activities to such a degree that a city cannot function without them is called the

(A) base ratio
(B) hierarchy of central places
(C) sprawl
(D) infrastructure
(E) urban influence zone

UNIT SEVEN FREE-RESPONSE QUESTION

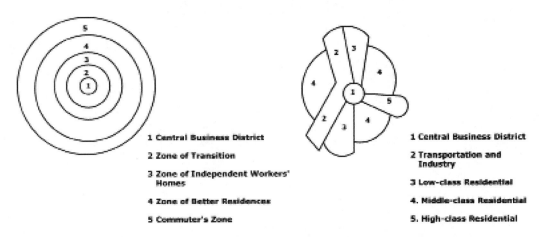

1 Central Business District

2 Zone of Transition

3 Zone of Independent Workers' Homes

4 Zone of Better Residences

5 Commuter's Zone

1 Central Business District

2 Transportation and Industry

3 Low-class Residential

4. Middle-class Residential

5. High-class Residential

The two models above provide explanations for urban land use.

a. Identify the model on the left. Identify the model on the right.

b. Explain two similarities between the two models.

c. Explain two differences between the two models.

SECTION II:
SAMPLE EXAMINATIONS

This section includes two full sample examinations. Each exam has 75 multiple choice questions and 3 free-response questions.

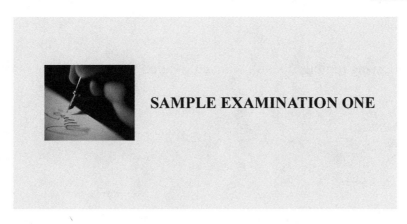

SAMPLE EXAMINATION ONE

Section I: Multiple-Choice Questions
Allow 60 minutes for these 75 questions.

1. Which of the following is an accurate statement about population distribution on a global scale?

(A) About half of all people live north of the equator; about half live south of the equator.
(B) More than half of all people live on about 5% of the land.
(C) Almost 9/10 of all people live on about 10% of the land
(D) Most people live in areas that are more than 1000 feet above sea level.
(E) In the past, most people lived near oceans or river valleys, but this is no longer true.

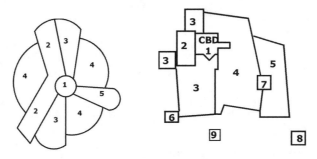

Hoyt's Model   Harris and Ullman's Model

2. In contrast to Hoyt's model of urban land use, Harris and Ullman's model

(A) does not differentiate urban neighborhoods according to social class
(B) has more than one center of urban growth
(C) shows that cities develop in a series of sectors
(D) includes a zone in transition
(E) describes the central city's relationship to edge cities

3. Geographers usually categorize cultural diffusion into the two broad categories of

(A) expansion diffusion and relocation diffusion
(B) contagious diffusion and stimulus diffusion
(C) migrant diffusion and hierarchical diffusion
(D) expansion diffusion and hierarchical diffusion
(E) relocation diffusion and migrant diffusion

4. In which of the following regions does shifting cultivation produce manioc, sweet potatoes, yams, and beans?

(A) central North America
(B) southwestern Africa
(C) central Asia
(D) northern South America
(E) Southeast Asia

5. Wallerstein's model of the capital world economy is based most directly on

(A) modernization theory
(B) dependency theory
(C) self-sufficiency theory
(D) locational theory
(E) central place theory

6. An example of a stateless nation in the Middle East is provided by the

(A) Egyptians
(B) Turks
(C) Kurds
(D) Iraqis
(E) Syrians

7. Which of the following is a disadvantage of a map based on the Mercator projection?

(A) Shapes of land masses in the middle latitudes are greatly distorted.
(B) South America and Africa appear to be much larger than they really are.
(C) Land masses in the southern hemisphere appear to be much smaller than they really are.
(D) True direction is difficult to determine.
(E) Sizes of areas, especially those close to the North and South Poles, are greatly exaggerated.

8. Which of the following is a limitation to the usefulness of arithmetic density for population studies?

(A) It does not calculate density by dividing the total number of people by total land area.
(B) It does not include rural areas in its calculations.
(C) It gives us only a broad idea about the strain the population puts on the land area.
(D) It includes only arable land in its calculations.
(E) It takes into account natural resources but not carrying capacity.

9. Which of the following directly challenges Alfred Weber's least cost theory?

   (A) substitution principle
   (B) space-time compression
   (C) value-added productivity
   (D) sustainable development
   (E) location theory

10. Demographic transition theory is concerned with which of the following concepts?

   (A) population growth
   (B) economic development
   (C) migration patterns
   (D) territoriality
   (E) core-periphery relations

11. Which of the following is an accurate comparison of subsistence and commercial agriculture?

   (A) A larger percentage of people in less developed countries are subsistence farmers.
   (B) The use of machinery is equally important for subsistence and commercial agriculture.
   (C) New breeds of plants and animals are more important for subsistence agriculture than for commercial agriculture.
   (D) Average farm sizes for subsistence agriculture are much larger than for commercial agriculture.
   (E) The total percentage of land space devoted to farming is much larger in countries where subsistence agriculture is practiced.

12. The type of culture that emphasizes artifacts is called

   (A) non-material culture
   (B) a culture system
   (C) a culture trait
   (D) a cultural hearth
   (E) material culture

13. Which of the following is a fragmented state?

   (A) Hungary
   (B) Thailand
   (C) Chile
   (D) South Africa
   (E) Indonesia

14. According to the U.S. Bureau of Statistics, a central county or counties with at least one urbanized area of at least 50,000 people, plus adjacent outlying counties with a large number of resident that commute in is called a

(A) megalopolis
(B) physical city
(C) nucleated settlement
(D) metropolitan statistical area
(E) primate city

15. Which of the following was one of the first geographers to accurately calculate the circumference of the earth?

(A) Eratosthenes
(B) Ptolemy
(C) Idrisi
(D) George Perkins Marsh
(E) Carl Sauer

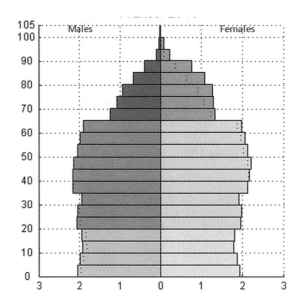

16. The population pyramid above reflects the population distribution of

(A) the United States
(B) Afghanistan
(C) Iran
(D) France
(E) India

17. In comparison to primary industry, secondary industry is less dependent on

   (A) transportation lines
   (B) labor costs
   (C) resource location
   (D) friction of distance
   (E) energy costs

18. The form of plant cultivation in which new plants are produced by direct cloning from existing plants is called

   (A) shifting cultivation
   (B) vegetative agriculture
   (C) seed agriculture
   (D) horticulture
   (E) labor intensive agriculture

19. The practice of judging another culture by the standards of one's own culture is called

   (A) cultural relativism
   (B) syncretism
   (C) ethnocentrism
   (D) acculturation
   (E) cultural transmission

20. Which of the following types of terrain is most likely to serve as shatter belts?

   (A) desert
   (B) shoreline
   (C) mountains
   (D) peninsula
   (E) river valley

21. The main reason that Nigeria moved its capital from Lagos to Abuja was to try to resolve differences between

(A) native Nigerians and Europeans
(B) the Muslim north and the Christian south
(C) American businessmen and Nigerian political leaders
(D) those who support international trade and those who don't
(E) populists and conservatives

22. By about 1000 C. E., all of the following were major cities in the world EXCEPT:

(A) London
(B) Constantinople
(C) Baghdad
(D) Kyoto
(E) Chang'an

23. The phenomenon of distance decay helps to explain the tendency for people to

(A) reject intervening opportunities when presented
(B) stay fairly close to home when they migrate
(C) choose cities as their destinations
(D) make international moves when they are young
(E) move away from an area when a new group begins to move in

24. The concept of territoriality is most central to the study of

(A) political geography
(B) urban geography
(C) cultural geography
(D) demography
(E) physical geography

25. Two examples of extensive subsistence agriculture are

(A) hunting and gathering and mixed crop agriculture
(B) lowland rice farming and pastoral nomadism
(C) shifting cultivation and pastoral nomadism
(D) intertillage and crop rotation
(E) grain farming and dairy farming

26. The country where the Industrial Revolution first began was

(A) Britain
(B) the United States
(C) Germany
(D) Italy
(E) Japan

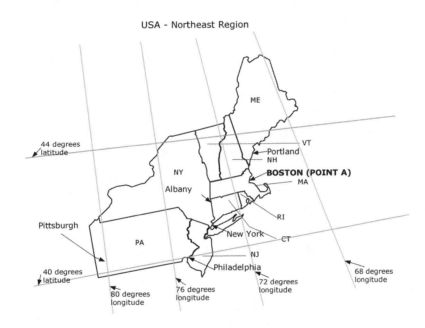

USA - Northeast Region

27. Which of the following is NOT illustrated in the map above?

(A) Point A's absolute location
(B) Point A's distance from the prime meridian
(C) Point A's distance from the North Pole
(D) Point A's distance from the South Pole
(E) Point A's relative location

28. Linguistic geographers map the area in which particular words are spoken, marking their limits as

(A) isoglosses
(B) toponyms
(C) artifacts
(D) dialects
(E) diasporas

29. Which of the following people is most likely to have the largest activity space?

   (A) an 8-year old boy who lives in the suburbs
   (B) an older man who has retired
   (C) a young professional woman who lives in an urban center
   (D) a middle age man who lives in a suburb
   (E) a middle age woman who lives in a rural area

30. The main purpose of gerrymandering is usually to

   (A) assert the power of the legislative over the executive branch
   (B) create congressional districts of approximately equal size
   (C) improve the chances of the dominant political party in the state to win seats in the legislature
   (D) challenge the authority of the courts to weigh in on political questions
   (E) improve the ratio of representatives to citizens in order to better serve constituents

31. Which of the following is an accurate statement regarding urban growth in the world today?

   (A) Cities are large and growing in developed countries, but less developed countries have few cities.
   (B) Urban growth in Latin America has been greater than urban growth in Africa.
   (C) The percentage of people living in urban areas in Africa and Asia is larger than the percentage living in urban areas in Europe and North America.
   (D) In most areas of the world, manufacturing cities are growing faster than mercantile cities are.
   (E) The proportion of people living in cities is rising in most countries.

32. The "world's breadbasket" is a name most commonly given to the

   (A) pampas region of South America
   (B) hilly region around the Mediterranean Sea
   (C) farming areas of the southeastern United States
   (D) prairies of North America
   (E) farming areas of northern China

33. As oil and natural gas became important sources of energy during the mid-20th century, new economic power was vested in oil and gas-producing countries such as

   (A) Saudi Arabia, Peru, and Japan
   (B) Kuwait, Egypt, and Australia
   (C) Iran, Russia, and Britain
   (D) Iran, Mexico, and Nigeria
   (E) Argentina, China, and Mongolia

34. The system that measures the position of an object on earth and stores different types of information about it in layers is called a

(A) physical landscape
(B) GPS
(C) map projection
(D) GIS
(E) space-time prism

35. Chain migration is most directly encouraged by

(A) step migration
(B) awareness space
(C) higher education levels
(D) dislocation
(E) kinship and friendship ties

36. The main purpose of the Security Council of the United Nations is to

(A) represent the democratic will of the member-states
(B) provide social and cultural benefits
(C) regulate global monetary policies
(D) adjudicate quarrels between citizens of different countries
(E) establish peacekeeping forces in "hotspots" around the world

37. Examples of modern lingua franco languages are

(A) Latin, Spanish, and English
(B) Mandarin Chinese, Spanish, and French
(C) Russian, Hindustani, and Mandarin Chinese
(D) Hindustani, German, and French
(E) Russian, English, and Swahili

38. Which of the following is NOT generally categorized as a newly-industrializing country today?

(A) Mexico
(B) South Korea
(C) Singapore
(D) Nigeria
(E) Taiwan

39. Which of the following agricultural products are most often associated with truck farming?

(A) milk and bread
(B) apples and lettuce
(C) grapes and cotton
(D) beef and chicken
(E) tobacco and coffee

40. The basic sector of a city's economy consists of

(A) goods and services produced for residents of the city itself
(B) special functions in mining, manufacturing, and recreation
(C) goods and services produced for areas outside the city
(D) functions that support the city's infrastructure
(E) functions that shape the urban influence zones of a city

41. Which of the following are areas that people believe to exist as part of their cultural identity?

(A) formal regions
(B) uniform regions
(C) functional regions
(D) perceptual regions
(E) nodal regions

42. According to the rank-size rule, if the largest city in a country has a population os 1,000,000, the 5th largest city will have a population of

(A) 500,000
(B) 400,000
(C) 300,000
(D) 200,000
(E) 100,000

43. The housing styles pictures above originated during the 17th century in

(A) southern England
(B) Scotland
(C) France
(D) the southern United States
(E) New England

44. The combination of natural change and net migration to summarize population change over time is called

(A) the epidemiologic transition
(B) demographic momentum
(C) demographic equation
(D) the gravity model
(E) spatial interaction

45. Footloose industries have negligible total costs for

(A) transportation of both resources and finished products
(B) finished products
(C) parts
(D) labor
(E) management

46. According to von Thünen's model of land use, the outermost ring is characterized by

(A) suburban living
(B) slums
(C) extensive agriculture
(D) dairy farming
(E) edge cities

47. In which of the following ways did the early southern ghetto differ from other ghetto models?

(A) B;acks tended to live nearby the white communities.
(B) Spatial and social segregation was complete.
(C) Blacks lived in high-density, deteriorating housing on the margins of the central business district.
(D) Whites strongly resisted blacks moving into their areas.
(E) Ghettos were overcrowded, contributing to the deterioration of the housing.

48. Which of the following religions have direct roots in Judaism?

(A) Daoism and Christianity
(B) Christianity and Islam
(C) Sikhism and Islam
(D) Hinduism and Eastern Orthodoxy
(E) Shintoism and shamanism

49. If a traveler crosses the International Date Line going from America to Asia, (s)he will set the time

(A) 12 hours ahead
(B) 24 hours ahead
(C) 48 hours ahead
(D) 12 hours back
(E) 24 hours back

50. The two most populous countries in the world that have actively applied restrictive population policies are

(A) China and India
(B) the United States and Japan
(C) Russia and China
(D) India and the United States
(E) Mexico and Russia

51. The phenomenon of space-time compression has been most directly promoted by

(A) social development
(B) modernization
(C) globalization
(D) value added productivity
(E) irredentism

52. Which of the following accurately compares urban transportation systems in the United States to those in western Europe and Japan?

(A) The U.S. government provides more funding for urban transportation systems than governments in European countries and Japan do.
(B) U.S. cities are more likely to have subway lines, whereas European and Japanese cities are more likely to have buses.
(C) Public transit is much more developed and funded by governments in most European countries and Japan.
(D) People in European and Japanese suburbs are much more dependent on motor vehicles than are people who live in the suburban U.S.
(E) The percentage of people who travel by bus is much higher in the U.S. than in Europe or Japan.

53. Wet mud mixed with straw is one form of building with

(A) wood
(B) wattle
(C) stone
(D) bricks
(E) plant products

54. Which of the following is generally encouraged by folk cultures?

(A) cultural diversity
(B) uniform landscapes
(C) increased demand for natural resources
(D) increased pollution
(E) large numbers of chain stores

55. All of the following are secondary industrial regions in the world today EXCEPT:

(A) Brazil
(B) Eastern Asia
(C) South Africa
(D) Ganges River area of India
(E) southern Australia

56. The British economist who was the first critic to note that the world's population was increasing faster than the food supplies was

(A) Ernst Ravenstein
(B) Alfred Weber
(C) Immanuel Wallerstein
(D) George Perkins Marsh
(E) Thomas Malthus

57. The main purpose of zoning ordinances is to

(A) support the development of a city's infrastructure
(B) prevent mixing of land uses within the same district
(C) insure racial desegregation
(D) promote smart growth
(E) promote gentrification

58. The map above illustrates

(A) important North American milksheds
(B) the "world's breadbasket"
(C) the core North American manufacturing belt
(D) areas where manufacturing spread during the 20th century from its North American origins
(E) concentrations of multi-lingual Americans

59. Which of the following best describes a recent global trend in domestic politics?

(A) movement toward two-party systems
(B) more power centered in the head of the executive branch
(C) movement toward market economies
(D) fewer internal nationality problems
(E) revival of communist ideologies

60. A countertrend to fragmentation in global interactions today is

(A) globalization
(B) democratic consolidation
(C) corporatism
(D) radicalism
(E) privatization

61. Nucleated settlement patterns are most likely to result in the formation of many

(A) mid-sized cities
(B) large cities
(C) towns
(D) hamlets
(E) megacities

62. The three major branches of Christianity in the world today are

(A) Baptist, Roman Catholic, and Methodist
(B) Roman Catholic, Eastern Orthodox, and Episcopalian
(C) Protestant, Eastern Orthodox, and Pentecostal
(D) Roman Catholic, Protestant, and Eastern Orthodox
(E) Baptist, Methodist, and Presbyterian

63. Which of the following countries has the largest percentage of people who live in public housing?

(A) the United States
(B) France
(C) Mexico
(D) Germany
(E) Britain

64. Which of the following areas of the world currently have net in-migration?

(A) Latin America and Asia
(B) Australia and Africa
(C) Latin America and Europe
(D) Europe and Asia
(E) North America and Australia

65. Like the earliest industrial heartlands in Europe, the earliest industrial heartland in the Northeast District of China centered on the region's

(A) access to seaports
(B) coal and iron deposits
(C) political stability
(D) access to rapidly moving rivers
(E) supply of skilled labor

66. Which of the following is an example of a centrifugal force within a nation-state?

(A) a separatist movement that demands independence
(B) a strong national economy
(C) ethnic homogeneity
(D) a strong sense of nationalism
(E) economic equality among regions

242 SAMPLE EXAMINATION ONE

67. Which of the ten major languages shown on the map above has the fewest number of people who speak it as a first language?

(A) English
(B) Spanish
(C) German
(D) Hindi
(E) Mandarin Chinese

68. As the distance increases from the center of the city, the density of residents and houses decreases, a change called the

(A) base ratio
(B) density gradient
(C) complementary effect
(D) multiplier effect
(E) urban hierarchy

69. Currently, the three most important trading blocs in the world are

(A) the European Union, the Middle East, and North America
(B) East Asia, South Asia, and North America
(C) North America, the European Union, and East Asia
(D) South Asia, North America, and South America
(E) Central Asia, Northern Africa, and the Middle East

70. The metes and bounds land survey system is most likely to make use of

(A) rivers
(B) roads
(C) natural features
(D) rectangular grids
(E) primogeniture

71. Push and pull factors explain reasons why people

(A) adopt cultural beliefs
(B) migrate
(C) create cultural landscapes
(D) try to promote sustainable development
(E) seek to form political states based on nationalism

72. Which of the following religions has the second largest number of adherents (after Christianity) in the world today?

(A) Hinduism
(B) Buddhism
(C) Judaism
(D) Islam
(E) Chinese traditional

73. Which of the following countries currently is NOT a member of the EU?

(A) Portugal
(B) Greece
(C) Hungary
(D) Lithuania
(E) Croatia

74. One important goal of smart growth is to

(A) produce more nutritious food
(B) stimulate the growth of suburbs
(C) encourage the growth of a city's basic sector
(D) limit overall population growth
(E) curb urban sprawl

75. The Columbian Exchange vastly changed global trading patterns as a result of the

(A) industrialization of countries in Asia and Africa
(B) Neolithic Revolution
(C) Green Revolution
(D) first sustained contacts between the Western and Eastern Hemisphere
(E) first demographic transition

Section II - Free-response Questions
Allow 75 minutes for these three questions.

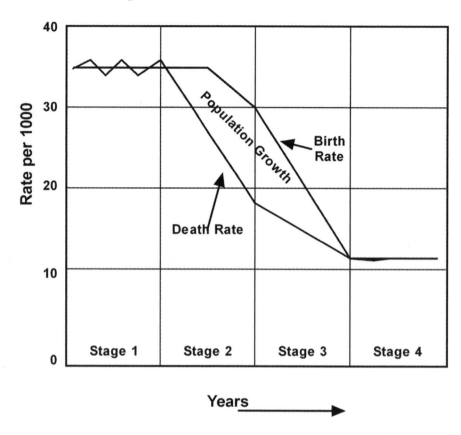

1. The chart above illustrates the stages of population growth, according to the demographic transition theory.

   a. Briefly explain demographic transition theory.

   b. Describe the population pattern that occurs in Stage 2, and explain one reason why that pattern occurs.

   c. Describe the population pattern that occurs in stage 4, and explain one reason why that pattern occurs.

2. Burgess's model and Hoyt's model were created to explain different land uses within cities.

   a. Describe Burgess's model, and describe three zones that exist within this model.

   b. Describe Hoyt's model, and explain one similarity and one difference between Hoyt's model and Burgess's model.

   c. Explain one way that the process of invasion and succession illustrates BOTH models.

3. Several secondary industrial regions lie south of the world's primary industrial region.

a. Identify two of the world's secondary industrial regions.

b. For each region you identified in part a, explain one reason specific to the region for recent industrial growth.

c. Define the term, "international division of labor," and explain how it has stimulated industrial growth in ONE of the regions you identified in part a.

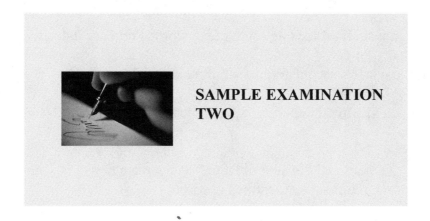

SAMPLE EXAMINATION TWO

1. In contrast to wealthy Americans, wealthy Europeans are more likely to live in

   (A) rural areas
   (B) inland cities
   (C) single-family homes
   (D) suburban areas
   (E) areas close to center city

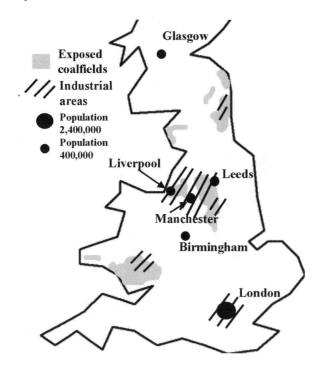

2. The map above shows industrial Britain by about

   (A) 1750
   (B) 1800
   (C) 1850
   (D) 1900
   (E) 1950

3. If a country has an arithmetic density of 78 and a physiological density of 3500, it most likely has

  (A) a very small population
  (B) a very large population
  (C) a high carrying capacity
  (D) little arable land
  (E) very few cities

4. The branch of Buddhism with the largest number of adherents is

  (A) Theraveda
  (B) Tantrayana
  (C) Baha'i
  (D) Shinto
  (E) Mahayana

5. Which of the following effects does the practice of primogeniture generally have on land settlement patterns?

  (A) It encourages nucleated settlement patterns.
  (B) It encourages settlement close to rivers and lakes.
  (C) It often results in large land parcels that are tended individually.
  (D) It divides land into narrow parcels that extend from major roads.
  (E) It encourages settlement in large urban areas.

6. Which of the following is NOT true of edge cities?

  (A) They have their own central business districts.
  (B) They generally have few transportation connections to older inner cities.
  (C) They often organize their own services rather than pay city taxes for them.
  (D) They often have businesses that provide jobs for residents within their boundaries.
  (E) They exist is most areas of urbanized Anglo America.

7. Which of the following pairs of countries are both multicore states?

  (A) Japan and the United States
  (B) France and Japan
  (C) Nigeria and the United States
  (D) France and Nigeria
  (E) France and the United States

8. The geographical perspective is distinct from that of other fields in its emphasis on

  (A) spatial analysis
  (B) cultural traditions
  (C) political relationships
  (D) urban lifestyles
  (E) sustainable development

9. Industry shapes economic activities that make up the

(A) primary sector
(B) secondary sector
(C) tertiary sector
(D) quaternary sector
(E) basic sector

10. The fiddle was featured at dances, and fife-and-drum bands were popular in the early years of the Republic in the

(A) Northern song area
(B) Southern song area
(C) Appalachian song area
(D) Western song area
(E) Black Song Style Family

11. Wattle building most commonly occurs in

(A) northern China, Mexico, and the Middle East
(B) Southeast Asia, Africa, and the Amazonian River Basin
(C) the Andes Mountains, Middle America, and the South Sea Islands
(D) Europe, North America, and Russia
(E) southern China, India, and central Asia

12. Which of the following developed an important model that explained different land uses within cities?

(A) E.W. Burgess
(B) Walter Christaller
(C) George Perkins Marsh
(D) W.W. Rostow
(E) Carl Sauer

13. Which of the following countries are majority Shiite?

(A) Turkey and Syria
(B) Iraq and Jordan
(C) Iraq and Iran
(D) Saudi Arabia and Qatar
(E) Iran and Saudi Arabia

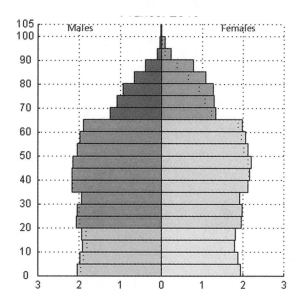

14. The country represented by the population pyramid above is most likely characterized by

   (A) inadequate health care for the elderly
   (B) ready access to birth control
   (C) high death rates for women in childbirth
   (D) persistent warfare
   (E) low rates of heart disease and cancer

15. Which of the following is a model of economic development that suggests that any country that wants its economy to grow should study the paths taken by industrialized nations and follow them?

   (A) modernization model
   (B) dependency theory
   (C) self sufficiency model
   (D) substitution principle
   (E) location theory

16. The ability of a state to carry out actions or policies within its borders independently from interference either from the inside or the outside is called

   (A) territoriality
   (B) integration
   (C) irredentism
   (D) devolution
   (E) sovereignty

17. Which of the following is the best explanation for why one parent households are more likely than two parent households to live near central cities?

(A) less need for physical space
(B) ghettoization
(C) the feminization of poverty
(D) more reliance by one parent households on automobile transportation
(E) cultural attractions of the city

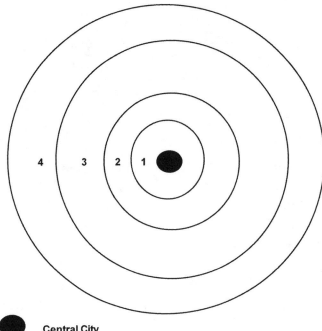

⬤   **Central City**

1   **Market Gardening and Dairy**

2   **Forest**

3   **Field Crops**

4   **Animal Grazing**

18. The model above for rural land use was devised by

(A) Johann Heinrich von Thünen
(B) Ernst Ravenstein
(C) Immanuel Wallerstein
(D) Louis Wirth
(E) Thomas Malthus

19. Core countries, countries of the periphery, and countries of the semiperiphery are types of countries that fit into the global economy, according to theory by

(A) W.W. Rostow
(B) Walter Christaller
(C) Alfred Weber
(D) E.L. Ullman
(E) Immanual Wallerstein

20. The province of Quebec is unique from other provinces in Canada because it has

(A) the largest overall population
(B) the mildest weather
(C) control over the largest share of the country's economy
(D) more young people under the age of 21
(E) a majority of inhabitants who speak French as a first language

21. Which of the following is NOT a region of high population concentration?

(A) South Africa
(B) East Asia
(C) South Asia
(D) Southeast Asia
(E) Eastern Europe

22. Which of the following theories is based on a landscape divided into noncompeting market areas called complementary regions?

(A) the rank-size rule
(B) dependency theory
(C) modernization theory
(D) central place theory
(E) locational interdependence theory

23. Bulk-reducing industries generally locate factories close to

(A) large bodies of water
(B) transportation hubs
(C) their markets
(D) raw materials
(E) labor supplies

24. Brazil's decision to move its capital from Rio de Janeiro to Brazília reflects the country's desire to create a(n)

(A) forward capital
(B) primate city
(C) world city
(D) urban hierarchy
(E) cultural landscape

25. The movement to practice farming based on principles of ecology that attempt to integrate plant and animal production practices that will protect the ecosystem is called

(A) subsistence agriculture
(B) sustainable agriculture
(C) industrial agriculture
(D) extensive agriculture
(E) biotechnology

26. Which of the following churches is most prominent in the southern United States?

(A) Lutheran Church
(B) Presbyterian Church
(C) Church of Jesus Christ of Latter Day Saints
(D) Episcopalian Church
(E) Baptist Church

27. According to urban geographers, as a city grows, a multiplier effects takes hold in which

(A) the ratio of basic sector workers to nonbasic decreases
(B) the ratio of basic sector workers to nonbasic increases
(C) smaller cities grow more rapidly than larger cities
(D) special-function cities increase in numbers whereas manufacturing cities decrease in numbers
(E) urban influence zones increase more rapidly than the size of the actual city

28. The art and science of mapmaking is called

(A) ecology
(B) cartography
(C) epidemiology
(D) topography
(E) physical projection

29. The theory that population patterns vary according to different levels of technological
    development is called

(A) the gravity model
(B) stationary population theory
(C) demographic transition theory
(D) the demographic equation
(E) dependency theory

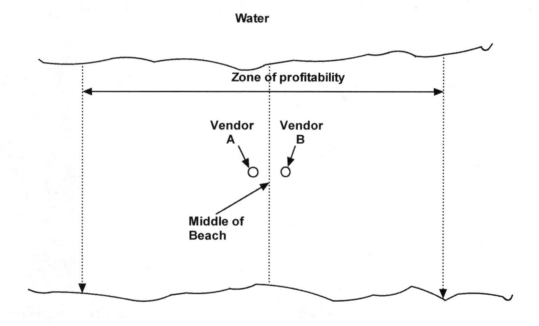

30. The diagram above illustrates

(A) least cost theory
(B) variable revenue analysis
(C) the substitution principle
(D) the rank-size rule
(E) the multiplier effect

31. Which of the following is an accurate description of commercial agriculture in the modern world?

(A) It is practiced mainly in industrialized countries.
(B) It is practiced mainly in newly industrializing countries.
(C) It is practiced in North America, but not in Europe or South America.
(D) It is becoming less common, since organic agricultural practices are becoming more common.
(E) It has spread to virtually all areas of the world , and almost all economies have adjusted to it.

32. A unitary state in one in which political power is concentrated in

(A) the hands of a one person
(B) a central legislature
(C) sub-governments
(D) one central geographic place
(E) the hands of those who also control the economy

33. Which of the following is NOT one of the ten largest megacities in the world?

(A) Tokyo
(B) Mexico City
(C) Seoul, South Korea
(D) Chicago, Illinois
(E) Delhi, India

34. Meridians and parallels are most helpful in determining

(A) relative location
(B) spatial organization
(C) the "why of where"
(D) physical site characteristics
(E) absolute location

35. Which of the following is computed by subtracting the crude death rate from the crude birth rate?

(A) total fertility rate
(B) mortality rate
(C) life expectancy
(D) natural increase
(E) migration rate

36. Most major industrial areas in eastern Russia are located on or near

(A) coastlines
(B) Moscow
(C) St. Petersburg
(D) the Trans-Siberian Railroad
(E) the Volga River

37. Which of the following is most likely to be a fundamental force promoting devolution?

(A) geographic diversity
(B) democratization
(C) economic development
(D) politicization of religion
(E) ethnonationalism

38. Today the top three export grains are

(A) potatoes, tomatoes, and beans
(B) beans, wheat, and potatoes
(C) wheat, yams, and rice
(D) rice, wheat, and corn
(E) corn, rice, and beans

39. Which of the following is a language sub-family?

(A) Indo-European languages
(B) Afro-Asiatic languages
(C) Niger-Congo languages
(D) American Indian languages
(E) Romance languages

40. Which of the following are primate cities in their respective countries?

(A) Paris, London, and New York
(B) Paris, London, and Seoul
(C) London, Seoul, Beijing
(D) New York, Montreal, and Mexico City
(E) Berlin, Shanghai, and Mumbai (Bombay)

41. The 19th century geographer who focused on the impact of human actions on the natural environment was

(A) George Perkins Marsh
(B) Carl Sauer
(C) W.W. Rostow
(D) Immanuel Kant
(E) Thomas Malthus

42. If current trends hold, which of the following countries will probably surpass China as the most populous country in the world by 2050?

(A) Russia
(B) the United States
(C) Japan
(D) India
(E) Saudi Arabia

43. The earliest country in East Asia to industrialize was

(A) China
(B) Singapore
(C) Korea
(D) Taiwan
(E) Japan

44. A country in which subsistence agriculture is commonly practiced is most likely to have a large

(A) secondary economic sector
(B) tertiary sector
(C) quaternary sector
(D) primary sector
(E) urban sector

45. Mackinder's heartland theory argues that the world will eventually be ruled by a

(A) land-based power
(B) country located on the Eurasian rim
(C) country located in the Americas
(D) sea-based power
(E) small country with colonies around the world

46. A hybrid that serves as a second language for everyone who uses it is called a

(A) creole
(B) lingua franca
(C) pidgin
(D) isogloss
(E) dialect

47. Religion distinguishes itself from other belief systems by its emphasis on

(A) the existence of gods
(B) supernatural intervention
(C) the sacred and divine
(D) the ability of human beings to guide their own lives
(E) profane, or ordinary, experiences

48. The size of ancient cities was limited to a few thousand inhabitants mainly because

(A) transportation between major cities was limited and slow
(B) they had an undeveloped social class system, so they had no powerful elites
(C) existing systems of food gathering, storing, and distribution would not have supported a larger population
(D) their inhabitants developed no systems of writing and record-keeping to help organize resources
(E) few early civilizations codified laws to ensure that society functioned smoothly

49. A term that describes the shapes, sizes, and relative locations of states is

(A) spatial interaction
(B) settlement variations
(C) density gradation
(D) territoriality
(E) territorial morphology

50. An advantage of the Peters map projection is that it

(A) does not distort shapes
(B) does not exaggerate the size of areas to the extreme north and extreme south
(C) accurately compares land masses in terms of area
(D) represents lines of constant compass bearing
(E) has curving meridians that curve gently and avoid extremes

51. By 8000 B.C.E., major migrations of hunters and gatherers had taken place to many parts of the Eastern Hemisphere that originated in

    (A) Australia
    (B) Europe
    (C) Southeast Asia
    (D) Central Asia
    (E) eastern Africa

52. The concept of distance decay best illustrates which of the following of Ravenstein's laws of migration?

    (A) The majority of immigrants only move a short distance.
    (B) Migrants who move longer distances tend to choose cities as their destinations.
    (C) Each migration produces a counterflow.
    (D) Families are less likely to make international moves than young adults.
    (E) Spatial interaction is directly related to the size of the populations.

53. Core-periphery distinctions in Europe have led to internal devolutionary forces within some countries, especially in

    (A) France and Britain
    (B) Norway and Sweden
    (C) Switzerland and Germany
    (D) Spain and Italy
    (E) Denmark and Ireland

54. The process in which an innovator country produces something new, which in turn is made better and cheaper by another country that exports it back to the innovator country is called the strategy of

    (A) export-oriented industrialization
    (B) the international division of labor
    (C) locational interdependence
    (D) space-time compression
    (E) sustainable development

55. Intertillage is most likely to be practiced by people whose main form of raising food products is

    (A) intensive subsistence agriculture
    (B) pastoral nomadism
    (C) agribusiness
    (D) shifting cultivation
    (E) vegetative planting

56. Three social characteristics of urban areas identified by Louis Wirth during the 1930s were

(A) large size, strong social class systems, organized governments
(B) high density, large size, and social equality
(C) agglomeration, transportation, and friction of distance
(D) large size, high density, and social heterogeneity
(E) secondary economic activities, tertiary economic activities, and primary economic activities

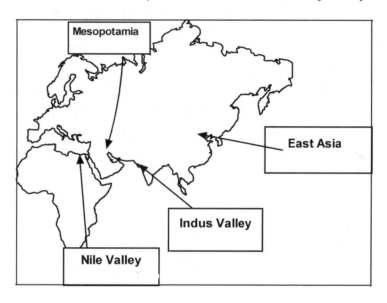

57. The map above identifies the earliest

(A) geographic regions
(B) cultural hearths
(C) areas of industrialization
(D) cultural landscapes
(E) areas of pastoral nomadism

58. After the middle of the 20th century, most African and Asian colonies received their independence, largely as a result of

(A) the formation of the United Nations
(B) the impact of World War II, which weakened European nations' ability to maintain colonies
(C) strong efforts by non-governmental organizations that promoted independence movements
(D) industrialization of large parts of both continents
(E) migrations of Europeans and Americans to settle in colonial areas

59. As Islam spread to Sub-Saharan Africa, its first converts were the elites, while ordinary people usually retained native religions. This phenomenon illustrates the process of

(A) hierarchical diffusion
(B) time-distance decay
(C) stimulus diffusion
(D) relocation diffusion
(E) migrant diffusion

60. Which of the following is an economic pull factor that encourages migration?

(A) lack of job opportunities in the land of origin
(B) plentiful jobs in the destination area
(C) religious persecution in the land of origin
(D) similar cultural practices in the land of origin and the destination area
(E) physical features that halt or slow migration from one place to another

61. For which of the following would a large scale map be most helpful?

(A) determining the best highway to travel between nearby cities
(B) showing the relationship between two continents
(C) navigating rough terrain with significant changes in altitude
(D) determining which way to turn on a small street
(E) mapping a route to circumvent traffic in a large city

62. One disadvantage that dairy farmers have in comparison to mixed crop and livestock farmers is that dairy farmers

(A) receive little income from cheese and butter products
(B) have to make more intense use of soil
(C) have to purchase all feed
(D) aren't usually able to sell products to large manufacturers
(E) face more competition, since the number of dairy farms has increased in recent years

63. The deindustrialization trend is most evident today in

(A) China and Japan
(B) Sub-Saharan Africa and the Middle East
(C) the United States and Europe
(D) Latin America and Canada
(E) Southeast Asia and Latin America

64. "Bosnywash" is best described as a(n)

(A) micropolitan statistical area
(B) megacity
(C) physical city
(D) megalopolis
(E) urban hierarchy

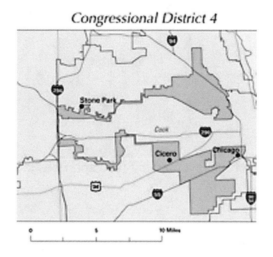

Congressional District 4

65. The map of Congressisonal District 4 in Illinois reflects the common practice of

(A) malapportionment
(B) gerrymandering
(C) irredentism
(D) fragmentation
(E) perforated politics

66. Which of the following is NOT an important region for livestock ranching?

(A) northern Africa
(B) the pampas or Argentina and southern Brazil
(C) the western United States
(D) Australia
(E) South Africa

67. As Buddhism spread from its origins in India throughout Asia, it came into areas where Confucianism was strong. Both Buddhism and Confucianism continued to be important forces, with a more or less equal exchange of cultural traits, a process known as

(A) cultural relativism
(B) assimilation
(C) acculturation
(D) transculturation
(E) cultural transmission

68. Place names may also be called

(A) toponyms
(B) perceptual regions
(C) site factors
(D) isoglosses
(E) artifacts

69. The *maquiladora* district in Mexico produces goods primarily for consumers in

(A) Mexico City and Guadalajara
(B) California and northern Mexico
(C) China
(D) the United States
(E) the European Union

70. "Balkanization" is said to occur when a country falls apart based on

(A) ethnicity
(B) geographical regions
(C) economic differences
(D) political affiliations
(E) disputes over the proper authority of the government

71. Which of the following is currently a major global migration flow?

(A) Europe to East Asia
(B) North America to South America
(C) Asia to North America
(D) South America to East Asia
(E) Africa to North America

72. During the late 20th century, immigration to the United States increased dramatically from

(A) Sub-Saharan Africa and Australia
(B) Asia and Latin America
(C) southern and eastern Europe
(D) Latin America and western Europe
(E) Asia and northern Africa

73. In the Caucasus region of Eastern Europe, several thousand languages are spoken by fewer than 2 million people, a characteristic known as

(A) independent invention
(B) linguistic diffusion
(C) language extinction
(D) syncretism
(E) linguistic fragmentation

74. Today, most plantation farming takes place in

(A) the southern United States, Mexico, and Africa
(B) Europe, Central Asia, and the Middle East
(C) the southern United States, Australia, and Latin America
(D) Africa, North America, and East Asia
(E) Asia, Latin America, and Africa

75. If people believe that a devastating flood was caused by the displeasure of the gods and respond by building an alter, the interaction between humans and the land best illustrates which of the following schools of thought in cultural geography?

(A) the "why of where"
(B) environmental determinism
(C) possibilism
(D) environmental perception
(E) cultural determinism

Section II - Free-response Questions
Allow 75 minutes for these three questions.

1. A state is separated from its neighbors by boundaries.

   a. Define boundary, and explain how a boundary is different from a frontier.

   b. Describe two types of boundaries.

   c. For each type of boundary you identified in part b, explain one problem that it may
      present for the country that set the boundary.

2. The map above shows areas of Africa that currently are experiencing a food supply crisis.

   a. Describe the Green Revolution.

   b. Identify one technology that has shaped the Green Revolution, and explain how it has
      shaped the Green Revolution.

   c. Explain two reasons why the Green Revolution has not provided famine relief to
      Sub-Saharan Africa.

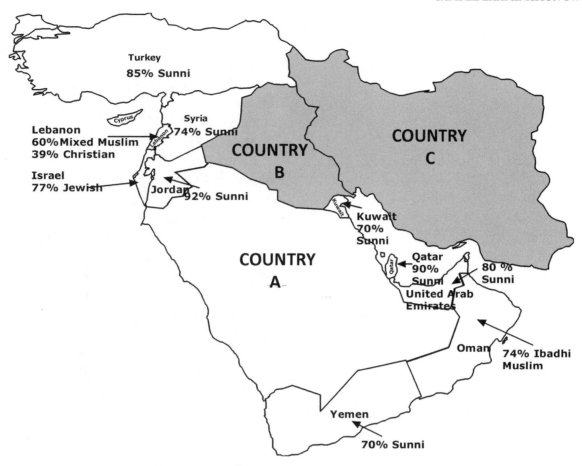

3. Both Sunni and Shiite Muslims have long inhabited countries in the Middle East.

   a. Identify Countries A, B, and C on the map above.

   b. Explain the major reason for the original split between Sunnis and Shiites.

   c. Describe the Sunni/Shiite proportions in one of the countries you identified in part a, and discuss one impact that these proportions have on

     i. social relations

     ii. political stability

INDEX

 # Order Information

Several ways to order:

1) **Fill out and send this form to:**
   WoodYard Publications
   285 Main Street
   Germantown, NY 12526

   Full payment must accompany the order. Make checks payable to WoodYard Publications.

2) Purchase Orders (for schools only) - Send purchase order to the above address
   or Fax to 610-372-8401.

3) Use your credit card (Visa, Mastercard, American Express, Discovery) when you call
   610-207-1366

4) Order from Amazon. Go to www.amazon.com for order information.

5) Pay for one student book through PayPal at
   http://woodyardpublications.home.comcast.net

Want more information?

Phone: 610-207-1366

E-Mail: woodyardpublications@comcast.net

Order Form

Please send _____copies of AP Human Geography: A Study Guide, 3rd edition, to:

Name_____

Mailing Address_____

City, State, Zip_____

Phone_____

E-mail Address_____

School_____

School Address_____

City, State, Zip_____

Please check one: Please send book(s) to _____Home Address
or
_____School Address

Prices:

     1 book - $17.95 + $5.05 Priority Mail shipping = $23.00

     2-9 books - $14.95 + 8% shipping

     10 books or more - $12.95 + 8% shipping

Mail this form with check payable to WoodYard Publications, 285 Main Street, Germantown, NY12526. School purchase orders also accepted.